Developments in Psychoanalysis

Developments in
PSYCHOANALYSIS

LEON SALZMAN, M.D.

Professor of Clinical Psychiatry, Georgetown University School of Medicine, Washington, D.C.; Visiting Lecturer, Medical College of Virginia, Richmond; Consultant, St. Elizabeths Hospital, Washington, D.C.

GRUNE & STRATTON   New York • London

Library of Congress Catalog Card No. 61-18528

Copyright © 1962
GRUNE & STRATTON, INC.

381 Park Avenue South

New York 16, N. Y.

Printed and bound in U.S.A. (B)

Contents

Acknowledgments

Acknowledgment is hereby made to the following publishers for permission to quote from various books and journals.

American Journal of Psychiatry, for "Psychoanalytic Treatment," 116: 323, 1959.

American Psychological Association, for American Psychologist 10: 520, 1955.

Basic Books, Inc., for Ernest G. Schachtel, *Metamorphosis*, New York, 1959.

Harper & Bros., for Erich Fromm, *Sigmund Freud's Mission*, New York, 1959.

Hogarth Press, for Sigmund Freud, *Ego and the Id*, London, 1927.

International Universities Press, for R. D. Fairbairn, "On the Nature and Aims of Psychoanalytic Treatment." International Journal of Psychoanalysis 39: 74, 1959.

Routledge and Kegan Paul, Ltd., for Martin Buber, *Between Man and Man*, London, 1947.

Oxford University Press, for Paul Tillich, *Love, Power and Justice*, New York, 1954.

Sheed and Ward, for Joseph Nuttin, *Psychoanalysis and Personality*, New York, 1953.

Springer Publishing Co., for William V. Silverberg, *Childhood Experience and Personal Destiny*, New York, 1952.

Tudor Publishing Co., for *Albert Einstein: Philosopher Scientist*, edited by P. A. Schlipp, New York, 1951.

Viking Press, for *A Portable Medieval Reader*, edited by James B. Ross and Mary M. McLaughlin, New York, 1949.

World Publishing Co., for M. K. F. Fisher, *Art of Eating*, Cleveland, 1954.

The author would also like to express his appreciation to Dr. Sandor Rado, Grune & Stratton, Inc., and to the widow of the late Dr. Bernard Robbins for their cooperation in placing source material at his disposal. He would also like to acknowledge the great debt he owes his wife, Ann, who played an invaluable role in the preparation, development and final production of this book.

Introduction

THE CONTRIBUTIONS of Sigmund Freud have touched on all areas of human learning and endeavor. From the original revulsion and rejection of most of his ideas came a fairly rapid, uncritical acceptance of all his views which reached an almost idolatrous state. In the past 30 years there has been a continuing appraisal of his work in a critical but respectful atmosphere.

The application of Freud's theories to psychology, psychiatry and psychoanalysis has been enormously fruitful and has stimulated the most energetic applications of his concepts to the practical problems of personality theory and the therapy of mental disorders. Consequently, we find the same divergences in the therapeutic applications as we find in regard to his theoretical formulations with greater emphasis on the essential agreements. In this book I propose to present some of the developments in psychiatric and psychoanalytic theory that have grown out of Freud's original contributions. The history of most scientific innovations is roughly parallel; the initial impact may be enormous, but subsequent decades or centuries will have modified and placed these ideas in a proper perspective. Psychoanalytic theory is now in the process of being modified, revised, and in some instances rejected as being invalid or not representing the true picture of human development or behavior. The modifications of Freud's work occurred early in his career by some of his own outstanding students, Jung, Adler, Stekel, and others. This book will deal largely with the later innovators who were more concerned with the development in Ego Theory, as contrasted with the earlier alterations in id theory, or the nature and contents of the unconscious. This group is frequently called the Ego Theorists, or neo-Freudians, or Culturalists. This group is highly diverse, and individuals in it range from those who have developed a consistent, integrated theory of personality (Horney, Sullivan) to those who have elaborated certain aspects of Freud's theory (Rado, Robbins, Ferenczi). Some psychoanalysts feel that any revision of Freud's original work is either heretical or frivolous, since Freud had already said it before and said it more clearly. I doubt whether this notion regarding the alteration of existing theories will satisfy the student in behavioral sciences who enters the field with few prejudices and a fresh curiosity for what he proposes to study. It is neither frivolous nor heretical to re-examine existing theory in any science, since some reward is inherent in every fresh approach to an old problem.

Victor F. Lenzen, in an article on Albert Einstein, quotes Einstein as saying: "Concepts that have proved useful in the constitution of an order of things, readily win such an authority over us that we forget their earthly origins and take them to be changeless data. Such concepts then become stamped as necessities of thought, as given 'a priori' so that the path of scientific progress often becomes impassable for a long period. Einstein declared that it is no idle play, therefore, if we engage in analyses of concepts that have been long current, and show on what their justification and usefulness depends.

The book is directed to all students in the behavioral sciences who are cognizant of the formidable meanings and applications of Freud's psychoanalytic theories and are concerned with their fullest development and expansion. It will attempt to present some details about the recent developments and contributions of some of the workers in the field, but will also deal with the developments of some of the concepts in psychoanalysis and how they have unfolded in recent years. It is the hope of the author that the reader will be impressed with the dynamic nature of Freud' original work and its capacity to stimulate many novel and fresh approaches to personality development. The understanding of man in all his complexities was begun in a scientific sense with Freud's work. It did not end with him, and will continue, hopefully, for centuries to come. Although I believe psychoanalytic theory and practice will continue far into the future, its form and content may be unrecognizable from today's *New Yorker* notion of the couch and the cliché. The developments presented here are only slight rumblings of the quakes and convulsions which will transform psychoanalytic theory as history has done to all meaningful views about man. However, the bedrock of Freud's discoveries will penetrate and permeate all future personality theories, and his influence will long continue to frame the direction of research in human motivation and behavior. The developments in theory described in this book have grown out of Freud's undoubted and now universally accepted contributions but have taken issue with some of his extrapolations and speculations in philosophy and science.

This book grew out of a series of lectures given at the Washington School of Psychiatry and the Catholic University Graduate School.

LEON SALZMAN

Washington, D.C.

THE PHILOSOPHICAL science of man must take as its starting point the consideration of the subject, "man with man." If you consider the individual by himself, then you see of man just as much as you see of the moon; only man with man is a completely outlined form. Consider man with man and you see human life, dynamic two fold, the giver and the receiver, he who does and he who endures, the attacking force and the defending force, the nature which investigates and the nature which supplies the information, the request begged and granted, and always both together, completely one another in mutual contribution, together showing forth man. Now you can turn to the individual and you can recognize him as man, according to the possibility of relation which he shows; you can turn to the aggregate and you recognize it as man according to the fullness of relation which he shows. We may come nearer to the answer to the question, what man is when we come to see him as the eternal meeting of the One with the Other.

MARTIN BUBER
Between Man and Man

I

Accepted and Disputed
Freudian Concepts

PSYCHOANALYSIS is not only a theory of personality development but also a therapeutic technique, and by implication, a philosophical statement about man—his needs, desires, goals and aspirations. Although one can deal with these aspects separately, they are necessarily closely interrelated. It is difficult, in spite of the protests of many psychoanalysts, to distinguish philosophy from theory and morality from practice.

This is especially true at the present time when the theories and practices of psychoanalysis are less than 100 years old and its founder and most prolific contributor is dead less than 30 years. At the early stage of development of any science, the original theories occupy the focus of interest of the students, and a massive literature accumulates in an effort to elaborate and validate these hypotheses. In these efforts, theory draws on practice, which rests heavily on a philosophical attitude that underlies the original formulations. In the early history of a science there are many concepts which remain open and require major alterations and others which are still beyond verification. This is particularly true in psychoanalysis, in which theories depend upon a broad understanding of man ranging from biology and physiology to epistemology and aesthetics. Since the original formulations of Freud, there have been major advances in the science of anthropology, ethology, biology and history which have drawn upon Freud's work but which have also shed new light on his original hypotheses. Each new advance in the social and physical sciences opens up new insights which either confirm or demand alterations in the existing psychoanalytic theories.

In order to appreciate some of these newer developments more adequately, we will have to take a brief look at Freud's contributions to psychiatric theory and practice. Some of his contributions are so manifestly valid and fruitful that practically all behavioral scientists, whatever their theoretical bias, accept and utilize them. On the other hand, many of his hypotheses, theoretical constructs, and metaphysical formulations have stimulated a variety of alternative theories and explanations. Without examining all of Freud's theories in detail, we will focus on those theories which are the basis for current controversies and modifications by students of the behavioral sciences.

Personality Development

Sixty years after Freud's first publications in the field of psychoanalysis we can appraise some of his contributions with great clarity. His development of a dynamic theory of personality is undoubtedly one of the great contributions in the field of psychology for a century. The significance of this rests in the recognition and formulation of the ongoing nature of personality development. Prior to Freud, personality was viewed as the collection of traits or attributes which characterized the individual. These traits appeared by virtue of innate physiological characteristics which were described as part of the individual's character structure. The characterstics were classified and the individual's personality was visualized as the totality of these described traits. Freud's early work with Breuer in 1885 and his description of the relationship of symptoms to the experienced events in the lives of his patients, firmly established the conception of personality as a developing and unfolding process based on the interaction of the hereditary substrate of the individual with his cultural milieu. Personality was the result of the interaction between the person's inner needs or instincts, as Freud called them, with the outside world. The individual unfolded his instinctual desires through the environment, which could either fulfill, impede, or deny these needs. Although it was a dynamic interaction, Freud visualized the environment as acting in a rather simplified fashion of either frustrating or satisfying these needs. Though the culture grew out of the necessity to restrain the instinctual demands, it also made demands on the growing individual in accordance with its own set of standards and values. The major developments in this growth occurred in the very early years, and Freud believed that in the fifth or sixth year the character structure of the individual was fully formed. Although much remained to be learned and experienced prior to maturity, the basic outlines were already established. He felt that all subsequent experiencing occurred within the confines of the patterns laid down prior to the sixth year. The scaffolding for the structure called personality was assembled on a solid foundation, and although there were still many possibilities about how the structure would be finished—in terms of the decorations and contents—the basic architectural form was fixed and final. This description of personality development was intricately bound up with the libido theory. Although there is almost universal agreement on the dynamic nature of personality development, there is considerable difference with regard to the nature of this development. Freud considered the libido and its energy to be the major instrument through which the infant and child reacted with the world. Subsequent theorists have presented alternative theories. Alfred Adler visualized the major integrating forces as related to the need to overcome inferiorities that are felt particularly in early infancy and childhood but effect the individual throughout his life. Others, like Carl Jung, described the libido as a force similar to Henri Bergson's *élan vital*, devoid of any specific content or direction. Still others postulated the need to fulfill one's potentialities or to communicate and relate adequately to one's fellow man.

Freud's formulations concerning personality development revolved essentially about his libido theory. This theory stated that the libido resided in various somatic zones at particular times in the individual's life, and that its life history constituted the individual's personality. Since the libido moves from the oral zone to the anal zone and finally to the genital zone, the phases of personality development move from one area to another. At about the time of the development of the Oedipus complex, the libido is concentrated around the genital zone. After the resolution of the Oedipus complex, which occurs around the age of five or six, the formal development of personality ceases. At this time the essential patterns of behavior are established, and subsequently, the additions to the personality are merely accretions with some refinements of the basic structure. Many theorists have raised objections to this notion, and take issue with the libido theory most strenuously. They do not accept the notion that personality ceases to develop at five or six years of age. They extend Freud's original dynamic view of personality development and conceive of the personality as undergoing development throughout the life of the individual in spite of the fact that some periods are more significant than others.

The Unconscious

It has long been a commonplace among novelists, philosophers, and even psychologists prior to Freud, that human motivation extended beyond the confines of the state of awareness. Parapraxes, slips of the tongue, everyday errors, and other vaguely understood activities of man were thought to have some significance, although they were considered largely accidental or magical in nature. It was one of Freud's great achievements to have explored and given meaning to this area of human functioning which is out of awareness. He made it possible to recognize that a great deal of so-called meaningless or seemingly unmotivated and undirected behavior derived from sources out of our immediate awareness. This area of mental activity was called the unconscious. For many people this is Freud's greatest single piece of work, for it pulled man down from the pinnacles of rationality and presented him with evidence of his irrational functioning. It showed man to be pressed and pushed by interests and ideas that were outside of his conscious and deliberate choice.

Freud felt that the unconscious was many things. It was a reservoir for primal urges of sex and aggression as well as a hotel for repressed ideas, needs and affects. In addition, it was a useful topological area where unsolved or contradictory problems of motivation could be assigned and stored and could influence behavior. The unconscious became a repository for a multitude of feelings, attitudes and ideas which seemed to be operating in the individual but was beyond his immediate awareness. From this notion came the idea of unconscious guilt, unconscious anxiety, latent homosexuality, etc. These conceptions have raised serious semantic difficulties as well as structural ones, since they implied that a feeling (guilt or anxiety) which was described as a felt need could exist outside of awareness or conscious feeling. Although the notion of the pre-conscious was an attempt to deal with such confused concepts, the unconscious soon became crowded with transient and permanent residents who were present only by virtue of the difficulty in placing them elsewhere. Whenever it came to one's attention that some forces seemed to be at work that could not be accounted for in consciousness, it was presumed to be present in the unconscious. The vital notion, however, was the recognition that there are tendencies, attitudes and feelings which influence our daily behavior that are outside of immediate awareness. Although Freud peopled the unconscious with primitive demons and unstable, unsatisfied sex needs which many individuals took exception to, he nevertheless firmly established the notion that human interests, needs and desires have roots outside of our immediate awareness and often more strongly determine our behavior than our conscious attitudes or feelings.

The problem of the unconscious is deeply involved in philosophical, epistemological and scientific issues. The structuring, labeling, and consequent utilization of the concept as if it were a "thing-in-itself" has produced many difficulties. It implies an area of functioning produced by the necessity of keeping out of awareness certain experiences and feelings that would, if present, produce distress or anxiety. As a repository, however, it involves concepts of memory, and in order to understand this aspect of its functioning fully, it should be subsumed to a large extent under the laws pertaining to memory. Memory is not only related to repression, which Freud emphasized, but also to such factors as the intensity or persistence of an experience, the recency of an experience, its relevance to prevailing interest, and the extremes of emotional states, i.e., the unusual versus the habitual. Freud tended to minimize all these elements except the last and developed his theory of recall primarily around the emotional elements in an experience. Currently, alternative theories of recall, particularly those of Ernest Schachtel, create doubts about this classic view of the unconscious as a repository of memories which are under repression.[2]

Freud spent the largest part of his life studying this area of mental functioning which was later identified topologically as the id, and the bulk of his writings concerns itself with rich and penetrating descriptions of the contents and activities of this area.

Although few current theorists seriously doubt the validity of Freud's unconscious, there are many sharp differences with regard to its nature, contents, and methods of influencing human behavior.

It is generally accepted that human behavior is influenced by attitudes and feelings which lie outside of immediate awareness. However, some theories minimize the effect of unconscious attitudes, laying greater stress on the conscious, volitional elements in behavior, and others take a firm position regarding the predominant role of the unconscious. Many theorists have accepted a middle position, which acknowledges the position of the unconscious in the mental life, but which questions the topological and reservoir functions of the unconscious as described by Freud. However diverse or extreme the theory of the unconscious may be, all recognize that there are forces in the mental life of an individual that may be outside of awareness but which still influence his decisions and behavior.

Significance of Early Years

That the child is father to the man is an axiom which was brought to life by Freud's dynamic conception of personality development. It is implicit in his theories that the influences, experiences and interactions which occur in the earliest years of infancy and childhood play a significant role in the future personal history of the individual. Today this is a commonplace idea and is part of practically every theory of personality. However, some question remains about the quality and timing of these influences, for some theorists do not accept Freud's dictum about the dominating influence of the first five years. Others have disagreed about the types of experiences which are most influential in the infantile period.

For example, traditional psychoanalytic theorists have emphasized the role of breast sucking as the basis for the ultimate development of tenderness and affection. A fascinating piece of research was done recently by Harry F. Harlow and his associates which raises serious questions about this generally accepted idea. Surrogate mothers were contrived for newborn infant rhesus monkeys by building two elongated figures, one made of welded wire and surmounted by a wooden head with a crude face. The other, a cylindrical figure of welded wire, was cushioned by a sheathing of terrycloth. Each figure had a protruding nipple attached to a nursing bottle. The two mothers were equally acceptable physiologically, but psychologically the cloth mother was the more acceptable mother. The monkeys spent more time on the cloth mother, and although they may have used the wire mother for feeding, they very quickly turned and clung to the cloth mother. This tended to contradict the notion that affection is a learned response in association with feeding, and attested to the overwhelming importance of bodily contact as opposed to the mere fulfillment of the physiological needs of the infant monkeys. In the same experiment it was illuminating to observe that whether the monkeys had fed at the wire or cloth mother, under stress they overwhelmingly sought comfort and security from the cloth mother.[3] This clever experiment raises many questions about the significance of the oral area in infancy, particularly in relation to the question of breast feeding. It points to the role of contact as a prime requisite in the developing relationship of security in the nursing area.

It is this type of research as well as the detailed observations of researchers such as Piaget and Gesell which has stimulated alternative theories about the nature and effect of infantile experiencing upon adult behavior. Although in general terms there is a tendency to acknowledge the importance of infantile experiencing, some feel that learning and basic patterning extend far beyond age five, and some insist that the most crucial experiences occur under the age of six months (Melanie Klein).

BIOLOGICAL ORIENTATION

There is a large area of disagreement regarding Freud's biological orientation and the development of his theories in a mechanico-causal system, using physics as a model. Freud's theories were framed in the philosophic-scientific atmosphere of the late 1800's and early 1900, when the mechanical view of the physical sciences was in the ascendency. David McK. Rioch[4] stated that, "It was not accidental that Freud's theory of psychotherapy and the theory of personality development derived from it, was part of a language of science in which he was trained . . . a language of fixed time and space, energy, mechanics, and biological absolutes." There was great stress placed on causality and the demonstration of cause and effect in a simple mechanical fashion. Energy mechanics, which was part of the mechanico-causal concepts, involved the assumption about the flow, impedence and transformation of energy and used hydraulics and electricity as the basic physical models. In this atmosphere the science of man was primarily influenced by the assumption of a biological base for human behavior, determined by man's instincts. The totality of man could be understood by some hypotheses concerning his fundamental instincts which motivated all his behavior. Although Freud altered his instinct theories on at least three occasions, he maintained throughout his life the predominant role of sex (libido) as the major impelling force towards activity and fulfillment in the human animal. The libido, although primarily sexual, included all the impulses which motivate man toward contact with other human beings, with pleasure as the goal. The biological assumption about man did not exclude the influence of culture, but minimized its role in man's development. It clearly implied that the forces operative in man's behavior were intrinsically bound up in his instinctual energies and impinged against the world, which either encouraged or resisted its fulfillment. It postulated fixed hereditary sources of energy which predetermined his psychological events as ubiquitous participants in his life. Certain events, such as the Oedipal situation, castration anxieties, penis envy, etc., were innate, biologically organized experiences which were universal and inevitable. Such points of view were prevalent centuries ago, and in the 13th Century, the historian Salimbone wrote of Emperor Frederick II:

. . . he wanted to find out what kind of speech and what manner of speech children would have when they grew up if they spoke to no one beforehand. So he bade foster mothers and nurses to suckle the children, to bathe and wash them, but in no way to prattle with them, or speak to them, for he wanted to learn whether they would speak the Hebrew language, which was the oldest, or Greek, or Latin, or Arabic, or perhaps the language of their parents, of whom they had been born. But he labored in vain because the children all died. For they could not live without the petting and joyful faces and loving words of their foster mothers. And so the songs are called "swaddling songs" which a woman sings while she is rocking the cradle, to put a child to sleep, and without them a child sleeps badly and has no rest.[5]

The focal role of sex was neither a frivolous nor a fanciful decision but arose out of Freud's early experience in the treatment of the hysterical neuroses. Much of the current psychoanalytic formulations raise serious doubts about the view of man as an exclusively biological animal and question the significance of instincts in human behavior. They specifically take issue with some of the formulations about the role of the libido and its derived theoretical formulations. The emphasis on culture has superceded the emphasis on sex and instinct, and recent existential analytic theories propose an alternative view of man which de-emphasizes both biology and objectivity.

It is not entirely fruitless to speculate about the framework in which Freud might have cast his theories had he begun his work in the 1920's, after the impact of Einstein's work on relativity and the reorganization of physics. This may shed light on some of the more questionable hypotheses which are dependent upon the limitations of Freud's knowledge of man and the universe. One cannot overlook the fact that Freud was a first rate scientist who was very familiar with most of the work being done during his lifetime, and who was well grounded in neurology and the scientific method.

However, Freud the philosopher (in spite of his own denials of interest in philosophy) and Freud the scientist are two different people. The scientific system which he established must be examined from the framework of a scientific methodology. His philosophical system, which subscribed to the notion that the resolution of man's problems were ultimately unsolvable, needs no verification or validation and can be accepted or denied without denying his scientific contributions. They must be judged exclusively on their capacity to elucidate the essential nature of man and the innate contradictions of his existence.

Libido Theory

Freud's early experiences with Breuer and with several hysterical patients convinced him of the major role of sexual trauma in the development of mental disorder. He noted that the symptoms of these patients were related to forgotten sexual experiences. This encouraged him to make an intensive study of the role of sex in the formation of personality and gave rise to the libido theory which ultimately involved Freud's biological and instinctual orientation. It is the most widely known, distorted, and controversial of all his contributions. Although it will not be examined in detail at this point, it is necessary to have a sufficiently clear picture of it in order to follow some of the objections and modifications of this theory.

Freud conceived of the infant as having a certain fixed amount of libido which participated in his ultimate development by being attached (cathected) to bodily areas of primary significance in his development. At first the libido was attached to the oral zone, and gratifications were derived through this area. Freud believed that sucking, biting, and other pleasures related to orality had libidinal origins. The libido, being capable of free movement, after a time shifted to the anal area, which then became the main source of pleasurable contact with the environment. At about age three, the genitals became the focus of the libido, and this was called the phallic phase of development. During the long period of latency, the libido remained dormant and inactive and then became reestablished in the genital area, and this was called the genital stage of personality development. In this way he accounted for some self evident notions about zones of interaction in human development as well as amplifying his notions of the primary motivations of development being related to pleasure. It is obvious that the infant is "all mouth" and derives its nourishment and sustenance through its mouth. Since ingestion is the infant's primary concern, it is the focus around which all contacts with the environment take place. After a year or more (depending upon the culture) the interest shifts to the excretory apparatus in terms of sphincter control and this, for a short while, takes over the focus of interest. What is striking about Freud's contentions is that this sequence is determined by the presence of the libidinal energy and that the biological and physiological development of the infant is determined by its activity. It introduces the notion of pleasure, and particularly sexual pleasure, in physiological performances. The consequences of this theory are manifold and are the source of much controversy. Although Freud viewed this theory as an hypothesis, some of his followers deal with it as if it were a fact and speak of the libido theory as though it were an immutable issue in human development. Wilhelm Reich, who was a prominent student of Freud, and who later developed his own conceptions which he called "Orgone Biodynamics," took Freud's theory literally and claimed to have isolated the libidinal energy which he called "Orgone." Although this work has never been substantiated, it has remained an adventurous episode in the history of psychoanalysis.

The libido theory was a very fruitful concept for the development of psychoanalytic theories since it embodied the notions of a dynamic development of personality and supplied many clues to a variety of psychopathological disorders. It was an excellent heuristic theory which enabled the psychologist to explain what he could see in the present and make some predictions about the future. It was an invaluable tool for the study and comprehension of the psychology of infants and childhood that heretofore had been cloaked in sentimental fantasy or scientific ignorance. However, it appeared to have many deficiencies which current theorists have attempted to overcome.

Can it be assumed, since there is no direct evidence through observations of infants, that the expressions of pleasure in feeding are analogous to sexual pleasure? Are there alternative explanations which would not require the postulation of a theory which is so highly generalized? The most serious question that it raises is in connection with the instinct theories that attribute all character traits, strivings and attitudes other than those involved in self-preservation to a libidinal source. Validation of this theory is not the crucial test. Its value in stimulating further inquiry into human motivation and behavior is the real test. It is in this connection that current theorists take strong issue with the libido theory.

A corollary to the libido theory is Freud's theories regarding the basic motivations of human behavior which reside in the instincts. Although he altered the instinct theories several times, he maintained his essential view of human behavior as being derived from the instincts—Eros and Thanatos—either as pure expression of these instincts or modifications of them. The instincts could be altered in terms of their aims as well as their objects. This alteration became the basis for the ultimate development of the character of an individual.

Many related formulations grow out of the constructs involved in the libido theory. The Oedipal situation is a case in point. Here, if circumstances are unfavorable, it became an Oedipal complex directly dependent upon the conceptions of libido and libidinal energy. Freud maintained that the attachments of children for their parents were libidinal in nature. The regular constellation of the attachment of a child to the parent of the opposite sex, with the accompanying feelings of danger from the parent of the same sex involved in this romance, constituted a ubiquitous event in all human existence.

For the male this development constituted a particular risk since he was in danger of castration from the father for attempted seduction of his wife. The castration fear finally overcame the Oedipus struggle in the male child. The concept of castration anxiety has created considerable dissension and is a curious misnomer, for

Freud meant that the infant fears loss of his penis, although castration is the loss of the testicles. This error is not without its significance, since castration would not necessarily rob the child of his sexual capacity, but only limit its procreative powers. The attachment of children for their parents is self-evident. The reasons for this attachment and the intensity of the relationship is presumably explained by the libido theory. However, there are alternative explanations for this phenomenon, which are equally illuminating and fruitful to a science of psychology. The supposition that every infant is first attached to the mothering one is related to its dependency upon an adequate source of physiological and psychological support. The subsequent history of the child's relationship to the parent of the opposite sex may depend upon other factors, such as the seductiveness of the parent or the authority figure in the family who would be the major source of security to the child. Some of the newer theories described here indicate that the basis for strong attachments, which may be sexual in nature, can also be understood in terms of the cultural milieu of the infant. These explanations do not require a biological hypothesis which is based on very limited evidence of man's instincts or the universality of the phenomenon.

Another major offshoot of the libido theory is its implicit assumption regarding the primacy of the male genital apparatus over the female. It has been said that Freud's theories are male-centered; that is, they develop out of the assumption that the male, genitally and otherwise, has greater biological significance and preference. Freud's theories regarding female psychology are the weakest elements in his entire psychological system. They not only expose his bias and culture-boundedness, but they reveal his limitations in comprehending the social and political forces that mold man. This was certainly due to his preoccupation with biology and instinct, and consequently, he had little time or energy for a broader look at the issues which specifically affect the female in our world. It is important to note here that the psychology of the female, for Freud, rested very heavily on her desire and inability to obtain the penis. This was not viewed symbolically, but literally, and accounted for a great variety of neurotic disorders.

The development of personality was intimately involved in the fate of the libidinal energy as it focused on the oral, anal, and genital areas. The character structure of an individual depended upon the way he dealt with his libidinal drives. One way was to inhibit the aim of the drive, and this aim-inhibited drive would produce character traits which would be minor versions of the original drive, such as striving for power, or self assertion which is an aim-inhibited aspect of the aggressive instinct. A more important and far reaching modification of the instincts resided in the capacity to sublimate, which is a device for making certain instincts socially acceptable. This was an expression of desexualized libido and played a most important role in the artistic, aesthetic, and other creative instincts of man. Still other character traits represent a reaction-formation to libidinal impulses and were expressed in traits opposite to the original impulse. In short, character was the result of the expression or modification of the libidinal impulse and was directly attributable to the historical development of the libido. This conception of character was almost exclusively dependent on the history of the forces which reside inside the individual. The culture and forces operating outside the individual were only accidental or coincidental elements in either sustaining or frustrating the libidinal impulses. It also encouraged and perpetuated the notion, in spite of all disclaimers, that sex is the major force operating in the development of personality.[6]

More recent theorists have proposed formulations for comprehending character structure which arise out of the techniques and defenses designed to deal with anxiety. The character structure of an individual involves the perduring ways of dealing with the individual's social needs as well as his physiological needs. The typical ways in which he attempts to fulfill these needs constitute his character. They develop out of an interaction with the culture and the individual's experiences in his development. It is largely a phenomenological process and while certain zonal areas are involved, such as the mouth, anus, and genitals, their importance lies not in the presence of libido, but in the significance of these zones as areas of intimate relationship with the parents and the culture.

Most of the concepts proposed by Freud to develop his system of personality theory have been taken issue with in subsequent years. Several basic formulations which underlie the specific propositions, however, seem to have received very wide acceptance since

Freud's original work. In summary, there appears to be widespread agreement on the following:

A. Personality is the result of a dynamic development of the individual which is related to the personal history and experience of the individual.

B. The definition of unconscious and its manner of influencing behavior may vary sharply, but most behavioral scientists agree that our living is influenced by factors which are outside of immediate awareness.

C. The significance of childhood experiences in shaping personality is a notion that has raised more contention from a therapeutic point of view than a developmental point of view. There are different points of view concerning the necessity to explore and revive infantile experiences for the ultimate resolution of neuroses. Some feel this to be essential and crucial, although others view infantile recall as having value only as confirmatory data regarding observations obtained from current living.

D. Although emphasis on man and his biological substrate and instinctual requirements has stirred up considerable controversy, it has been the source of very fruitful debate among philosophers as well as among scientists regarding the essential nature of man. Whatever one's ultimate position, Freud has pointed up the biological heritage of man which Darwin first presented to the world. Every theory of personality must take this into account. Although some theorists reject Freud's extreme biologistic view of man's behavior and place the major emphasis on the culture, every useful psychological theory must rest to some extent on man's biological needs and requirements.

The theories which developed from Freud's biological, evolutionistic and mechanistic orientation are the source of continuing discussion and polemic. The libido theory, with its implications for character development, rests on the instinct theories of Freud with the ancillary hypotheses of the Oedipal triangle, castration anxieties, and penis envy in the female. The theories of anxiety which Freud developed arose directly out of his instinctual view of human behavior and have also been the sources of debate and modification.

NOTES

1. Breuer, J., and Freud, S.: Studies in Hysteria (1896). New York, Nervous & Mental Disease Publishing Co., 1936. This was one of the first studies in which the behavior of a patient was made comprehensible by the recall of previous episodes in the life of the patient.

2. Schachtel, Ernest G.: On memory and childhood amnesia. Psychiatry, 10:1-26, 1947. This paper is a refreshing examination of the whole matter of recall as it relates to psychoanalytic theory. It suggests the notion that individuals may remember childhood experiences which are unusual and painful

instead of repressing them. The pleasant and successful activities tend to be forgotten and are revived only through associative processes.

3. The authors limit their interpretation to the notion that the experiment contradicts the idea that affection is a response which is learned or derived in association with the reduction of hunger or thirst. They also assert that bodily contact and tactile sensations are decisive factors in eliciting the infant's attachment to his mother. Experiments of this type will help elucidate many of the so-called obvious notions about human development. While direct analogies cannot be made between animal and human behavior, the striking characteristics of these studies are the extent to which they point up the similarities. In the nature of love. Am. Psychologist, 13:673, 1958.

4. Rioch, D. McK.: Current Trends in Psychological Theory. Pittsburgh, University of Pittsburgh Press, 1951. See also:

Colby, Kenneth M.: Energy and Structure in Psychoanalysis. New York, Ronald Press, 1955.

Rappaport, Anatol: Operational Philosophy. New York, Harpers & Bros., 1954.

Frank, Phillip: Philosophy of Science. New Jersey, Prentice Hall, 1957.

Reichenbach, Hans: The Rise of Scientific Philosophy. Los Angeles, University of California Press, 1951.

5. Ross, James B., and McLaughlin, Mary M. (eds.): Salimbone, in A Portable Medieval Reader. New York, Viking Press, 1949 p. 366.

6. The libido theory has aroused considerable controversy inside and outside of psychiatric circles. Almost all serious psychoanalytic students from Jung and Adler to the current theorists such as Heniz Hartmann, Ernest Kris, Franz Alexander, Sandor Rado, Karen Horney and Jules Masserman have contributed to the debate. However, several recent books touch on this problem particularly. They include:

Monroe, Ruth L.: Schools of Psychoanalytic Thought. New York, Dryden Press, 1955.

Masserman, Jules H.: Principles of Dynamic Psychiatry. New York, W. B. Saunders, 1961.

Szasz, T. Z.: Pain and Pleasure. New York, Basic Books, 1957.

Schachtel, Ernest G.: Metamorphosis. New York, Basic Books, 1959.

Hartmann, Heinz: Technical implications of ego psychology. Psychoanalytic Quart. 20:31-43, 1951.

Freud, Anna: The Ego and Mechanisms of Defense. New York, International Universities Press, 1946.

Kris, Ernest: On preconscious mental processes. Psychoanalytic Quart. 19:540-560, 1950.

Lowenstein, Rudolph M.: The problem of interpretation. Psychoanalytic Quart. 20:1-14, 1951.

Hartmann, Heinz; Kris, Ernest; Loewenstien, Rudolph: Comments on the Formation of Psychic Structure. In psychoanalytic study of the child, Vol. II. New York, International Universities Press, 1946.

II

Review of Disputed Concepts

A REVIEW of some of Freud's concepts and some of the objections to them is necessary in order to get a clearer perspective of the more recent theories of personality development. It has been suggested that the newer theories merely emphasize single elements in Freud's original formulations and offer no new insights into the process of human development.

Are these newer theories merely semantic alterations? Is there a valid basis for dropping some of the language, such as "libido," "cathexis" or "defense," which has become so intimately involved in the traditional theories that one cannot evolve new conceptions without a new language? Do the new views draw on the more recent scientific developments in other sciences? Are the newer theories capable of elucidating the processes of pathological development as well as normal development? Do they yield data which can illuminate those areas of human functioning such as creativity, for example, which Freud's theories had great difficulty in comprehending? And, finally, can these theories stimulate new hypotheses which will maintain an expanding science of personality?

The current theories tend to emphasize motivational and adaptational elements in experiencing and consequently draw heavily on other sciences such as sociology, ethology, anthropology and philosophy. Freud and the early revisionists like Carl Jung, Alfred Adler, Sandor Ferenczi and Otto Rank remained in a genetic, instinctual framework and contributed to these ancillary sciences rather than drawing from them. Although Freud's genius for observation and description is without parallel, the interpretation of his observations and his conceptions of the dynamics of behavior have been expanded. This was inevitable, since he lived in a three dimensional world and in an era in which the physical sciences were dominated by a mechanistic, oversimplified conception of cause and effect.

When we evaluate the work of the theorists who followed Freud and the early revisionists, we notice not only practical and theoretical differences, but also major philosophical and scientific disagreements.[1] Some of Freud's students, such as Alfred Adler and Carl Jung, expanded his theories by altering the conception of the role of sex and instinct in personality development. They recognized more explicitly the influence of culture on personality development. Spiritual and ethical values became more than mere sublimations of the libido. Later, other psychoanalysts discarded the instinct theories and evolved theories of personality development which were not wedded to any mechanical or biological bias. In agreement with most anthropologists and sociologists, psychoanalysts viewed man as more than an instinct-ridden animal. Personality development was linked to the innate dichotomies in man's existence. Man was an animal and part of nature while he was also human and alienated from nature. In man's development from infancy into childhood and adulthood, the problems of maintaining security, esteem and independence were determined not only by his biology but also by his relations with his fellow man.

The developments in psychiatric theory and practice have proceeded in two directions. One was physiological, and the other was psychological. The physiological research and development drew on Freud's descriptive classification of mental illness and less on his psychological theories. It concerned itself largely with attempts to relate mental disorder to physiological disturbances in the brain, endocrine system, and other related organs. It produced a large number of physiological therapies with typical cycles of exaggerated and overly optimistic expectations, followed by sobering and modest reappraisals. From the excision of the large colon to the use of a variety of convulsive agents, culminating in excision or ablation of parts of the cerebral cortex, these procedures were all pragmatic and were unsupported by adequate theorizing. We are currently witnessing a drug cycle, which while it may be less harmful in some ways, will probably have the same denouement. These therapeutic approaches have enlarged our grasp of the value of milieu therapy and have contributed much to the neurophysiological understanding of human behavior. Recent biochemical research has the aim of discovering specific chemical causes for the major mental illnesses. So far there have been many claims but only limited validation of these claims. These approaches may have considerable influence on the psychological theories of the neuroses and psychoses, but whatever the findings and however valuable the pharmacological aids may be, they will not supplant or minimize the effective insights of the psychological theorists.[2]

Much of the theoretical value of these studies, aside from the undoubted practical value of these therapies, has been to encourage a greater integration of the physiological aspects of human development with the psychological processes that accompany them. Such integration is manifested in the exciting and promising developments in psychosomatic research. It has served as a major impetus to the growth and application of cybernetic and field theory approaches to human behavior. Such developments are subsumed under the rubric of communication theory, or systems theory. The researchers in these areas have generally been well trained in the psychodynamics of human behavior as well as in the neurophysiological correlates of such behavioral activity, and they are striving towards a unitary approach to the understanding of mental functioning as well as mental disorders.

The other direction of research restricts itself largely to the extension and amplification of the original theories of Freud and his co-workers. Its path is strewn with many dedicated and discarded disciples, such as Wilhelm Reich, who in accepting the libido theory went far beyond Freud in emphasizing sex as the core issue in human psychology. Others, although essentially accepting all of Freud's formulations, have recognized the necessity of broadening some of the original conceptions to conform with the newly discovered data about man's behavior. This group is exemplified by the work of Heinz Hartmann, Ernest Kris, and Rudolph Loewenstein, who have made many significant advances in ego psychology while retaining the essential framework of the libido theory and Freud's topology of the mental apparatus. They are the bridge between the extremists, who refuse to alter a single syllable of Freud, and those psychoanalysts who view Freud's work as the great exploration in human behavior, and who feel free to refine and recodify his notions when increasing skill and knowledge seems to indicate that this might be useful. They have attempted to fill the gaps in Freud's psychological system and to take into account the deficiencies of some of his theories.

Another group of psychological researchers are those theorists who have found it necessary to abandon some of Freud's hypotheses and to move in new directions. They all subscribe to the basic formulations regarding personality development, which were described in Chapter 1. Theorists such as Karen Horney and Harry Stack Sullivan have developed complete and consistent theories of personality development. Others, although developing only partial conceptions of personality, have presented novel and fruitful theories regarding the therapeutic process. They will all play a role in the final formulations regarding personality, but particular attention will be given here to the major theorists and systematizers.[3]

PSYCHOLOGICAL RESEARCH AND PHYSIOLOGICAL OVERTONES

Wilhelm Reich will be considered here because of the significance of his work in relation to the libido theory. Although he followed the classic tradition in his early years, and wrote an outstanding book called *Character Analysis,* he later undertook a direction of research that led to the most astounding consequences. He was either a genius or a madman, depending on one's point of view.[4] His significance rests on the validity of his vegetotherapy technique and his orgone discoveries. Strange to say, he was the only psychoanalyst who attempted to validate the libido theory. He claimed to have done so by the discovery and isolation of the libidinal energy, which he called orgone. His work can be divided into two phases; the pre-orgone, and the orgone phase. In the pre-orgone phase Reich was a brilliant, traditional analyst, and his work on masochism and the techniques of character analysis were milestones in psychoanalytic theory. Although he disagreed with the death instinct theory, most of his work during this period has been incorporated into psychoanalytic theory and practice. His description of character armoring amplified the understanding of the neurotic structure and paved the way for character analysis as opposed to symptom analysis. He identified the role played by the individual's character structure as a defense against change, which constituted the chief resistance to treatment. As a consequence, he developed a systematic approach to the uncovering of these resistances.

However, at a time when there was a growing dissatisfaction with the libido theory, Reich, taking the libido theory literally, began to search for the substance that heretofore was considered a hypothetical construct. He not only accepted the "mythological conception of libido," but claimed to have isolated the substance. Although he was profoundly interested in social and political matters, he conceived of human behavior as being exclusively and biologically determined by the presence of "orgone" substance.

In 1934 he linked character disorders with biophysical behavior and entered the orgone part of his work. In that year he was expelled from the International Psychoanalytical Association. In 1939 he claimed to have discovered a "visible ubiquitous cosmic energy" which he called "orgone." His rigid adherence to Freud's earliest theories proved him to be the only "true believer," and resulted in his claimed isolation of libidinal energy. The orgone theory of Reich is an expression of the extreme, mechanical, biophysical view of man as a functioning animal. Activity, experiencing, and the intricacies of interpersonal activity were seen as merely vehicles for the distribution of orgone energy. This served to reduce the focus of interest to the study of orgone rather than of man as a functioning being. This was reminiscent of the early years of Freud's work, when his preoccupying interest was in the vicissitudes of the instincts to the neglect of ego activity. All the deficiencies of Freud's theories were magnified in this approach.

The objections to Freud's explanatory conceptions of values, morals, and spiritual ideals as sublimations of sexual energy were elevated by Reich to a position of prominence. For Reich, man was not a complex individual with productive capacities on all levels, but a simple biological animal whose productivity was based upon his capacity to absorb and utilize orgone, and upon society's permissiveness to enable him to do so.

Since his philosophical orientation forced him into a physiological approach to mental phenomena, Reich occupied all his time with research in physics and chemistry. As a result, he developed the orgone accumulator, the orgone blanket, and other devices designed to concentrate orgone in the body. These devices were enjoined for interstate traffic, and his failure to comply with these restrictions led to his arrest, imprisonment and conviction, and finally to his death while in prison.

Although the validity of his orgone discovery is extremely doubtful, the *cul-de-sac* at which Reich arrived, and from which he could no longer withdraw, was produced by his position as a true Freudian whose theories pressed to the ultimate the earliest conceptions of Freud. Being philosophically and scientifically outdated, he became a martyr to an outgrown era of the history of the development of psychoanalytic theory. However, in the morass of his orgone bio-physics one can recognize significant contributions to an ultimate psychosomatic theory. As an offshoot of his work on muscular rigidity and armoring, he approached a true understanding of many of the bodily functions and their ultimate association with tension and anxiety. In spite of the difficulties, both cultural and profes-sional, in treating patients in the nude as he did, there is no doubt that anxiety and tension manifest themselves in other parts of the body besides the face and hands. Whether the loss outweighed the gain in studying the fully dressed patient remains an academic question, since the practice of psychotherapy cannot proceed in the atmosphere which Reich advocated. His elaborate studies of the orgasm have done much to clarify this aspect of the sexual function. It is doubtful that it is at the core of all successful mental func-tioning, or that it is an index of maturity, as Reich implied. However, his notion that the orgasm is not only a culmination, but the state of a pure somatic phenomenon from which the psyche is entirely removed is an intriguing and fruitful notion which has not been sufficiently examined or understood.

TRANSITIONAL GROUP

Hartmann, Kris and Loewenstein represent the thinking of many classic psychoanalysts who have attempted to reorganize the de-ficiencies in Freud's formulations rather than relinquish any of the concepts that are responsible for these deficiencies. They are a gifted trio and have presented some fascinating material with regard to ego development, the area largely neglected by Freud. They developed some concepts which avoid the postulate of the helpless, defenseless ego that draws its energy from the id. They postulated an undifferentiated id from which an autonomous ego can develop. Although their work has been far more extensive than is here indi-cated, it is also too technical for consideration here. It is of interest to notice at this point the necessity for some of the classical theorists to alter and expand and at times to negate (as with the death instinct) some of Freud's hypotheses in order to be more in accord with the data which is currently available to psychoanalysts. However, they remain classical theorists who maintain the basic orientation of the libido theory, and simply add to it whenever it appears deficient. At times this patchwork becomes quite confusing, but it avoids relinquishing the libido theory.[5]

NEO-FREUDIAN GROUPS

These groups represent a large number of theorists who are involved in a continuing reappraisal of Freud's theories. Most of them have substituted a variety of hypotheses to replace the libido theory. Some are system builders, such as Horney and Sullivan, while others expand on single concepts or broaden the base of therapy. The first group which, in addition to Horney and Sullivan, includes Erich Fromm, Sandor Rado, and others, has a common set of questions and concerns about the classical theories of Freud. They all take issue with Freud's mechanical and biological orientation and recognize the focal role of culture in personality development. They have abandoned the libido theory as having lost its usefulness in the further development of psychoanalytic theory and have offered alternative explanations for the mainsprings of human development. They acknowledge the role of values in the maturing process and deal with it as a positive force in personality growth. They view personality as the consequence of the interaction of the individual with his biological capacities and potentialities to the world he encounters. The world includes not only the intimate environment of the family, but the social, economic, political, and religious influences which bear on the family unit. They all agree that man's destiny is determined by more than his biology, even though it may ultimately be limited by it.

Freud's biological orientation incorporated his broad scholarship in the scientific philosophy of his time. He established psychoanalytic theory in the tradition of the physical sciences, which had many methodological and medical advantages. Although he clearly brought psychoanalysis into the realm of the medical sciences, it was restricted in its development by a too rigid application of the notion of constitutional or hereditary factors in personality development. Freud's biological bias introduced the notion of instincts into the libido theory and the hereditary nature of the libido, with its mechanical, developmental history. Freud's concerns about grounding psychic phenomena in biology led to his emphasis on the innate nature of certain human attitudes, such as the role of femininity and the ubiquitous nature of certain relationships between parents and children, which he called the Oedipus complex. This tended to obscure and neglect the cultural situation which also played a role in the development of such attitudes. Once a biological basis was established for the passivity of the female, for example, the cultural situation served only to validate this notion and eliminated the possibility of being the cause of it. Although it is evident that man is ultimately limited by his biologcal capacities, it is still an open question as to whether these capacities are all inherent in his heredity, or whether his heredity supplies only the raw materials which are developed and expanded by the social situation. This is the root of the neo-Freudian objections to Freud's biological orientation which minimizes the effect of culture and in the long run does not represent a valid picture of man. The neo-Freudians believe that Freud's view of man is only a partial one and that behavior is derived from sources beyond the physico-chemical forces that reside in the instincts.

A significant outgrowth of Freud's biological orientation was the assumption that biological sex differences were reflected in the psychology of the sexes and were based solely on these anatomic differences. This notion was already apparent in the bisexuality theory of sexual development. In his *Three Contributions to the Theory of Sex*, Freud, as his predecessors Krafft-Ebbing, Magnus Hirschfield, and a host of earlier workers in the field of sexology, accepted the concept of the bisexual constitution of human beings. This implied that in the course of development of the sexual apparatus, the sexual potentialities of both sexes are present. They felt that at a specific time, development proceeds in one direction, but the physiological and psychological remnants of the other sex remain to a greater or lesser degree in the adult individual. This conception, Freud said, "merely carried the notion of bisexuality into the mental life," and was based on rudimentary embryological remnants of the opposite sex in the individual's anatomy as well as a host of poorly formulated data about male and female characteristics.

While the conception of bisexuality had its origins in biology, biologists have recently denied it most emphatically. Frank P. Lillie, an eminent biologist, said: "Sex of the gametes and sex in bodily structures or expression are two radically different things."[6] Sandor

Rado, in a paper entitled "A Critical Examination of the Concept of Bisexuality," dealt with this problem and arrived at the same conclusion. He said: "To sum up this biological survey: using the term bisexuality in the only sense in which it is biologically legitimate, there is no such thing as bisexuality, either in man or in any of the higher vertebrates. In the final shaping of the normal individual the double embryological origin of the genital system does not result in any physiological duality of reproductive function."[6]

Based on the concept of bisexuality, Freud stated that in each sex there are not only the embryological rudiments of the opposite sex, but the inherent psychological characteristics of the opposite sex. Thus the male and the quality of maleness which is biologically associated with aggressiveness, activity, and other characteristics related to the pushing, forcing, and penetrating aspects of the male genital, also manifests to a greater or lesser degree the characteristics of the opposite sex. It is assumed in this theory that there lie dormant in every individual sexual needs, attitudes and psychological characteristics of the opposite sex. Implicit also in the bisexual theory was the primacy and higher value of the masculine apparatus and the inferiority of the female genitals. This notion was incorporated in Freud's concept of penis envy. The aggressive, pushing quality of the male genital was considered a greater virtue psychologically as well as physically. This conception was based exclusively on Freud's intuitive notions of the primacy of the male genital and was influenced by pagan ideas and Judaic and Christian theology. It resulted in many extraordinary ideas about the psychology of the female.

The neo-Freudian group of theorists have taken cognizance of this curiously prejudiced view of the male and the female and have drawn upon anthropological data to indicate that masculine dominated societies have not been a universal, biologically predetermined fact. They point up the evidence of cultural factors which place high value on aggressiveness as opposed to passivity and which give value to the "so-called masculine traits" as opposed to the feminine ones. They have raised strong doubts, as Rado does, about the bisexuality theory, indicating that embryological remnants are hardly conclusive evidence of the presence of psychological traits of the opposite sex. In addition, they feel that the penis, which has the capacity to deliver sperm, has no special pre-eminent role in the reproductive process and no privileged status in biological terms. Some point out the opposite, and indicate the privileged role of the female, who is capable of bearing and delivering the child.

There seems to be much evidence accumulating in recent years to support the thesis that women are not biologically inferior, but are, on the contrary superior, both physiologically as well as psychologically.[7]

Another widely established notion that has grown out of the bisexual theory is the concept of latent homosexuality, which has served as a catch all concept to account for a great deal of human behavior. The concept of latent homosexuality plays such a vital role in Freud's scheme of personality development that it will be dealt with later at greater length. Suffice it to say here that those investigators who have uncertainties about the bisexual theory are also uneasy about the concept of latent homosexuality.

PHILOSOPHICAL CONSIDERATIONS

Since Freud matured in an atmosphere that accepted Darwin and his evolutionary theories as well as the mechanical conception of physical phenomenon, Freud's view of man was in accord with these ideas. Man as an animal evolved out of the animal kingdom and in accord with the Christian view struggles to control his animal instincts which are base, destructive and lecherous. This view of man stresses the animal heritage rather than the human and views culture as a suppressing rather than an expressing force. Many of the theorists who object to the view of man as an instinct-ridden animal have been called sentimental humanists, since they picture man in terms of a tender, cooperative human, striving to fulfill his potentialities. Who are the realists and who are the sentimentalists remains an open question. There is increasing evidence that tends to refute the Darwinian thesis of the competitive struggle for existence. This sheds new light on the values of cooperative living as the basis for the evolution and development of the human species.

Freud's evolutionistic thinking is also manifest in his assumption that personality arises exclusively out of the past. This was expressed in his view that personality development ended at the age of five and that everything that occurred after five was merely a repetition or an accretion on the basic structure rather than a fundamental alteration. This is at variance with other theories of personality which visualize the process of development as continuing throughout the life of an individual and as dependent only upon one's capacity to benefit from life's experiences.

In spite of Freud's disdain for philosophy and philosophizing, he was a competent philosopher. Like Hegel and other dialecticians, Freud's theories evolved in a dualistic framework and were constantly involved in the pairing of opposites in his characterological types and dynamic formulations. Although this dualism is characteristic of the neurotic individual who sees life only in the extremes, Freud presumed it to be representative of all human performance. This duality concept influenced his notions of sexuality, hostility and ambivalence and was an essential part of his instinct theories. More recent theorists who have grown up in an era when the mechanical view of physical behavior was supplanted by the Einsteinian revolution posed their theories in terms of interactional or transactional processes, rather than in terms of energy, forces, or precise cause and effect relationships. Human performances are studied as operating in the context of a culture in which a great many forces operate and influence the organism. Although this has complicated theory, it has also brought it closer to a more valid view of the nature of the influences which impinge on man. The theory of relativity introduced the notion of the observer as a relevant factor in scientific operation, and this influenced psychoanalytic theorizing by stressing the non-neutral role of the therapist. It brought new insights into the investigations of personality development as well as in therapy. Most of the neo-Freudian theorists implicitly utilize these operations in their formulations. They tend to view man as more than animal in his ability to achieve a capacity for self-consciousness, no longer requiring harness or restraint.

LIBIDO THEORY AND INSTINCT THEORIES

The libido theory and the instinct theories were developed around the concepts of energy as a mechanical force which could be dammed up or allowed to flow freely. This accounted for the notion of fixation of libido under special conditions of stress or trauma, as well as the tendency to go back to established libidinal sources as in the process of regression. The libido theory was useful in developing therapeutic principles as well as developmental concepts. However, it is a hypothetical construct based on very limited evidence. It arose out of the genius of Freud's capacity to conceptualize in physical terms. A major objection to the libido theory is that it tries to explain too much. It becomes an explanatory concept for too many varied and dissimilar phenomena and is too inclusive and overgeneralized. For example, libido became not only the explanation of the source of all sexual activity but even included all artistic activity, spiritual interests, and intellectual pursuits. It was felt that these activities all derived from the libido, either directly, or through a sublimatory or altering force. The libido became the explanation for the source of all pleasureable activities.

Many theorists feel that the theory is insufficiently documented; that attempts to validate it have been largely negative. It has not yet been adequately demonstrated that the focus on the zonal areas of the mouth, anus, and genitals occurs by virtue of a concentration of libido rather than a sequence dictated by the essential needs for human survival. The concept of sublimation as an explanatory theory for the development of artistic pursuits and spiritual endeavors is largely undecided. Although it remains an attractive idea at times, on other occasions it reduces creativity to such absurdity that it sounds simple minded to espouse it.[8] The libido theory and the instinct theories are still metapsychological concepts and not undisputed facts. The fate of the death instinct is clearer, since most analysts have abandoned it entirely. This final formulation of Freud's instinct theorizing followed the first World War, when he was amazed and shocked by the extraordinary manifestation of aggression. This forced him to acknowledge the strength of the aggressive instincts, which were incorporated in his final instinct theory, as the life versus the death instincts, or Eros versus Thanatos. Freud postulated this instinct in a most fascinating volume, *Beyond the Pleasure Principle*, which is a brilliant sample of his skills in propounding and developing an idea. This imaginative flight, which utilized biological data to serve his thesis, makes this an invaluable book in understanding some of the other metaphysical concepts which have been considered inviolate in classical theory. The death instinct is more than a simple recognition that man will ultimately die. It is part of the concept of homeostasis that Freud favored and an example of the tendency to repeat, which Freud called the *repetition compulsion*. The death instinct incorporates man's aggressive instincts which are expressed as sadism or masochism and which represent the tendency to return ultimately to the inorganic state of death. This concept implies a constant state of warfare between man's instinct for survival and perpetuation of his relentless urge to reinstate his former inorganic self. The objections to this idea come from various sources and various theorists. Primarily, it is beyond validation in spite of all the evidence that clearly demonstrates man's hostile, aggressive impulses. However, hostility and aggression can be understood without having to postulate an instinct to account for it. Some theorists view hostility as the result of frustrated or denied needs and consequently see these as secondary developments rather than primary ones. The postulate of a primary aggression has encouraged a looseness about assuming responsibility for one's hostile actions as well as justifying the expressions of the feelings in the service of freeing one's self from instinctual bondage. It becomes a rationalization for one's destructiveness. Although this notion coincided with Freud's view of the essential nature of man, it ran smack against the humanistic view of man as a cooperative animal rather than an aggressive one.

The problem of masochism and sadism, which was so easily settled by the postulate of a death instinct, can also be understood in other terms. Since the problem of masochism is so widespread in the neuroses and psychoses in our culture, it will be considered in detail in a later chapter. Masochism, like hostility, can be viewed as a defense secondarily produced in response to anxiety of a particular kind. It develops in the interaction between people rather than as a primary basic instinct. Is there any justification for proposing complicated theories to explain phenomena that can be comprehended in simpler terms?

One interesting sidelight to the death instinct dilemma was the tendency in therapy to encourage the expression of hostility. This came to be considered a sine qua non of psychoanalytic therapy, and the better one became in expressing hostility, the better the analytic work was considered to be going, and the healthier the individual was becoming. This principle came to be applied very energetically in the treatment of depressive disorders. There is very little evidence that the expression of hostility, in itself, is useful in the resolution of mental disorders. Like any unacceptable feeling or impulse, its free expression is accelerated by the analytic process, which in turn, helps the analytic therapy to move along. However, the expression of hostility as such, often makes the patient more guilty and makes him feel less acceptable and consequently more defensive. Rather than accelerate the therapeutic process, it often slows it down or terminates it. It is hoped that the analytic work would, by uncovering the needs which produce such hostility, reduce the necessity for its expression, rather than accelerate it.[9]

CHARACTER STRUCTURE

The theory of personality development and the character structure of the individual was one of Freud's contributions to the science of psychology. On the basis of the libido theory, the development of personality rested on the vicissitudes of the libidinal energy as it fared in the zonal areas where it tended to concentrate. For various reasons, the libido might become fixated, or sublimated or manifested in ways other than a direct expression of its energy. This concept of character was an expression of the emphasis on the fate of the internal forces (instincts) as they shaped man's destiny. However, many anthropologists have described cultures in which character traits were dependent upon and derived from the specific cultural factors under which that community was organized. This has broadened the notion of personality development to include not only the hereditary or constitutional elements, but also the special requirements of a culture that may enhance or glorify certain values and deprecate others. It puts more emphasis on the study of child-parent interaction and child-community interaction rather than on the study of the intricacies of the unfolding libidinal organization. The study of personality in the hands of current theorists has been in the direction of recognizing personality as the result of the interaction of the individual with his culture. This notion has encouraged the interdisciplinary research by psychologists, sociologists and anthropologists. Sociological as well as anthropological findings are valuable in expanding conceptions of character, rather than in verifying or validating existing theory. The area of character structure has been the greatest impetus in involving psychology and psychoanalysis with the other social sciences.

OEDIPUS COMPLEX

Except for the association of Freud's name with sex and psychoanalysis, his concept of the Oedipus complex is the concept best known by both the lay and professional public. Although the description of the Oedipus situation is relatively simple, e.g., the development of a relationship between the child and the parent of the opposite sex, the implications, amplifications, and connotations of this notion are enormous. It has had a most salutary effect on the development of psychoanalytic therapy, even though its influence on theory has not always been as fruitful or illuminating. It is necessary at the outset to make clear that no observer, whether he be psychologist, psychoanalyst, sociologist or anthropologist, could fail to discover that what Freud described as the Oedipus situation occurs very frequently in all cultures with a variety of effects on the ultimate mental health of the individual. What is at issue is the interpretation of the phenomenon. How do we account for this phenomenon, and is it primarily sexually organized? Is it universal and biologically ordained with a history that is identical at all times and in all cultures? The most direct evidence for the influence of culture has been observed around the study of the Oedipus situation. At the same time, the validity of Freud's biological premises have received some severe blows in the attempts to verify Freud's universalized conceptions of the Oedipus complex.

Freud not only described this phenomenon with remarkable clarity and perceptiveness but presumed that it was a biologically determined event which was inevitable in the personal history of every human since the advent of man. Since it involved the libido, it had sexual roots and overtones. The successful resolution of the Oedipus complex was considered to be a crucial factor in achieving maturity. In the male it is resolved through the fear of castration caused by the child's concern about father's jealousy. The father's anger stirs up this castration fear, which forces the child ultimately to yield his interest in mother. The female child has greater complications in dealing with her Oedipal situation, and must make complicated readjustments in the process. Its faulty resolution or perpetuation leaves permanent and damaging effects on the personality. Consequently, its clarification in therapy is of utmost significance.

What are the concerns of many current theorists regarding this formulation? As was pointed out earlier, there can be no doubt about its existence. What is questioned is its nature and its destiny. Many analysts seriously doubt its universality and ubiquity. The question of its biological, hereditary nature is of the utmost importance, since it has been observed to be absent in cultures where parent-child relationships do not foster strongly dependent attitudes. This observation has strengthened the position of the culturalists, and the possibility of understanding the Oedipal situation from a cultural point of view has reduced the necessity for clinging to a biological theory of psychosexual development. The sexual nature of the attachment of the child for its parents, which may occur, can be understood in other than libidinal terms.

What are the alternative explanations for the presence of an Oedipal situation? It is hardly surprising that every child, male or female, develops its first strong attachment to the mothering figure, who is usually the female. This initial element in the Oedipal development can be simply understood in terms of dependency and the fulfillment of the basic nutritional and emotional requirements of the completely helpless infant. How is it that the female child frequently (for Freud, always) becomes noticeably interested and attached to the father while the male child remains attached to the mother? Many theorists feel that this is not a normal occurrence, but is evidence of some disturbed family constellation. Frequently there are seductive parents who play out their unsatisfactory sexual adjustments on the children and actively try to win over the child of the opposite sex. This may even result in sexual attachments developing in the child, and be precisely what Freud described in his Oedipus complex. Such seductiveness, which may be apparent to either of the marital partners, may arouse resentment and hostile attitudes toward the child. On those occasions it would be apparent that tenderness was lacking between the marital partners and that their relationship would be characterized by discord and mutual hostility. The play for the child would be an expression of frustration, irritation and revenge. Under these circumstances strong attachments, sexually tinged, might occur, but these would result essentially from a malevolent attitude toward the marital partner, and not from love. Although this is a possible basis for the development of an Oedipal complex in a child, it is not intended to account for its frequent occurrence.

Some theorists see this situation developing out of the need for the child to relate to the dominant individual in the family in order to get the maximum of security. It becomes a matter of security, and not sex, and the child relates to the parent that guarantees the greatest security.

The Oedipal situation can be understood on cultural terms, particularly in relation to the family constellation, its inner strains, and the neurotic needs of the parents. A mother who has little regard for her husband or the marriage may focus all her interest, time and affection on the child, who might be a male. She will communicate her primary interest in the child while discarding or neglecting the husband, which would arouse his resentment toward the mother as well as the child. Such neurotic needs of the parents often force the children into excessive attachments, for if the child is a girl, such a mother will push aside the child, who will then be forced to become attached to the father. In a family of male and female children, it is not too difficult to see the alignments occurring with exaggerated attachments to the parent of the opposite sex. Many such possibilities could be detailed, that would bring us to the familiar picture of the Oedipal situation. Consequently, a situation described by Freud as biologically determined could be produced by cultural factors unrelated at times to sex and determined largely by the security needs of the child. It could be a response to anxiety rather than an expression of the libido. The major objection of many current theorists is that the biological libidinal basis for the Oedipus complex cannot be validated and requires an additional hypothesis for the explanation of a phenomenon that can be understood on simpler grounds.

INFANTILE SEXUALITY

The basis for the Oedipus complex rests on many factors, but foremost among them is the assumption of sexual interests and concerns in the infant. Although much evidence has been presented to indicate its prevalence, closer examination reveals this evidence to be based on a prior acceptance of the existence of sexual interest in the infant and child. Much of the evidence for infantile sexuality is based on the notion that the infant's and child's play with his genitals is analogous and consequently the same as adult masturbation. It is also presumed that the pleased expression and quiet sleep which follows feeding is analogous to the orgasm, and so the oral area is thought to have libidinal aspects and that feeding has sexual overtones. This was reinforced by the knowledge that the adult frequently uses the oral area for sexual satisfaction in fellatio and cunnilingus. There is considerably more evidence adduced from reminiscences, phantasies and associations derived in adult analytic therapy. In recent years there has been greater hesitation in attributing sexual or libidinal interest in the infant for want of direct evidence of its presence. Reasoning by analogy and the forced reconstruction of the early years (forced by theory and not by deliberate design) has not satisfied many serious behavioral scientists. The activities of children which resemble adult activities, even when it is clearly genital play, may be a reflection of a more ubiquitous tendency noted in all mammals—that of curiosity and play devoid of sexual elements. Recently, the behavior of children has been observed and described rather than interpreted on the basis of a pre-existing view, and in this way a new perspective on the origins of this behavior has been achieved. Many theorists feel that it is unlikely that sex in any form enters the individual's life until the maturation of the gonadal apparatus. From this viewpoint, the Oedipal situation, whenever it occurs, is not viewed as having any relevance to libido, but to anxiety and security.

It should be noted that the documentation for any theory regarding human behavior is extremely difficult, and is complicated by the absence of statistical evidence. It is not always apparent that an Oedipal situation exists or that a piece of behavior has sexual elements until one has done a rather intensive investigation of the individual or the phenomenon. If one approaches a phenomenon with a predetermined explanation of cause and effect, then it is a fairly simple matter to identify such elements and interpret them as evidence for the theory. If one accepted the notion of the libidinal nature of infantile activity, then one could see many elements of sexuality in the attachment of a child for the parent of the opposite sex. On the other hand, if we examine the relationships between the child and his parents from a fresh viewpoint, many factors can be seen at work, sex among them. Although statistics are not definitive evidence in personality studies, they cannot be altogether discarded. Theoretical formulations should not be turned aside for lack of statistical evidence. Other criteria must be used for validation. One should however, avoid prejudicing the data by preconceptions. This applies particularly to the studies on infantile sexuality.

FEMININE PSYCHOLOGY

The psychology of the female as described by Freud is the least tenable and the most forced aspect of his theorizing. It was not only based on the biological differences between the sexes, which must inevitably account for some of the major differences in the psychology of the sexes, but it made an assumption about the superiority of the male as a biological entity. This resulted in the charge that his views were male-centered and that the female was viewed from the perspective of the male. Maleness and masculine traits have been the standard from which femininity was compared and contrasted. This resulted in many striking hypotheses about the female which are open to serious doubt and contention. Freud believed that woman has an incurable desire to possess the penis, and from this view he developed the concept of penis envy. Since it is impossible for woman to possess the penis, he said, she must accomodate herself in some way, either by relinquishing the desire, or substituting for it by having a child. Although Freud stated that this notion was based on the biological fact of the primacy of the male genital and the theory of bisexuality, it was determined largely by evidence of the apparently inferior role that the female played in all cultures throughout history. But in what ways is woman inferior? Why, in view of the possession of a very adequate genital apparatus of her own, does she desire the penis? In what way and at what time does she discover the superiority of the male genital? And most of all, from whose point of view is the male genital a most prized possession? Is it related to some of the apparent cultural privileges of the male? These questions are all relevant to Freud's description of the psychology of the female, since it rests most heavily on this desire and inability to obtain the penis. The evidence for this concept is extremely flimsy, and is based on material which again is capable of interpretation in other ways. His attempt to fit this thesis into the libido theory required many theoretical excursions which made his views difficult to accept.

Freud's conception of the superiority of the male genital was based on nothing but the retrospective recall of his female patients about their feelings of inferiority and the discovery in early years that they lacked something that the boys had. At times, they expressed some desire to have a penis because it was so desirable. This was coupled with the clear and present evidence that the female is envious of the privileges, prerogatives and cultural superiority of the role of the male. The envy was attributed to envy of the genital rather than envy of the male privilege in conformance with the libido theory. Although the phenomenon of envy can be clearly observed, it has been explained in different ways. The envy of the male can be understood in terms of the cultural advantages of being a male. Curiously, however, the area of sexual function is least likely to stir up female envy. Although culturally she may be more restrained in the expression of her sexual activities, her genitals are better equipped in many ways for more frequent and more satisfactory sexual experience than the male. The cultural differences and advantages are clear-cut. Karen Horney and Clara Thompson, as well as others, have developed this thesis very convincingly.

The result of the concept of penis envy was to draw many conclusions about the female in terms of passivity, masochistic tendencies, dependency, etc., and to ascribe it to biological inevitabilities which presumed that the female was more prone to neurotic disorders. This might be very significant if true, but the facts are somewhat at variance with these conclusions. Recent studies reveal that in most physical respects, except for muscular power, women are better adapted for their function than men. In addition, as the culture becomes less prejudiced toward women, and as opportunities open, it becomes clear that the women have capabilities and capacities that, while different, are formidable, and hardly inferior to the male.

Yet, the question still remains as to whether woman desires the male genital as well as the opportunities available to the male. What makes the male genital more desirable—its size? Its aggressive potentialities? Its ability to become erect? There is nothing intrinsic in any of these things to make the organ more desirable. On the contrary, its tendency to require a refractory period to enable it to function sexually renders it less formidable and efficient than the female genital.

Recent theorists have abandoned the biological basis for the understanding of the female and have recognized the major role that the culture plays in encouraging or discouraging some of the classically described female tendencies such as jealousy, passivity, etc. They account for many of the differences on the basis of the opportunities and handicaps that the culture imposes on woman. On the other hand, they do not overlook the fact that biological differences in terms of the role the male and female play do account for many characterological differences. It is obvious that the role of child bearing and rearing forces some needs such as security and dependency to be more an issue for the female. The requirements of settled, established modes of living have forced the female to have broader social perspectives. Man and woman are not equal. They are different, and their differences are biologically determined and culturally endowed. Motherhood is a social role destined only for the female, with whatever rewards and sacrifices it entails. It is a social necessity, and the female rarely resents the role. What she does resent is the prejudiced subservient status that motherhood endows on her.

TOPOLOGY

The divisions of the mind into ego, superego, and id were extremely valuable categories to simplify the complexities of mentation and the operation involved in any mental act. Although at first they were clear-cut and separate, it soon became apparent that any attempt to artificially schematize mental activity over-simplified as well as distorted the fantastically complex operations involved in human mentation. Although most current theorists have maintained the terminology, they do not use the topological classification in the schematized fashion as the classical therapists do. They do not, for example, describe neurotic events as being a conflict between the id and the superego, but rather speak of the patient's ideals and values coming into conflict with unconscious needs. This change in language is more than semantic pettiness, for it allows for a broader conception of the neurosis than the id-superego framework.

In addition, there are many aspects of Freud's description of these areas that are not wholly acceptable to current theorists. It was indicated earlier that Freud's preoccupation with the id and its content left the ego area largely unexplored. Most of the recent developments in psychoanalytic theory are attempts to fill this gap.

Freud's ego was a confusing conglomeration of desexualized instincts, sublimated instincts, and the organized part of the id. Its essential character, however, was its weakness and its dependency on the id, superego, and the external world. This notion of the ego may be applied clearly to the neurotic who behaves as if he had no control over his behavior or his destiny. It is a distortion of the activity of the non-neurotic whose ego does not conform to this description, since he does not appear to be controlled by forces outside of his immediate control. Consciousness and our knowledge of the ego and its structure and functions are still largely unknown and require extensive research. Current theorists have attempted to reduce this gap through their investigations into ego psychology.

There is even more disagreement in considering the id. The nature of the unconscious, its contents and functions are all matters of dispute. The id is not considered to be the mainspring of human motivation as it was for Freud. This is seen as residing in man's need (which can be described biologically, physiologically, or existentially) to express and fulfill his potentialities. Freud saw the ego as dependent and at the opposite pole of id and at war with the id. It was a battle between good and evil, or the animal nature versus human nature. Current theorists see the id as an expression of man's deeper, unrecognized need, and not in opposition to the ego. They are usually conjunctive and cooperative.

This philosophical difference has had profound consequences for the ultimate development of alternative hypotheses in personality development.

The concept of the superego represents the incorporated moral standards of the significant adults in the individual's life. For Freud these standards represented rigid, stringent requirements which forced the individual toward perfection and was synonymous with conscience except that it was more strict. This concept of morality and guilt did not account sufficiently for the prevalent phenomenon of pseudo-guilt, in which the individual uses guilt and guilt feelings as a defense against change. Current theorists find the concept of superego useful, but limiting, since it seems to be a mixture of a healthy conscience with a neurotic, compulsive one. They have distinguished between values, morality, and standards as formulated by the individual's goals and his mode of living as opposed to the incorporated attitudes and standards of the parental figures which may be acting as neurotic foci of conflicting standards and ideals. The importance of values and standards has been emphasized by current theorists and given a central role in personality development.

NOTES

1. These differences are systematically explored in several books:

Horney, Karen: New Ways in Psychoanalysis, New York, W. W. Norton & Co., 1950.

Mullahy, Patrick: Oedipus, Myth and Complex. New York, Hermitage Press, 1948.

Hall, Calvin S., and Lindzey, Gardner: Theories of Personality. New York, John Wiley & Sons, Inc., 1957.

2. It must be emphasizezd, however, that the drug therapies, unlike the earlier and more destructive physiological therapies, can play a most important ancillary role in the psychological treatment of the mental disorders. These drugs are quite useful in controlling the behavioral manifestations of the disorders even when they have no specific or etiological effect. The excessive and undisciplined use of drugs has tended to detract from their value as amelioratives rather than curative agents.

3. There is some virtue aside from brevity in concentrating on a few theorists rather than making a cursory survey of all of them. This has already been done by several authors, notably: Harper, Robert: Psychoanalysis and Psychotherapy —36 Systems. New Jersey, Prentice-Hall, 1959.

A superficial sketch of the extent and variety of these theories cannot convey the depth or suggest the validity of these views, and can become sufficiently confusing to force the student to attach himself prematurely to one theoretical approach, rather than get an adequate taste of the others. Consequently, I will limit myself to those which can be presented in a brief chapter, and whose theories are more direct outcomes of Freud's original contributions, as well as those which promise to be most useful in the ultimate development of a unified personality theory.

4. Although his later work has appeared largely in the journals of his Orgone Institute, the extent of his ultimate illness can be gauged from two illuminating volumes called: The Murder of Christ, and People in Trouble. Maine, Orgone Institute Press, 1953. These books, alternately dull, accusatory, repetitious, and polemical, reveal the extent of his messianic fervor and his alienation from psychology as a science of human behavior.

5. This point of view is shared by the adherents of the classical Freudian theories. Anna Freud has led the way towards the study of the ego and its role in personality development. The psychoanalytic journals, namely, *the Journal of the American Psychoanalytic Association* and *Psychiatry, the Journal of Interpersonal Processes*, regularly publish articles which are attempts to bridge the transition from classical theory to neo-Freudian theory.

6. Psychoanalysis of Behavior. New York, Grune and Stratton, 1956., also

Lillie, F. R.: General biological introduction. In Sex and Internal Secretions. E. Allan, Ed. Baltimore, 1931.

7. The evidence has been collected and presented in a most controversial book by Ashley Montagu entitled: The Natural Superiority of Women. New York, MacMillan Co., 1953. The qualities of superior and inferior are not moralistic judgments, but refer entirely to the adaptive capacities of the sexes to fulfill their biological roles. The female appears to be better equipped physiologically to fulfill her role than the male; however, the greater muscular capacity, social flexibility and freedom from periodic physical limitations has enabled the male to assume a primary and superior social role in most cultures.

8. See Schachtel's *Metamorphosis*. Creativity may be related indirectly to sublimatory processes, but the impetus for all forms of artistic activity, plastic or verbal, or for the multitude of activities that characterize man, is sparked by man's need to utilize his capacities. The ability to express oneself freely, spontaneously, and independently must be a total expression of one's personality and not the simple transfer of libidinal energy.

9. A colleague, Dr. Marianne H. Eckardt, in an unpublished manuscript, has put it rather succinctly. She says: "Repeatedly, I run into what I call the gut theory of analysis. Briefly stated, it means that whatever makes my guts feel good is good. It is mostly encountered in connection with the need to express rage. If rage fills the gut with tension then this discharge is healthy from a mental hygiene point of view. The added reasoning is that repression of anger would allow it to emerge in a more subterranean fashion and be even more destructive. This theory is stupefying. We are never justified in using other people as receptacles for our vomitus. Sometimes this cannot be helped and we apologize, but we cannot lift it to the status of a beneficial therapy. The rage is a problem usually of undue impotence, and the answer lies in finding one's capacity for potent action and not making a ridiculous spectacle of oneself.'

III

Early Revisionists and Karen Horney

KAREN HORNEY's system of psychoanalytic theory constituted the first major attempt to reformulate Freud's theories into a consistent total theory of personality. There had been other major defections from the original theories on both ideological and philosophical grounds before this, but they remained largely in the framework of the libido theory even though libido was defined somewhat differently.

After a prolonged set of disagreements with Freud, Alfred Adler broke with the traditional psychoanalytic group in 1911 and established his own school of psychoanalysis which he called Individual Psychology. Adler took issue with the notion that the libido was primarily sexual and that personality development was determined exclusively by the fate of the instincts. He maintained that power and the need to overcome one's deficiencies, both constitutional and environmental, determined the motive forces for human development. He recognized that the influence of man's goals and values played a crucial role in this process. Man's goals were expressed in terms of a "guiding function," which laid the guide lines for the individual striving to fulfill his destiny. Sex was only one tool among the many whch were available to the individual in his struggle to achieve superiority. Since Adler's psychological theories were male-centered, he derived the concept of masculine protest as the explanation for much of the activity of the female, which seemed to be directed toward achieving the status of the male. In recognizing the significance of the culture in determining the areas of superiority with which man was endowed, he implied a major role to cultural issues in determining his development. This finally led to a set of conceptions revolving about the need to socialize one's activities and to participate cooperatively in a "community." He tended to minimize the intrapsychic forces and emphasized the social pressures in adaptation. He established a theory of personality which went beyond merely explaining the behavior and character of human beings. Adler's theory, although radically different from Freud's, maintained the libidinal basis of development and operated in Freud's mechanical, dualistic and biological framework. Although he put the role of sex into the perspective of another operation of human activity, he assigned the role of power in human performance to the exalted role that sex had previously held. This was a similarly oversimplified view of the sources of human behavior. Although Adler emphasized the role of the culture, he was still tied down to the biological substrates of organ inferiority, in spite of the fact that he recognized that human adaptive activities were involved in what Freud considered to be constitutional. His therapeutic innovations stressed the future rather than the past and eliminated some of the sacred rituals of technique to shorten the whole process. It seems clear, however, that although Freud considered Adler's views unpsychoanalytic because he felt that Adler had relinquished the concept of the unconscious and stressed the ego aspects of personality, this would not be considered as such a striking deviation today. Adler's theories constituted a new theoretical system, and his major heritage was the recognition of factors other than the biological in organizing the personality. He presented a vivid picture of neurotic development based on motives and sources other than the sexual, and he was a forerunner of the later developments in ego psychology.[1]

Carl Jung, having developed and expressed dissenting views of Freud's theories, was the next to disassociate himself from Freud in 1912. Although Jung's views did not vary greatly from Freud's, he ultimately developed them into a system which bears little resemblance to psychoanalysis or psychotherapy. Adler, who was respected by Freud to a lesser extent than was Jung, made a firmer impact on psychoanalytic history. For the past 25 years Jung had been more of a mythologist, semanticist and comparative anthropologist than he had been a psychologist or therapist. His views were developed in the same mechanical mold as Freud's, and Jung tended towards an even more rigid dualistic view of human behavior. He saw libido as a more generalized life force and considered it to be an undifferentiated energy, sexual and nonsexual. His view of the development of personality rested heavily on the archetypical concepts he developed rather than on the zonal distribution of libido, but it was an even more schematized and mechanical unfolding than Freud's. Although Jung put greater emphasis on the role of the mother in early development, his view of personality development was dependent on fixed, instinctual tendencies and inherited ancestral archetypes and collective memories.

Jung emphasized many of the positive aspects of the personality as opposed to Freud and recognized that the artistic, aesthetic and spiritual interests of man have sources beyond the mere sublimation of the sexual interest. He also recognized that the process of repression affected positive elements as well as negative ones in personality development.

Although at first he introduced some valuable therapeutic innovations such as the notion of therapy as a mutual, interactional process of patient and therapist, it soon became an exercise in unrestrained phantasying, which resulted in the undue emphasis on dreams and their interpretations.

The later work of Jung and his followers consisted in extensive research in comparative mythology and semantics, with only a suggestion of their applications to the therapeutic process. Jung's system was not a radical departure from classical theory at the outset, but later on it became totally divorced from the main line of psychoanalytic theorizing and practice. Jung's contributions were very significant in extending the concepts of countertransference and in stressing the creative, positive aspects of the personality. On the other hand, his more rigid application of Freud's theoretical and scientific framework extended and glorified the symbol as a personality tool and elevated the unconscious and its mechanized role in personality to a higher level than Freud ever conceived it to be. Although Jung was a first rate mythologist and cultural anthropologist, he added little to the role of culture in personality development except in terms of the clarification of the early parent-child relationships. His background finally led him to develop a semi-mystical religio-philosophical system of psychology which is very important in studying myths, religions, phantasies and semantics but has little application to the field of applied psychology.

During the early years of the development of psychoanalytic theory, encouraged and stimulated by the enormously productive and provocative concepts of Freud, his colleagues extended and reaffirmed his formulations. At the same time other colleagues were raising serious questions about some of his concepts, but these were centered largely on the instinct and libido theories. It is important to note some of these for historical reasons.

Otto Rank made the greatest impact on social work theory and technique with his concept of will therapy. He also contributed greatly to the psychoanalytic therapeutic process. Rank dignified the status of the neurotic by showing that it was the efforts of the neurotic to overcome his deficiencies and limitations which produced the neurotic symptoms. The creative artist however, had already succeeded in overcoming his limitations. The so-called normal individual was the most maligned and was considered to be unproductive. Rank felt that the normal person had merely accepted his limitations without attempting to surmount or transcend them. He gave dignity to the neurotic, and to the neurotic process, which heretofore had been viewed as either a constitutional weakness or degeneracy. He saw the neurotic process as one of repair or adaptation and as a striving toward a fuller and more productive existence. Although Rank accepted the libido theory, he postulated the birth trauma as basic to the neurosis rather than the Oedipal situation. His contributions to therapy are most significant. His attempts to shorten the process produced novel and exciting experiments. One of these was to set a termination date to the therapeutic process by analogizing therapy to gestation which should be completed in 9 months. In Rank's hands, therapy became a more active process in which the patient was encouraged to assert himself and strengthen his "will." He clarified the cultural status of the analyst with *his* "power possibilities," and focused on the dynamic aspects of the doctor-patient relationship. In Rank's concept of will, he envisaged the development of personality as extending beyond the scope of the instinctual demands. This implied the necessity of developing a "counter-will," in order to overcome the demands of the culture symbolized by the authority of the parental figures. The stress was in the direction of acknowledging the role of the cultural situation in inhibiting creativity and fostering the neurotic development. He was another forerunner in the growing trend towards an ego psychology, and he greatly influenced the client-centered therapeutic approach of Carl Rogers.[2]

Sandor Ferenczi was another innovator, particularly in the philosophy of therapy. He, too, remained within the framework of the libido theory, and was an active experimenter in the problems of variations in the analytic technique. He felt that the therapist must be flexible and fulfill the needs of the patient. Although some of these variations were often extreme, he left the heritage of the therapist who is responsive to the needs of the patient, rather than to the technical rules of theory.

Karen Horney's contribution to the expansion of psychoanalytic theory lies in the bold step which she took in formulating a dynamic, psychoanalytic theory of the neuroses based on Freud's basic principles, but differing in many essentials. Although making a complete break with Freud's instinctual orientation, she developed a consistent theory of personality without the libido theory and other doubtful psychoanalytic concepts. Her theories draw heavily on other contributors to psychoanalytic theory such as Rank, Jung, Ferenczi and Reich. Her foundations are closest to Adler's ideas, although her work has a broader base.

Karen Horney was trained in the classic psychoanalytic tradition in Germany. She came to the United States in the 1930's and published extensively shortly after her arrival. Her views developed during her lifetime, and she made many alterations in her conceptions as the results of a greater familiarity with American culture and a dissatisfaction with her earlier formulations. Her final views were presented in her book, *Neurosis and Human Growth,* which was published shortly before her death. The following presentation of her views are drawn mainly from this book.

For Horney, neurosis is not only a deviation from healthy behavior qualitatively and quantitatively, but it is also antithetical to good health and opposed to productive, healthy development. The typical, neurotic vicious circle is one in which the individual shifts his energies toward developing an idealization of himself and sets up rigid systems of dictates in order to escape his anxieties. The neurotic development not only misuses energies in unproductive ways, but becomes the focus for further deviations and distortions of the individual's interests and goals. In this sense, the neurosis is unhealthy and encourages further unhealthy development. Her notions regarding the neuroses were related to her conception of morality. Any motivation or action which is conducive to human development is moral, while any action which impedes or obstructs this development is immoral. This underlying hypothesis regarding human development is a positive, humanistic and optimistic one in contrast to Freud's instinctual, motivational hypothesis, which regards man as an individual overcome by hostile and sexual needs which must be restrained and controlled.

Her basic hypothesis, which is subject to the same difficulties of validation as Freud's theory, is that there is an inner urge or drive toward the fulfillment of one's potentialities. If this urge is not interrupted or interfered with, the individual will develop what she calls his "real self." This hypothesis comes very close to the notion of a "self-expressive instinct," but it is not what Horney means to convey. It is more than mere self-expression. It is a total pressure towards overcoming one's deficiencies and anxieties which are inherent in human existence. This pressure is a positive force beyond the mere avoidance of pain and represents an active search for the full utilization of all one's capacities. This hypothesis implies that the cultural situation plays a crucial role in the search for security and that development proceeds out of more than the pressures of man's instincts.

Harry Stack Sullivan formulated the same concept in another way by emphasizing man's desire to fulfill his *innate* capacities. This stress makes the concept less mystical and metaphysical. He rooted this desire in man's ultimate biological heritage without postulating any instincts to account for it. This hypothesis, in one form or another, is the basic motivational framework of most of the neo-Freudian psychologies. Although this hypothesis has its own weaknesses and drawbacks, it avoids the very questionable instinct and energy concepts and the necessity for a multitude of second and third order assumptions of neurophysiological correlates of energy exchanges. Its formulations are more closely linked to observable data, which then form the basis of generalizations about human development.

Horney said that in order for the organism to grow and develop, it must have an atmosphere of acceptance, warmth, affection, and benevolent interest, as well as nutritional supplies. This requirement was firmly established in the highly significant research of Rene Spitz and Margaret Ribble.[3] Horney stated that the unfavorable atmosphere which is conducive to the development of a neurosis is one of hostile malevolence in which the anxieties of the infant are exaggerated and sustained. An atmosphere of out and out hostility is often the easiest parental attitude to deal with. Under circumstances of pretended affection or inconsistent affection, however, or where parents are involved in difficulties between themselves, the developing human may undergo considerable damage. The ultimate issue, therefore, is the family constellation and the varieties of relationship and attitudes which exist between the parents and towards the child. In an atmosphere of malevolence the child develops what Horney has called "basic anxiety," which is the feeling of helplessness in a hostile world. Since anxiety is a feeling which cannot be repressed or overlooked, it must be dealt with. The infant uses the only three possible alternatives available to it: a) avoiding situations which produce anxiety, and withdrawing from unnecessary exchanges with the environment. This is presumed to be the forerunner of schizophrenia and, if severe enough, can produce what Rene Spitz has called the anaclitic depression; b) attempting to force a change in the environment or the responsible individuals in the environment through whatever means are available to the infant. Horney calls this moving against the source, or c) compromising, or making adjustments to the situation, or making peace with it. Horney calls this moving towards the source.

These three techniques are utilized by all individuals throughout their lives in dealing with anxiety, and since they are often mutually contradictory, it becomes necessary to focus on one of the maneuvers in order to minimize the disruption caused by such conflicting tendencies. Although the ultimate personality structure will contain all three types of defenses, one will usually predominate.

In order to deal with the anxiety produced by the situation and the anxiety produced by the attempts at solution which create conflicts, Horney suggests that imagination begins to play its role in personality development. This begins as early as the second year, and may play a role in personality development for the remainder of one's life. The imagination, or the power of thinking to influence behavior was the discovery of Freud. This occurred at a crucial point in Freud's career, when he discovered that his patients were describing traumatic situations and sexual adventures which had never actually occurred. At that time he was faced with either abandoning his theories entirely, or accounting for this frequent occurrence. He suggested that the events themselves need not have actually transpired, but that the phantasies or imaginative mental play regarding these events were capable of producing traumatic effects, sometimes more severe than if the events had actually transpired. This became the cornerstone in all his subsequent discoveries. Horney added further meaning to the process of imagination or daydreaming by elucidating its role in the development of personality as a regular accompaniment of the maturing process. It can serve as a simple antidote to everyday frustrations and disappointments as well as become the focus for profound personality disturbances. Although daydreaming is most noticeable in the early years, it remains a part of our lives, and is utilized in positive and creative ways as well as in problem-solving which is often unconstructive and infantile. Horney recognized that the daydream is an attempt at a solution of a problem which the child has to face in dealing with his anxieties and insecurities. The daydream overcomes the problem by idealization, glorification or enhancement of the particular personality defect which appears to be producing the anxiety. This is the "Walter Mitty" syndrome which is recognizable in everyone. Horney has demonstrated that the particular daydream is highly personalized and deals specifically with the individual's needs. It reveals the details of the neurotic problems that he is attempting to solve. The propensity to phantasize is utilized in many projective tests, such as the Rorschach or Thematic Apperception Tests. Since anxiety creates conflicting tendencies, the daydreams are also contradictory and conflicting, and it becomes necessary to discard, or repress, or take out of focal awareness some of the daydreams, while maintaining and elaborating others. The basis for this selection depends on the nature of the most pressing need as well as the particular opportunities in the situation for potential fulfillment of the daydream.

The child, for example, who must always be the first and pushes other children aside, may have dreams which make him a monarch, a baseball hero, or a feared gangster. At the same time, he has a great need to be liked by everyone, and indulges in the daydream of the kind, retiring philanthropist. Such needs and daydreams are contradictory, and ultimately (depending on where the need is greatest), one must be pushed aside to avoid the more distressing situation of feeling torn by opposite feelings. Those needs which are pushed aside are not necessarily permanently abandoned and may play a role in one's life by the out-of-awareness activity which may represent the part of oneself that one longs to be. This notion makes many aspects of the neurotic process very clear, and like Adler's "guiding fiction," helps us to better understand the neurotic structure.

It helps us to recognize the neurotic's plaintive cry that he is not being what he wants to be or fulfilling his real self, since it has become necessary to discard aspects of his personality that are unacceptable and undesirable in some cultures in order to achieve security. Often these discarded tendencies are positive and productive. In our culture and in Western society in general, tenderness, softness and decency are frequently not highly regarded, and as a consequence they are pushed aside. Instead of developing tender feelings, one tends to present a front of being strong, unemotional and unaffected by other people's interests. Tender feelings that have been pushed aside have few outlets in our culture. They are often expressed toward pets or in secret passions for sentimental books and movies. There is a significant tendency in some cultures to repress the more positive, tender feelings and attitudes as opposed to the hostile, aggressive ones.

Freud's theories necessitated the repression of the animalistic instincts such as hostility, sexuality, etc., and it implied that cultures developed out of the repression of these basic animal forces. It is now becoming clear that at certain times and in certain cultural settings, fewer animalistic but more humanistic tendencies may be repressed. In our Western society this is certainly the case. Hostility is freely expressed, and the more brazen, aggressive, exploitative attitudes encouraged. To be strong, adventurous and without fear is a virtue. To be kind, sensitive, and soft (meaning attentive to people's needs) is unpopular, dangerous, and leaves one insecure. The free expression of tenderness is discouraged and in the male it is often maligned by the label homosexuality. Consequently, tenderness is often repressed in our culture. Horney's conception of neurotic development accounts for this phenomenon far more effectively than Freud's theories do by emphasizing the tendency to repress those aspects of our personality that will stimulate anxiety. This is in contrast to the implied assumption in Freud's instinct theories that certain drives, particularly those of sex and aggression, require repression since they automatically strive for expression. Certainly sex and hostility are frequently the focus of repression, but other feelings and attitudes may also be repressed if the culture does not value or reward them.

Horney recognized the need to select one daydream, or one type of solution to the anxiety problem and focus on it. Ultimately this idealization becomes the nodal point in the patient's living and all his energies go into the attempt to actualize, or to become the idealization. Idealization, or glorification is an attempt to overcome a defect which, in the neurotic structure, becomes a pillar of the neurotic's esteem. Even though it is associated with perfectionistic needs and standards it is still essentially an effort to enhance a particular character trait that the individual feels is deficient and which has become a source of anxiety.

Such idealizations are called neurotic because they are insatiable, relentless, compulsive and indiscriminate. The individual no longer has any choice; he must strive to fulfill his ideal under all circumstances and at all times, regardless of the significance of the situation. If a person must be first, then he cannot accept anything but first place, whether in school, in his profession, or in any area of his living. He simply must be first, though the achievement may ultimately be harmful. The compulsive aspect of this kind of behavior occurs in all the neuroses, not only in the compulsive neurotic. The individual is left with the feeling that he is not the master of his own behavior or destiny. He feels forced, pushed, and unable to do anything about this feeling, since he is unaware of what is causing it. There is simply the necessity for being or doing something to which he may have many objections. These strivings are quite distinct from healthy, self-assertive and competitive activities. The neurotic strivings are relentless in that one cannot alter or compromise them. Since they are idealizations and cannot ever be achieved, the individual is perpetually dissatisfied, even if he may momentarily feel successful and secure. The neurotic strivings are open-ended, never achieved, and consequently, are ultimately self-destructive. Though these strivings often seem to produce some success and are considered necessary by the individual, the success and creativity is flimsy and devoid of real satisfaction. It is quite different from the values and standards that come from the spontaneous, unforced activity of the truly creative individual. The output of one's labor may be the same if one is forced by an overseer, or by inner neurotic drives, or by spontaneous interest in the activity. The difference lies in the feelings of personal reward and satisfaction, and the quality of the work being done.

In order to support the personality structure of an individual who is attempting to be, or to actualize his idealizations, he demands recognition from the community. Reality has an unpleasant way of intruding itself into peoples' lives, much against their will. These idealizations are so extreme and so impossible of fulfillment that the neurotic is periodically forced to acknowledge that in reality, he has little likelihood of achieving them. One way of overcoming this discomforting awareness is through the claims that he makes on the environment. This concept of the claim is a very valuable addition to the understanding of the neurotic process and is a most useful concept in therapy. Although the concept originated with Dr. Schultz-Heincke, it is utilized to its fullest by Karen Horney. The neurotic attempts to maintain his idealization and overcome the evidences of its inadequate fulfillment by demanding that society deal with him as if his idealization were actually achieved or actualized. This is called a claim as opposed to a legitimate demand or request that an individual has the right to make on his environment. The claim is a neurotic demand and is super-imposed on our basic needs. These claims are exorbitant, exaggerated demands that are unrealistic, insatiable and indiscriminate. It does not seem unreasonable for an individual to want to be liked by everyone. However, for the neurotic, the claim is an insistence on being liked by everyone, at all times, under all circumstances, and in the manner prescribed by himself. This makes it a claim. Everyone has the right not to be excessively criticized for everything he does, since, as a human being, he has inevitable weaknesses and deficiencies. The neurotic not only asks to be immune from criticism, but demands that he be free of it at all times no matter what he does. These claims are valuable clues to the understanding of the nature of the neurotic's insecurities and the idealizations designed to deal with them. In addition, they serve to protect the idealization. This is particularly so in therapy, where the identification of a claim will reveal large segments of the nature of the neurotic process. However, this is only the beginning, for it is a very difficult problem to get the patient to agree that he is making a claim, rather than a legitimate demand. For example, if the patient makes the claim that he should be beyond criticism because his idealization requires him to be invulnerable and omnipotent, then one can assume that the problem being dealt with in the neurosis relates to anxiety in connection with the feeling of helplessness and inadequacy. This particular constellation, incidentally, is characteristic of the obsessive-compulsive neurosis. This type of individual insists on being invulnerable at all times, and this is achieved through a marked indecisiveness which prevents the person from making any decision which will then leave him vulnerable. By avoiding a decision and remaining uncommitted, he remains free of criticism and avoids making an error. He makes a choice only when he is forced to by the exigencies of living. Even when he does he will still remain in doubt or else will disown it. In this way he avoids responsibility for his living. The compulsive individual looks for all sorts of hedges and guarantees before he will commit himself. The claims are all made in terms of being freed from responsibility and criticism and in getting guarantees for any decision that is made.

This pattern can immobilize living to such an extent that often the individual, in his need to maintain his idealization, refrains from activities that are essential to his existence. One such patient started to buy a car many years ago. In order to get the best car for the money and a guaranteed purchase, he studied the literature and the specifications of all cars within his income bracket. By the time he had made his choice, the new cars were on the market, and the same process had to be repeated for the new models. After many years of studying the market and the consumer reports, and checking with friends, the prices on all cars had advanced to such a point that in desperation he stopped at the first dealer closest to his home and bought the first car he looked at. He had avoided making a decision, since this purchase was impulsive. He took no responsibility for this purchase, and remained free to criticize the automobile without recognizing his role in the entire project. The claim to perform ideally often prevents one from acting at all.

An interesting aspect of these claims is that they are generally secret, unexpressed and out-of-awareness, so that the individual appears to himself and others only to be trying to do the best he can. Consequently, such people are sensitive and touchy, and are easily hurt and resentful. Their expectations of others are not precisely formulated and are frequently unfulfilled. For example, they feel that they should not need to tell others about their needs and desires; these should be known and understood. They expect their mates to know precisely what they want. They will say: "If you loved me, you should have known, I shouldn't need to tell you." Their claim is for total understanding, which does not require verbal communication because in true love, the partners should know each other perfectly. What it most often comes to, however, is that the individual expects his partner, friend, or colleague to either read his mind, or to know how completely virtuous, honest, and loving he is without having to manifest such behavior. It should be taken for granted.

When the neurotic's claims are refused, he gets angry, and it is frequently possible to recognize a claim by the reaction to its denial. This is in contrast to the denial of a legitimate request which may result in reasoned and energetic behavior to help attain it. The reaction of rage which characterizes the response to a frustrated claim may not be openly expressed, since it will reveal the person's weakness. Instead, such resentments are stored up and maintained through an elaborate bookkeeping system, to be held in reserve and used as ammunition on suitable occasions.

If, after an extended process of therapeutic work, the patient agrees that he is making an unreasonable claim, there is the possibility that he is making a claim out of his agreement. He may then preserve his idealization or illusion of perfection by being willing to admit an error which serves to confirm his grandiose self. The bulk of the work in treatment often revolves about exposing these claims, and demonstrating their role in the neurotic process.

Although the claims are neurotic demands on the world, the "tyranny of the shoulds," as Horney calls it, is what the neurotic demands of himself. These "shoulds" are the inner, unreasonable, extravagant, and unrealistic demands he makes on his own performance at all times and under all circumstances. These inner demands consist of all the things his idealization requires him to be and do. These "shoulds" are often freely expressed by the neurotic, and they become statements of his goals or values, and the standards by which he constantly rates himself. Although they may encourage and promote activity on the part of the neurotic, and may be responsible for great bursts of energy, they differ quite clearly from productive work, which is motivated by a desire to express one's skills and capacities. Creative activity is devoid of the excesses and the inner dictates that characterize the activity of these "shoulds." The activity involved in fulfilling the neurotic "shoulds" are generally unproductive "make-work" which the individual must do and over which he has little choice or discrimination. The most frequently used and felt expression of the neurotic is: "I should," or "I must." These activities have no boundaries or limitations, and rarely take into account the essential weaknesses and limitations of the human organism. This problem is manifested in the neurotic's reluctance to seek help for himself, since it is admitting a weakness that he should be able to deal with himself. When he finally comes to a therapist, he strives at the outset to overcome his weakness by becoming more perfect, which in a sense is an effort to build a bigger and better neurosis without the defects that made it necessary to seek therapy. He feels that therapy should overcome his deficiencies and fulfill his neurotic idealization. This is the initial battle that needs to be overcome in the therapy of the neurotic.

The real damage from the rigid, impossible demands which the neurotic makes on himself comes from the inevitable failure to live up to the demands and strains that they impose on his physical as well as psychic structure. In order to fulfill these demands, he presses too hard. He frequently drinks too much, or plays too hard, or dresses inadequately, because even the weather should not restrict him. However, the inevitable failure to fulfill his expectations, coupled with the inability to recognize and acknowledge his limitations leads to a continual self-belittling and self-deprecating process in which he constantly tears down his pride and self-esteem. These "shoulds" have been likened to the superego, or to one's conscience, but they are different in many essential respects. Although conscience is a mechanism for maintaining the morality of the culture, the "shoulds" are designed to force the individual to extreme, superhuman activity beyond the cultural requirements. The activity produced has little relevance to morality, ethics, real ideals or values, but are attempts to sustain false value systems which are frequently immoral and inhuman and always unsuccessful.

The "shoulds" occupy a great deal of time and energy of the neurotic, and seriously impair his spontaneous activity. The inability to live up to the "shoulds" produces the self-hatred and self-contempt which are such an important part of the neurotic picture. These feelings are either on the surface or only slightly below the facade of the egocentric blustering or self-immolating activities of the individual. Although at times the self-destructive tendencies may be in the extreme, as in suicide, the self-accusations in terms of being a weakling, a fake and a phony are almost always present. These accusations result from the recognition of the discrepancy between the idealization, with its high standards, and the actual achievements, which inevitably fall far short of these superhuman goals. Self-deprecatory feelings are not only experienced towards himself, but are also directed to the world at large by a process Horney calls "externalization." By this process the neurotic not only feels that his activities are being observed and compared with his idealization, but that the failures he recognizes in himself are also recognized by everyone else. This enables him to develop great skill in discovering his own deficiencies in others. In this way he tends to observe and criticize in others those aspects of his own neurotic activities. This may serve many purposes, but essentially it allows him to feel less the failure by seeing greater failure all about him.

Although the neurotic is engaged in the contradictory process of tearing himself down at the same time that he is attempting to be superman and actualize his idealized self, he develops a pride system which centers about this idealization. Horney makes a distinction between true pride and false, or neurotic pride, which is of great value in understanding the neurotic process. She defines false pride as that which the neurotic develops about his idealization and his efforts and accomplishments in this direction. This is opposed to true pride, which is based on one's actual and realistic accomplishments. Although this distinction may not always be clear to the observer, it is always distinct for the neurotic, and he rarely confuses the two. He can generally verbalize this distinction most accurately.

False pride is maintained through a denial of the discrepancies between the idealization and actualization and the capacity to rationalize all the failures in his efforts to achieve his idealization. Consequently, false pride is highly vulnerable and requires constant affirmation and support from the environment which are not always forthcoming. The false pride system is a very loose and fragile structure, and requires such constant attention, that the individual hardly has any time, energy, or opportunity for achieving what he is really capable of doing. The values of the individual may be tenaciously adhered to, even though they may represent ideals which the individual does not really believe in, but which he must support in order to maintain his neurotic structure. This raises many interesting questions about guilt, which is related to true pride as opposed to guilt feelings which may arise out of failure to sustain the false pride of the neurotic. Such a distinction could be of considerable value to the theologian, philosopher, or moralist, who sets up categories of guilt without taking into account the individual's mental state. The pride system of the neurotic expresses his ideal goals and values as they are represented by his idealization, which requires superhuman efforts to sustain. When these efforts fail, or fall short of the ideal, deprecatory and belittling feelings are stirred up which result in self-hatred and self-contempt. No matter how successful, how competent, how moral and ambitious the neurotic might be, he can never be satisfied because his standards are impossible to fulfill. Consequently, his attempts to actualize his idealization are inevitably doomed to failure. Striving for perfection may be an admirable goal, but the necessity to achieve it without compromise or concession to reality produces the despair of the neurotic.

It is no wonder then, that the neurotic individual is described as being at war with himself, constantly attempting to achieve the impossible, and tearing himself down because he is unable to do this. He demands more and more of himself and, if through some insight, he becomes aware of a human frailty or limitation, he becomes even more self-derogatory. In this way the vicious cycle is again nourished by the self-sustaining conflictual system which we call the neurosis. What does the neurotic really hate and despise? In essence he despises those weaknesses in himself (as well as in others) that prevent him from actualizing (or being) his idealized self. He does not despise his real self, for this he does not know. The real self is pushed aside, denied, or covered up by the preoccupation and focus on the fulfillment of the idealization.

The neurotic process, although complicated, can be understood in rational terms. In attempting to deal with an anxiety situation, the individual develops an idealization which, in order to serve its purpose, must be actualized. At least attempts are made to actualize it. Since this is beyond the possibility of fulfillment, the neurotic is constantly failing, falling down on the job, and belittling and berating himself. This stimulates more anxiety which demands more activity to actualize the idealization to reduce the anxiety, and so on. In this process the real self gets pushed aside in the struggle to fulfill the idealized self. In this way the individual becomes alienated from himself. Although this notion of alienation has been current in theological thinking for some time, it has recently become more prominent in psychotherapeutic theory through the revival of interest in existential philosophy. In Horney's terms it is a rather simple concept, but it has all the richness of meaning and structure that the metaphysicians and philosophers have applied to it. The alienation in the neurotic expresses itself as a feeling of not being one's self, or knowing what one's self really is. The neurotic feels some separation and remoteness from himself as well as others and feels that he has no control over himself or his destiny and does not know what he really wants or wants to be. This feeling is not only experienced as separation, but is often described as being torn into two and pulled apart. This is often what the individual is describing when he speaks about his nervous breakdown. At these times he seems to have no goals or focus, and is unable to function. The process of alienation is an active one, and is self-imposed by forcing one's interest and attention away from one's real self as well as derogating and belittling one's self because the achievements fall short of the idealized self. This produces the strikingly low esteem with the accompanying absence of true pride that the neurotic feels for his own self. The false pride system produces an unspontaneous person who appears to be role-playing and phony without any real sense of direction.

The neurotic individual must deal with the constant tugs and pulls produced by demands made on himself and those he makes on others. He must attempt to fulfill his idealization and be on guard against being dethroned while keeping his anxiety level at a minimum. Consequently, he is rarely comfortable, and utilizes various techniques to deal with these discomforts which become part of his character structure. These techniques include: a) Alienation, which is one way of relieving tension by putting distance between one's real self and idealized self, and avoiding any entanglements. This is a false peace because it cannot succeed and ultimately produces more anxiety. b) Externalization—this is the process by which we minimize our failures by focusing on the deficiencies and weaknesses in others. It also permits us to account for our inability to succeed at a task by assuming a malevolent and uncooperative attitude from others. It partakes of "blaming it" on others. It is a much broader and meaningful concept than projection, which Freud described. c) Psychic fragmentation—which is a molecular aspect of alienation that compartmentalizes aspects of those personality characteristics that seem to contradict one another. We simply keep these aspects in separate categories, like the successful roué with wives in every port who never run into each other. However, like the wives, the compartmentalized ideas and attitudes do sometimes meet, and then there is trouble. d) Automatic control—this is a technique that the neurotic uses to avoid being torn apart. Here the individual always checks his own feelings and thoughts, so that he never becomes fully aware of his own discomforts. He does not really express his own emotions, or if he does, he keeps them well in check and under control. This seems contradictory to the popular conception of the neurotic who is seen as someone who is over-emotional and unrestrained. Although this is often the case, the emotions which the neurotic expresses are rarely aspects of his own true feelings and are either responses dictated by his idealizations, or else are exaggerated attempts at control. True feelings are kept out of his living as far as he possibly can in order to minimize his discomforts. Although all these tendencies seem to be present in all individuals, they are exaggerated in the neurotic.

Horney has not developed categories of specific character types, but rather she has described action types in terms of the ways they deal with the culture in which they live. They represent attempts at solution of one's neurotic conflicts and are a more dynamic expression of the way an individual with his constitutional endowments meets the challenges of his idealizations, claims, and "shoulds" when faced by particular problems in the culture. She did not see character as rigidly organized pieces of behavior, but rather as constellations of tendencies, determined by the particular problems one faces in the course of living. She preferred to describe types of solutions which correspond roughly to certain diagnostic categories and cut across the categories of the traditional character types:

1. *The Expansive Solution.* This is the type of person who identifies with his idealized, glorified self and in this identification tries to actually be that idealization. Life, for him, is an arena in which every obstacle must be overcome and everything mastered. He deals with anxiety by moving against it. His pride revolves around the issue of strength, and weakness is the thing which he despises most. He has no doubts or uncertainties about his grandiosity, and is often arrogant and perfectionistic. He insists that his ideals, values, or standards be acknowledged. He acts as if he deserves the recognition of being the perfect, ideal citizen. Although the elements of self-hatred and self-contempt are at a minimum, they are manifest in his relentness, demanding attitude. He appears to be completely independent and not to need anyone. In this way he belittles the need for love and affection. Although he is desperately in need of love, he is convinced that he is unlovable, and so must play down this need in himself. He will insist that he requires only respect from others. He has an exaggerated pride in strength, power, and independence, and he tends to minimize all his failures by blaming and criticizing others. This description may apply to any of the conventionally described nosological types, but it roughly resembles the hysterical, compulsive, or manic-depressive types.

2. *Self-effacing Solution.* This is, in many ways, the opposite of the expansive solution. Here the demand is always for love. This individual must never be independent and must always appear helpless and impotent. He expects that this will stimulate the concern and good will of others. He never threatens anyone, and his pride revolves about the notion of being inferior, weak, helpless and self-abnegating. He shuns success and refuses to be in any dominant position. He doesn't allow himself to have any ideas of his own. The ultimate effect is a shrinking of his personality. He never makes demands or expresses his own feelings or needs. This is a solution of weakness, and his anxieties are overcome by a

continuous supply of love, which he hopes to obtain through an expression of his pitiful need. Because of his desperate need for love, he is prone to accept substitutes, and to sell himself cheaply to others for any favors bestowed. This kind of person is easily taken advantage of and made a sucker of. In therapy these patients have no trouble in asking for help. Patients of this type are not really interested in learning about themselves. They try to present themselves to the analyst, as well as to others, as lovable, in order to stimulate good will. In therapy it is necessary to help such patients recognize that the charm and cooperative attitudes they manifest do not necessarily express their capacities or potentialities, but are simply techniques to get people to like them. Their claims are in terms of their right to be loved because they are such help-less, pitiful people. Since they are not always successful, they feel angry, abused, and put upon. The greatest source of pride for these individuals lies in their being lovable, and so they direct all their energies toward indiscriminately stimulating everyone's good will. How do they express the resentments which must inevitably occur? These are expressed in acceptable ways. The dramatizing of their misery and suffering has a large element of accusation against others. This is characteristic of the depressive reaction, which is common in this type of solution.

3. The third type of solution is called "the appeal of freedom" by Horney. This group deals with anxiety by "moving away" from it. Such a patient is resigned to the pain and dangers of existence, and he detaches himself from any emotional involvement. He makes no apparent claims or demands, and wants to be left alone, free of any emotional involvement. This is his greatest claim, that he be allowed to exist free of any entanglements or respon-sibility in his living. Freedom is his slogan, but it is freedom *from* living rather than freedom *to* live. His idealization is one of detach-ment and stoicism. Although Horney does not devote much time in describing the genetic development of this type of solution, she has indicated the directions for such research.

She feels that the expansive solution probably originates in a parental situation in which the child has few, if any good experiences with his parents. The possibility of obtaining genuine love and affection is abandoned as a way of establishing one's security. Con-sequently, the need for love, affection and tenderness is belittled. The self-effacing solution probably occurred under circumstances where the possibility of getting affectionate interest from others lay in the direction of completely subordinating oneself. Problems were solved by compromise, or moving toward people, subordinating all hostility, and concentrating on appeasing and appearing lovable to others.

The resigned group apparently develop in an atmosphere where there is no opportunity to express oneself, either to rebel, or to get any affection. The way to deal with the world then, under these circumstances, is to put some distance between oneself and the situation. Then one need neither rebel nor compromise, but simply remain aloof.

It is to be noted that Horney sees the beginnings of the neurotic development in the relationship with the parents and the atmosphere which prevails in the early years of development, with no special emphasis on sex, or other specific factors.

VIEWS ON THERAPY

Horney's most valuable contributions probably lie in her amplification and clarification of the therapeutic process. She has made many significant alterations in the technique of therapy. Horney's goals of therapy, although essentially similar to Freud's, are expressed in positive terms of helping the individual free his real self rather than in making the unconscious conscious. In order to achieve this goal the patient must relinquish his neurotic pride and acknowledge his idealization. To achieve this he must discover how his claims and "shoulds" support this idealization.

Horney utilizes the technical discoveries of Freud such as free association, dream analysis and transference. However, her conceptions of these phenomena are somewhat at variance with Freud's. Free association, the technique that Freud developed in order to explore the unconscious can be abused by the patient and therapist. Much time can be wasted in the fascinating search for related data which may or may not illuminate the life of the individual. Since the genetic reconstruction of the neurosis is not Horney's primary interest, she emphasizes the present situations that might clarify the neurotic's idealizations, claims and "shoulds." The process of therapy no longer emphasizes the tracing of childhood experiences or the exploration of it in great detail. She believes that the mere revival and illumination of infantile experiences does not eliminate neurotic behavior in the adult. Symptoms are the result of multiple, repeated experiences over long periods of time in a malevolent atmosphere and are not produced by single, isolated events. This is in contrast to the Freudian emphasis on trauma and fixation.

Horney has been frequently criticized for de-emphasizing the influence of childhood in the genesis of the neurosis. This is not entirely true. She has indicated that although the early years have great significance in the development of personality and neurosis, these are not the important years from the point of view of therapy. Though behavioral patterns are organized in early years, how the individual expresses his character today, and how it has developed through the years are crucial to the therapeutic process. A mere elucidation of its beginnings is the first thread in the finished garment which is the neurosis. Although it can be helpful to uncover the first thread, it is more useful to examine how the sweater has been made in order to unravel it. The earlier notion of exposing and reliving earlier experiences as if this in itself were therapeutic has been largely discredited and abandoned in recent years. If the genesis of a pattern of behavior can be elucidated through an actual recall, it can be an enormously convincing experience in therapy. Unfortunately, because of the nature of infantile amnesias, we are forced to reconstruct such memories through a combination of interpretation and preconceptions about infantile development. Consequently, such reconstructions are less convincing and forceful and rarely have therapeutic value in themselves. The clarification of the current distorted patterns of living, the role which they play in supporting the neurosis, and the effect they have on one's self-esteem, true pride and self-fulfillment occupies the major part of the therapeutic process. Genetic reconstructions are helpful, whenever they are possible, but they are not seen as crucial to the therapeutic process. Working with experiences that are within recall, either consciously or through the analytic techniques of free association, is a more meaningful, and consequently, a more therapeutically effective tool. Most early experiences are lost in the haze of years, and it is rare that we can validate such recall when it does occur. Reconstructions have the value of a novel, but rarely that of a scientific production. Horney's objection does not lie in the difficulty of such a reconstruction, but rather in its ineffectiveness in the therapeutic process.

The concept of repetition compulsion, which is so important in therapy, has similar difficulties. Horney modified this concept by denying its instinctual origins. The tendency for children and adults to repeat experiences and activities in order to master them is well known. However, such repetition, she believes, not only serves to alleviate anxiety but is also an expression of pleasure derived from the skill involved in effectuating these activities. There is a positive pleasure in utilizing our skills and the repetition of certain activities serves this purpose as well as to master our anxiety. Sports are an excellent example of this phenomenon. In the neurosis, however, this tendency to repeat unsuccessful patterns of living is an integral part of the structure of the neurosis. Horney feels that this occurs because of the nature of the character structure of the individual, not because of some instinctual compulsion. In addition, experiences are not repeated in the simple fashion in which they originally occurred. As they are repeated, there is some elaboration which comes from later experiencing. Although one could say that a patient has a tendency to fight with his superiors, one would notice that it is quite different from the way he fought as a child. It is not a mere repetition, and it contains the additions and modifications produced by later years. In addition to the modifications, the neurotic structure itself produces alterations in the responses to the authority. This relates to the development of devices and techniques which are an outgrowth of the neurotic process and produce a rather complicated expanding system of defenses or behavior patterns rather than the simple reactivation of earlier attitudes by repetition.

The transference phenomenon, which was Freud's major contribution to the technical problems in psychotherapy, was related to his concept of repetition compulsion. Freud felt that the transference was simply a revival of infantile attitudes toward the parents. One deals with others in terms of the major elements in one's relationship with parents and with the same set of affects and ideations that one had toward them. Horney pointed out that the attitudes one person develops towards another, whether in therapy or outside of it, has some relationship to the actual situation in the present as well as elements of transference. For example, although the patient has transference attitudes towards the doctor, he may also be extremely dependent upon him in order to get well, or to return to a productive way of life. This is more than a mere revival of the patient's attitude toward his parents. It is also related to the actualities of the present situation. Some therapists are petty, or unlikeable, while others are charming and very warm. The patient reacts to his doctor in terms of the present as well as the past, and it is much more than "only" past. Some attitudes towards psychiatrists are rational and realistic as well as irrational and unrealistic. Horney felt that Freud's utilization of the transference was too static, and while it might expose earlier relationships with the parents, it did not always clarify the present therapeutic situation. If a patient was becoming overly dependent on the psychiatrist, it might be partially related to his excessive dependency on mother. Does this really add to the clarification of why he is the way he is now? The patient can say, "I am this way because of my relationship with mother. How can I change this? I can't very well go back and revise the relationship with mother, can I," Or they will say, "I am hostile because I had a parent that I hated, and so I hate all authority figures." The transference is used to explain certain attitudes and the patient feels that once having explained it, there is no need to alter it further. Horney felt that the utilization of transference in this way was an obstacle to therapy. Transference, for Horney, was a special instance of the operation of a particular character structure in a special situation called therapy, which reflected his behavior everywhere else. This enabled the therapist to get a clear view of the way this patient functioned in the outside world by studying his behavior toward the therapist.

It is clear that Horney not only placed great emphasis on the analysis in the present situation but also on the goals of the patient. This is similar to Adler's "guiding fictions," which are the neurotic's false goals that arise out of his idealized self. These goals must be exposed, since they are a potent source of anxiety.[4]

SUMMARY AND APPRAISAL

Horney's conception of neurotic development was related to the cultural or familial situation in which the infant developed. Instead of developing confidence from the benevolent tenderness of the parent, the individual develops some anxiety which is a response to feeling helpless in a potentially hostile world. Anxiety, because of its extreme discomfort, must be dealt with and kept at a minimum. The person may "move toward" it and make peace with it, or "move against" it and fight it. Or he may "move away" and withdraw from it. These efforts become compulsive, and all three of them go on in the same person to a greater or lesser degree and produce conflicts. In order to deal with these opposing and contradictory feelings, which also produce anxiety, the individual selects one of the three ways, idealizes this approach and expands them in his phantasies and day dreams. The conflicts are solved by the imaginative idealization process, but the idealization itself is a damaging development and sets up a way of life that is dedicated to fulfill this idealization. All the energies and interests are focused on the attempts to actualize the idealization. These efforts are compulsive and are pushed within the individual by the "shoulds." They attempt to force the outside world to support their neurotic pride system by the claims they make. Coincident with the attempts to actualize the idealization, self-hate and self-contempt begin to pervade the individual's life because of his inability to succeed at this endeavor. The real self meanwhile is being pushed aside and the person feels alienated from his real self, which he begins to hate because it is a weak edition of his idealized self as well as a constant reminder of his neurotic phoniness and pretentiousness. While all these conflicting activities and feelings are going on, the individual tries to establish some mode of living in the real, practical world. At the same time he is involved in a wholly private, neurotic world of his own idealization. This is a picture of a fully developed neurosis.

In order to help the neurotic establish his real self and relinquish his false securities, he must get some assurance that this can be replaced by something better. The assurance can only come from someone for whom he has regard and a feeling of benevolent interest and acceptance. This is what characterizes the psychotherapeutic situation, or any situation in which one individual gets help from another in the healing process. Tenderness and sympathetic understanding do not overcome the neurosis. These only enable and encourage the neurotic to examine and entertain the possibilities of change. The process of changing is a further step in assuming responsibility for one way of life and taking steps to alter it.

The contributions of Karen Horney to psychoanalysis must be appraised in terms of her theory as well as practice. Horney was the first psychoanalyst to present, in an organized fashion, the theoretical objections to the biological and philosophical substrate of Freud's contributions. Her theories incorporate the insights of the social sciences, anthropology, and particularly the significance of culture on personality development. Although she followed some gifted analysts from whom she drew ideas, many of her contributions are milestones in the development of ego psychology. She highlighted the role of values and goals in neurosis, and emphasized the parent-child transaction as the basis for the development of personality. Her contributions to the psychology of the female were considerable in clarifying the role of the culture and its effect on sex differences.

Her major contribution to theory, I believe, is her recognition and elucidation of the contradictions and conflicts in the neurotic process which set up a vicious, self-perpetuating cycle that gradually draws upon more and more energy in the individual, leaving little time for any other activity. Like Adler, she had a vivid style in describing the neurotic process and brought it to recognizable life size. Although some of her hypotheses are subject to the same criticisms leveled at all social scientists, she has attempted to develop her theories in a more operational framework capable of being validated through suitable experimental designs. There is much distress about her concept of the "real self." This notion should not be viewed as a conglomerate of tendencies or capacities which exist in a definable way. This is the basis for much of the discontent about the concept. The "real self" should be visualized as the portion of one's personality that is overshadowed and buried in the neurotic, compulsive activities. It does not necessarily represent the best or most moral or creative aspect of the individual's personality that would be present if the neurosis did not hide it. It should not be made into a "thing-in-itself" but merely a collection of possibilities under certain conditions. This would avoid the tendency on the part of some critics to require that the "real self" be defined and localized. It would also avoid the embarrassing question as to how we know what the real self is.

Horney was a brilliant observer of the social scene. It was not long after coming to the United States that she recognized the cultural differences between Europe and the United States that produced different neurotic constellations. Her lucid style and capacity to move into everybody's life by her descriptions of neurotic behavior made her books very popular. Her popularity did not result from a watering down of the unpleasant truths of Freud, but rather from her skill in reducing neurosis to everyday terms minus the complicated technical language of the libido theory.

Her contributions to therapy were considerable and included her stress on the analysis of the current situation and the recognition of the reality aspects of the analytic process as well as the irrational transference aspects. She encouraged a very active, educating role in the therapist, whose task it was to help the patient unravel the complications in his attempts to deal with anxiety. It minimized the interest on genesis and emphasized the significance of studying one's living in the here and now. She developed many strategies and hints in dealing with the typical neurotic attempts to evade the real issue in his neurosis.

The criticism of Horney comes mainly from the classical analysts who feel that she abandoned psychoanalysis when she rejected the libido theory. Her contributions are considered superficial additions to ego psychology. There is the feeling that she oversimplified the entire process, and that in stressing the present, missed the whole point in the development and therapy of the neurosis. As is so often the case, her enthusiasm about examining the here and now did, for a while, cause her to neglect the genesis of the neurosis. However, this was a practical problem and not a theoretical one, and this criticism, I believe, is no longer valid.

More to the point is her inclination to focus on the evolution of the neurosis and its widening circles of involvement rather than on the genesis. This is particularly useful in therapy, since it is generally the only effective element in the treatment situation which is usually called the "working through." Historically, her major contribution may well be the delineation of the cultural factors in the neurotic process and the abandonment of the libido theory while retaining the essential discoveries of Freud.

Notes

1. Adler's concepts form an integral part of the neo-Freudian theories even though they reject the concepts Freud developed. His emphasis on the purposive and adaptive aspects of the neurotic symptoms is incorporated in current pesonality theories. His de-emphasis of sex and aggression and his focus on the social elements in man's living is shared by most contemporary theorists.

Although Freud could be called the father of dynamic psychiatry, Adler is certainly the first neo-Freudian theoretician. It is interesting to note that while Freud considered Jung to be a significant figure in the psychoanalytic movement, his influence today is very limited, while Adler, whose defection Freud felt was no loss to psychoanalysis, has been the intellectual prophet for much of the neo-Freudian innovations.

2. Otto Rank's approach was called "Will Therapy" and emphasized the conscious elements in man's functioning. Although it has influenced social work theory and practice extensively, its influence in psychiatric and psychoanalytic theory and practice is negligible.

3. The research of Rene Spitz, which was reported in a number of articles, and *The Rights of Infants,* by Margaret Ribble, established the fact that the infant required maternal handling and fondling as well as an adequate intake of food in order to survive. It helped explain the greater death rate of infants in circumstances of limited maternal care, as in hospitals or foundling homes as compared with adopted or natural homes. These studies emphasized the value of the physician's prescription of T.L.C.—tender, loving care—three times a day for the young infant. Not only was the disease of marasmus understood (this disease had been the cause of many infants' deaths), but the significance of human relationship, even in the earliest days of infancy was established. Human dependency became more than a mere physiological necessity, and survival depended upon factors other than the fulfillment of physiological needs. These findings were a milestone in the development of interpersonal theories of human development. See:

Spitz, Rene A.: Hospitalism: An inquriy into the genesis of psychiatric conditions in early childhood, *in* Psychoanalytic Study of the Child, Vol. I, New York, International Universities Press, 1945.

Anaclitic depression, an inquiry into the genesis of psychiatric conditions in early childhood, *in* Psychoanalytc Study of the Child, Vol. II, New York, International Universities Press, 1947.

4. Compare this conception of transference with that of Thomas M. French and Franz Alexander. They said: "The more we keep our attention focused upon the patient's immediate problem in life, the more clearly do we come to realize that the patient's neurosis is an unsuccessful attempt to solve a problem in the present by means of behavior patterns that failed to solve it in the past. We are interested in the past as the source of these stereotyped behavior patterns, but our primary interest is in helping the patient find a solution for his present problems by correcting these unsuccessful patterns." Psychoanalytic Therapy, New York, Ronald Press, 1946.

IV

Erich Fromm

Although Erich Fromm has not developed a complete system of personality development, he has had a significant influence on other neo-Freudian systematizers. His work has extended our understanding of the variety of forces which are brought to bear on the developing character structure of the individual.

Fromm is a psychologist who has modified Freud's biological orientation by demonstrating the effect of culture with its socio-economic, political and religious aspects on personality structure. Culture as the composite of the multitude of man's activities has its inevitable effect on the individual. Fromm has traced the relationship and interaction of sociological factors with the psychological elements and has thus expanded the existing theories of personality development. In so doing, he has added considerable understanding to the problem of neurosis through his concepts of conformity, freedom, and love. His concerns with the problems of morality and ethics have contributed to the philosophical as well as the psychoanalytic explorations in this area. Unlike Freud, who claimed that moral values are alien to the psychoanalyst's interests, Fromm insists that morals and values are essential elements in the therapeutic process and play a role in the production of neurosis. The therapist has his own set of values which he brings unwittingly, and often imperceptibly, to the therapeutic process. The therapist's attitude toward work, creativity, health versus illness, and particularly, toward the good and the bad in human behavior influences his reaction to the patient and his illness in spite of all the precautions he may take to avoid it. Fromm insists that the therapeutic process should concern itself with these very questions rather than pretend to avoid the issues of morality. Society, for Freud, was a suppressive and repressive force which restrained the destructive attitudes of an individual. Fromm, on the other hand, visualizes society as being in a dynamic interaction with the individual and tending to suppress the more creative as well as the destructive potentialities of the individual.

Although Fromm has retained many of Freud's original formulations, he feels that Freud was at times painfully ignorant of the social forces which beset human societies. Freud was largely outside of the political currents that raged around him. He was astonished and shocked at the aggression and destructiveness which were manifested in the First World War. The advent of Hitler and the anti-Semitic movement caught him in a web that he was ill prepared to deal with. His major interest was on the id forces that operate inside the individual, and on the whole, he was less well informed about the social forces which raged outside of man himself.

Fromm, on the other hand, is a social psychologist, and he is very much aware of what is happening in the world. He is even associated with major political movements. He is dissatisfied with the libido theory and feels that what Freud called instincts are simply physiological needs whose form and expression are culturally determined. He insists that man satisfies his basic needs in the manner in which the particular culture dictates. For Fromm, man is an animal that has gone beyond the instinctual necessities into the area of learning which is organized and determined by the cultural situation. Consequently, the study of man requires more than a familiarity with man as a biological animal who has physiological needs. It requires an elucidation of the cultural situation in which man lives and which shapes the form and content of these needs. In addition, Fromm has been influenced by existential philosophical thinking and recognizes that the state of being human creates its own contradictions and dilemmas which are a plentiful source of distress.

In contrast to other animals, man is capable of looking at himself from a distance and of visualizing his own existence in the present, the past, and the future, ultimately anticipating his death. These capacities have been a source of considerable distress, and he has attempted to overcome the inevitability of death, since the beginning of time, by the use of a variety of magical techniques and imaginative play. Because of his capacity for self-consciousness, he has become estranged from nature while still being a part of it. This has created singular problems for man, and has been responsible to a large extent for his developing a character structure which has replaced his instincts. It has enabled him to function in an economic fashion without being tied down to rigid, unchangeable, prefixed patterns of behavior. It has allowed him to have some choice and variability in the satisfaction of his physiological needs. His capacity to symbolize has broadened his skills in dealing with all these problems.

In the awareness of his separation from other animals, man strives to effect some reunion with nature which produces, as Fromm sees it, the key problem in psychology; that is, the need to relate to other humans as well as to the world in general. Thus, the major issue in the psychology of man is that of relatedness. The context of his theoretical formulations regarding character structure is based on the variety and specific modes of relatedness that an individual maintains towards himself and the world. Thus, man not only has physiological needs like other animals, but more significantly, he has a need to be related to himself and to the rest of the world.[1] Relatedness is a different concept from the herd instinct or the family behavior of certain animals. In animals the goal apparently is one of guaranteeing the fulfillment of their physiological needs. In man, however, relationship is required not only to expedite the fulfillment of his physiological needs but is essential to the satisfaction of his psychological requirements as well. In addition, the herd instinct is based on inborn patterns which the animal can neither alter nor disregard. Man is capable of great alteration and variation in the patterns of his psychological fulfillment in his attempts at relatedness.

The problems of relatedness can be viewed on two levels, the individual and the social. In the course of his development, it is essential in the maturing process to separate oneself from one's parents, to become independent while retaining some remaining dependencies. In a broader or social sense, relatedness refers to the family, the clan, and the religious or social groupings that one becomes part of.

Fromm's concepts rest on the hypothesis which states that man has a basic need to express and fulfill his potentialities. It is the same humanistic assumption which might be called the psychology of optimism that is implicit in the theorizing of Horney and Sullivan. In fulfilling his potentialities, physiological problems arise—food, sex, excretion—but psychological (or human) needs exist as well. Psychological needs include his philosophical, aesthetic, religious, and other social needs, which can be fulfilled only through human relationships.

There are certain factors in man's existence that he can alter and some that he has no control over. Although this is clearly an incontrovertible thesis, man, through the centuries, has not entirely accepted these limitations. Fromm distinguishes these two categories into: (a) existential factors, which are facts of our humanness and which cannot be altered, and (b) the historical factors, which are the accidental issues of existence, such as when and where we are born and in what financial and status circumstances we happen to be born into. On the whole, these factors are capable of being altered. Among the existential issues which plague human existence, the fact of being a part of nature yet separate from it, is most distressing. This inevitable separation can be productive of much anxiety. In addition, man has the capacity to visualize his limitations in being unable to utilize all his skills in his brief lifetime. He cannot alter his life expectancy, except in a most limited way, and he can never fully utilize all his capacities, yet he strives to do so. It is this dichotomy rather than some instinctual pressures, Fromm believes, that pushes man to function productively and creatively and to establish some meaning to his existence. He does not postulate inner drives pushed by innate needs, but rather the conception that man cannot remain static and is forced by the contradictions in his living to move forward and attempt to overcome these dichotomies.

Although Fromm's hypothesis appears to be identical with that of Horney regarding the innate drives toward self-realization, Fromm does not think of it in precisely the way Horney does. Horney conceives of some inner force or pressure which strives towards fulfilling man's potentialities. For Fromm, the inner force arises out of the need to overcome the contradictions and dichotomies in his existence. It avoids the postulate of an "inner, unidentifiable force" which has moral purpose and constructive goals. It is essential to any psychology of man to distinguish between the existential dichotomies which cannot be overcome from the historical dichotomies, that are contradictions and conflicts which occur in the course of one's living. Being born in a particular culture will determine the nature of the social and economic conditions an individual will confront in his development. These issues will vary markedly in different epochs and even decades. The problems of the depression of the thirties or of the institution of slavery in ancient Greece produced its specific effects on the structure of the personality of individuals developing under these historical conditions. The existential dichotomies, however, are rooted in the very nature of man and are contradictions which prevail at all times and in all cultures. They cannot be overcome, but man will deal with them in a variety of ways, depending upon his own character structure.

Man's psychic problems arise after he has satisfied his physiological needs. Although the psychological and physiological needs cannot always be clearly separated and are rarely satisfied by themselves, man's economic development, except in rare instances, has put him largely outside of the animal struggle for existence. Until man's physiological needs are sufficient and relatively stable, he cannot and does not concern himself with aesthetic, philosophical, or other "specifically human" interests. Consequently, the real problems of man, as human—as opposed to the animal—arise once these basic needs are fulfilled. The search for security, prestige, status, and the curiosity about art and religion are possible only when the basic, physiological requirements are met. Consequently, Fromm, unlike Freud, does not consider man's instinctual processes to be relevant to the problem of the neurosis.

Fromm visualizes the development of the individual in terms of the problems created by his separation from man and nature and the anxieties which this produces. This is not a novel thesis and was the basis for much of the work of Otto Rank. The infant and child, while relatively secure in his dependency on the parental figures, must, in order to achieve some maturity and independence, ultimately separate himself from them and attempt some form of independent existence. However, desirable it might be, it is rarely possible to remain entirely dependent on one's parents. There are pressures, both from the parents and from the child, to effectuate his inevitable growing up and away from parental influences. This separation, with its accompanying demands for independent action and living, produces its own pressures for the reestablishment of some form of intimacy and relationship with other humans. The difficulties encountered in this dependency-independency crisis depend largely on the atmosphere in which the child grows. The parents can encourage the process of growing up and leave the child with secure feelings about being independent, or the process may be frightening and threatening. In some families, these problems are at a minimum, and in others, the feelings of doubt, uneasiness, and uncertainty about being grown up are maximized. In either case, one must grow up and develop some measure of independent existence. Ideally, there would be a balance between the independent modes of existence and the individual's sources of dependent security. One cannot remain isolated or separated, and the individual makes great efforts to relate to others in order to overcome these unbearable feelings of loneliness, powerlessness, and separateness. The most effective way of relating is through a loving relationship in which one maintains a productive relationship with another person while also remaining independent. However, this solution is a difficult one and, unfortunately, is rarely achieved. Most people therefore utilize a variety of ways of relating. Some of the techniques for establishing a meaningful relationship with another person seem to be extreme and even bizarre. Fromm describes four alternative ways: 1. masochistic, 2, sadistic, 3. destructive, and 4. conforming. These techniques are pursued in a compulsive, indiscriminate and relentless fashion, which are the characteristics of the neurotic process. They arise when the maturing process is seen as menacing and dangerous, and where there is insufficient love in the relationship between the child and his parents.

1. *Masochistic Form of Relating.* Fromm views masochism as a phenomenon of relationship rather than as a sexual perversion or a derivative of the sexual instinct. Like Horney, Fromm believes that the masochist is attempting to make himself entirely acceptable to others by his self-belittling and non-aggressive attitudes. In order to establish some form of relationship, the masochist is willing to undergo and accept all forms of abuse. The attitude of submissiveness, dependency, complete inferiority and powerlessness prevents one from being entirely isolated and abandoned. This is a very common way of relating, and in minor degrees we find it as a part of most relationships. However, at times it is the predominant mode of relating to a partner who is a sadist. One can visualize the beginnings of this in the early history of the child. Feeling that he is unacceptable, he allows himself to be taunted, tormented and kicked about in order to be accepted by the group.

The masochistic way of relating will be reflected in all aspects of living. As a sexual phenomenon, it is quite rare, though it is widespread in the non-sexual aspects of living.

2. *Sadistic Way of Relating.* This type of relationship occurs most frequently in symbiosis with the masochistic type.[2] This is the converse of the masochist. While the masochist is utterly help-less and dependent, the sadist appears to be entirely independent. He relates by pushing others around and having no dependent needs; he is unconcerned about the effects of his behavior on others. Only the masochist will accept him, and so the symbiotic relation-ship develops. The term sadism, like masochism, has become so closely identified with sexual pathology that its widespread preva-lence in our everyday life is easily overlooked. It manifests itself in the callous and often smug insistence on needing no one and being affronted by an offer of help. Independence coupled with indifference for the feelings of others is considered a virtue. These people move about life taking, pushing, demanding and exploiting, and at the same time acclaiming their disinterest in others. Only the individual who is prepared and willing to accept such abuses will tolerate such self-indulgent behavior. Yet the sadist is a lonely, unattached soul, desperately attempting some relationship in the only manner he is capable of.

Many marriages are based on a mild form of this sado-masochistic symbiosis in which a relationship is continued that is clearly un-pleasant and destructive to both partners because the alternative is lonely isolation. Through fear of separation and loneliness, the partners in such a relationship spend their lives in mutual torment rather than seek relief, as long as their neurotic needs continue. Therapy or marriage counseling in these instances must touch upon both problems in order to effectuate any change, since both partners mutually require that one be sadistic while the other be masochistic.

3. *Destructive Way of Relating.* This type of relatedness depends on the need to destroy the object of the relationship. This can be accomplished by a total possessiveness or a martyred slavishness. It implies that one can never truly possess another person or thing until one has destroyed it or rendered it useless to anyone else. The relationship is not one of submission or domination but is un-friendly, hostile, and competitive. Individuals who pursue this kind of a relationship have probably grown up in an atmosphere where one is acceptable only by a repression of tenderness which leads to the development of nasty, malevolent and hostile attitudes. It is characteristic of the criminal or delinquent way of relating to the world.

4. *Conformist Way of Relating*. This technique of relating is most prevalent in contemporary Western culture. Conforming (though largely unproductive) is a safe and successful way of getting along. It produces the least turmoil, and is a relationship of the automaton. Fromm calls it "automaton conformity." One simply accepts the patterns of behavior which are most acceptable, wipes out differences and individuality and becomes part of the crowd. Although to some extent this is a normal and expected process in the adolescent in our culture, it can extend into adulthood. It may produce a variety of the "peace of mind" cult, and is often accompanied by a lack of originality and independence.

The productive mode of relating, or the relationship of love, allows for the greatest fulfillment of one's capacities. It is associated with a feeling of strength, power, respect and responsibility for the other person's independent needs. Fromm defines love in terms of the quality of the relationship that exists between the partners rather than on the basis of the existence of genital maturity of the partners. Love becomes a concept that is broader than sexuality, and the nature of a sexual relationship depends on the quality of the non-sexual aspects of the relationship, rather than the other way around. Love involves the recognition and respect for the other person's independent needs while at the same time not relinquishing one's own. It also involves the maximization of dependent security in a relationship without the sacrifice of an essential independent existence.

CHARACTER STRUCTURE

For Fromm, personality and character are determined by the ways in which the individual satisfies his needs and relates to others in doing so. Fromm distinguishes the physiological and psychological needs by drawing a distinction between assimilation, which involves the processes of acquiring the physiological necessities (biological requirements), and socialization, which includes all other needs of man which arise out of his humanness. The processes of assimilation and socialization are conjunctive and go on simultaneously. The physiological needs are frequently satisfied in a social situation, and vice versa.

Character structure, as Fromm defines it, is made up of the characteristic, enduring ways in which the individual assimilates and socializes, or the ways in which an individual satisfies his needs.[3] Personality is the totality of character structure plus temperament, which consists of the inherited psychic characteristics or modes of reaction of individuals. Thus, the choleric or phlegmatic temperament may be associated with a variety of character types. Personality is the sum of the acquired and inherited psychic characteristics. In the human, the development of character has obviated the necessity for instincts. These character types refer to the characteristic ways in which these individuals relate to their socializing and assimilating activities. This is in sharp contrast to the character types described by Freud, which develop around the historical developments of the libido. While the motive forces are markedly different, the character types are surprisingly similar. Horney does not think in terms of character types, but in terms of action types, or the solutions achieved by the individual in attempting to actualize his idealized image. Fromm's character types consist of: 1. receptive, 2. exploitative, 3. hoarder, and 4. marketing and 5. productive.

1. *Receptive Character.* This type of character structure is based on a relationship with the world in terms of taking. Everything one wants or needs, whether it be love, food or satisfaction, comes from the outside. If one waits long enough and offends no one, then all one's needs will be satisfied. There is a great dependence on authority. For this type of person, love means being loved, not loving. He becomes easily and adhesively attached to anyone who will supply his wants so that slight kindness or friendliness may result in exaggerated attachment.

He appears to have grown up in a candy factory atmosphere where one needs to be passive and unobtrusive, and a magic helper will come along and automatically fill his needs.

2. *Exploitative Character.* The exploitative type of character structure relates by doing and taking. He believes that nothing comes gratuitously and that everything must be fought for. He is convinced that "you get nothing for nothing"—not even love. Anything that comes freely, or easily must be suspect. He never allows himself to be caught in a position of weakness, for then he will be taken advantage of. Love is the bunk, and what really counts is what one can force out of another person by cunning, guile, or a display of power. Such a person undoubtedly grew up in a family situation in which nothing came freely and everything had to be fought for. Life was a rat race, and tenderness a phony gimmick.[4]

These character types are similar to those described by Freud and Horney and are never pure types. They are described in an isolated way only for purposes of clarity and description. One rarely finds the pure character type in life as he is described in a textbook. Consequently, one may find a person whose prevailing mode of relationship is receptive, though he may not quite believe that passivity will achieve his goals, and at times he will push and struggle. This will, of course, set up conflicts which will produce anxiety. A young lady who feels that if she is patient and good she will be rewarded by a Prince Charming, may grow impatient if he doesn't arrive after awhile, and may join clubs, or visit summer resorts where she may possibly hunt for a substitute. If she is unsuccessful, she will be doubly humiliated and may withdraw more strongly into her receptive, magical attempts at a solution of her needs.

In the contrast between the life histories of the receptive and exploitative character it is important to distinguish between the atmosphere of deprivation and overindulgence. It is conceivable that a child may grow up in an atmosphere of overindulgence and yet feel deprived. We must be careful not to confuse the assimilation needs or physiological requirements with the socialization needs, or psychological requirements. One frequently finds persons who grow up in wealthy or middle-class homes, where there may be an oversupply of material goods, who feel deprived of psychological or affectional supplies. It is also common to find overindulgent parents in homes where there is material deprivation; material deprivation is not the crucial question. There may be rich, generous affection for the children in a materially deprived home, and vice versa. Children of a wealthy but emotionally deprived family frequently have the conviction that nothing can be had in this world, and that they must hang on to everything they can get, because they can never get enough. This occurs in spite of the fact that there is more than sufficient wealth. This feeling clearly stems from emotional deprivation.

3. *Hoarding Character.* Such an individual relates by giving nothing and holding on to whatever he has. This may mean holding on to money, friends, etc. He has no faith whatever in the world and what he can get from it and feels that the only security is to hang on to what he has and never give it up. He is a miser, a hoarder, and a stingy person who behaves as if there were fixed

quantities of materials, as well as affection in the world, so that if one gives something away, one can never get it back. Security is what you have, not what you use or give away. To love someone means to give up something which you may never regain. He does not believe that love begets more love, but that one is impoverished by giving away love. It is the familiar complaint of the dissatisfied wife who says "my husband doles out only one kiss a week."

4. *Marketing Character.* This type of character is typical of 20th Century development. His character structure is a prime example of Fromm's thesis that character is intimately related to the socio-economic situation. He is the Madison Avenue type, motivationally directed by market values. He believes that personality is a commodity that is saleable. In his book, *The Lonely Crowd,* David Reisman has drawn on Fromm's development of this character structure for his "other-directed" personality, who is essentially a marketing character. This type of person has no standards or morality and feels that he must be whatever others want him to be. The ideal is conformity and uniformity, and the slogan is: "Here I am, as you desire me." Selling oneself is more important than being oneself. Under these circumstances, one relates by a combination of conformity and selling, which denies any individuality except that which is permitted in the marketplace, which has become the authority for him. The problem of authoritarianism is crucial to this character type, and Fromm has critically examined this whole area. He distinguishes between rational authority, which is based on competence, and irrational authority, which is based on power, intimidation, and the manipulation of others. To submit to an irrational authority is to yield to a neurotic dependency based on a sado-masochistic relationship rather than one based on a reasonable recognition of one's competence. Fromm believes that we submit too easily to the irrational authority of the marketplace, and his views on ethics and morality derive from this fact. The rational authority must represent true competence and can be a constructive and valuable force for the freedom, growth and development of the individual. Irrational authority is merely coercive and serves the purpose of intimidating others to satisfy its own neurotic needs. It is not concerned with the other person's development. Because we have strong inclinations to submit to the irrational authorities and to deprecate the rational authority, we

yield our potentialities for productive and creative living. This is the immorality of our culture as Fromm sees it.[5]

5. *Productive Character.* This is the rare individual who has realized his true self and has the capacity to be involved in relations where there is care, responsibility, and love for the other person's needs and requirements. These individuals attain the capacity to love themselves as well as others, and to have a responsible concern for the welfare of others. They have overcome the distinction between self love and selfishness, and in loving themselves, they have the capacity to love others. This is in contrast to selfishness, which is self-hatred and emptiness that needs to be constantly filled by a preoccupied concern for one's own needs, which makes it impossible to have any regard for others. The productive character who relates through the mode of love is capable of the most creative, energetic, and satisfactory living. It is on this formulation that Fromm is often called the optimistic humanist.[6] Competence in living, or the productive relationships which characterize this type of character structure is related to the capacity to love. A capacity to love may enhance sexual competence and satisfaction, rather than vice versa.[7]

Fromm's influence in psychoanalytic theory will, I believe, rest on his exploration and elucidation of the role of morals, values, and ethics in the development of personality and the neuroses. Freud maintained throughout his work that the question of morality and values were not the concern of the psychoanalyst. The physician was called upon to heal, not to judge, and his role must be that of an interested scientist who examines facts without bias, prejudices, or concerns for the ethics of a situation. This was reflected in his theories as well as his therapy. Although this is valid to a great extent for the physical scientist, it is apparent that the social scientist finds that morals, ethics, and values are not only his concern, but are often the main content of his interest. The psychoanalyst cannot avoid values, since for some theorists, the whole concept of neurosis is a value judgment varying from culture to culture and in periods of history. In addition, the therapist, try as he will, cannot divorce his own background, morality, and ethical judgments from his appraisal of his patient's mental health, since neuroses are products of social diseases in the social context, not diseases of an isolated organ enclosed in a skeletal framework. Kidney diseases, for example, can be examined, diagnosed, and treated in an identical fashion, whatever the background, ideas, values, and family history of the patient. This is patently impossible in the neuroses, in spite of our efforts to discover the panacea in our tranquillizing drugs. Fromm has explicitly raised the questions about the relationship of values to the psychiatric process.

Fromm believes that the therapist's values are communicated in spite of his efforts to restrain them. He cannot be a blank screen, and it is highly doubtful that psychoanalysis could be effective if he were. All theorists would agree that the therapist must believe that love is a productive human endeavor, and that he must have a positive orientation towards it. This immediately puts him in the position of having a morality regarding the worthwhileness of a loving attitude.

For Fromm, the basic ethic for man is the fulfillment of his potentialities. This is a humanistic thesis and reflects Fromm's own philosophical predelictions. What one does to oneself rather than what one does to others becomes the ultimate problem of ethics, since what we do to ourselves represents a truer, more honest motivation, while our behavior toward others may be overlaid with defensive techniques.

Self-fulfillment can be accomplished only through a relatedness with others. The efforts towards overcoming the dichotomy of man's loneliness and separateness are ordinarily productive and thus can be looked upon as a positive, constructive endeavor. In this sense, neuroses that interfere with man's fulfillment, creativity, and productivity can be considered an evil. In recent years this unproductive kind of living has been characterized by the existential philosophers as a state of non-being as opposed to the productive mode of existence which is called "being."

The relationship of non-being to sin in a theological sense has been explored in recent years by many existentialists and theologians. Paul Tillich has been particularly lucid and interesting on this matter.

Our comprehension of the process of productivity and creativity is still unclear. It has been alleged by psychologists and social scientists, as well as many interested laymen, that the creative process is helped, even instigated by the neurotic tendencies in the individual. Fromm's thesis supports the opposite view. Although there is much material at hand to indicate that creativity is possible in the neurotic, such as in Dostoievsky, Poe, Van Gogh, and Gauguin, etc., we have no evidence that the neurosis produced the creative activity. We can speculate that these people were creative in spite of their neuroses and imagine the enormity of their contributions if the obstacles of the neurosis were removed. This whole matter needs a more detailed examination.

The problems of morality are placed in a new light by posing questions in terms of what man does to himself rather than what he does to others. The insights of psychoanalysis have enabled us to recognize that one's overt behavior may be defensive, consequently hypocritical, and not a true indication of one's real feelings and attitudes. In examining an individual's behavior, we must be careful not to think of single items of behavior, although this may be the entire basis on which a man may be judged. Character structure, not single items of behavior, more truly reflect the total character, but may be the result of an extreme provocation or a defense against some other underlying force. A professional censor of public morals may have a true concern over the spiritual values of the community or an exaggerated curiosity about pornographic matters or a combination of both. His job and public behavior do not inform us of his motivation, but his character structure would. The person of deep integrity may be hostile and cantankerous, as opposed to the hostile individual who is forced by his neurosis to be compulsively good. In terms of behavior, hostile or angry behavior may be constructive and even considerate of another person's needs, while forced pleasantness may be ultimately destructive. This gives us a clue to the necessity of studying character structure rather than specific behavior items in our psychological tests and research designs, otherwise we cannot be sure what we are discovering. An individual's behavior may sometimes be the index of the real person, but sometimes the opposite is true. The prohibitionist or professional censor is not necessarily an individual who has strong negative feelings about liquor or pornography. He may be an individual who, in dealing with a strong inclination to drink, or having an interest in pornographic materials, becomes a professional reformer, and so overcomes these weaknesses by activity which is self-righteous and accepted by the community. The reformed alcoholic is often a person who becomes deeply involved in helping others reform, as in Alcoholics Anonymous, and sometimes becomes a self-appointed saint. This allows him to spend much time in a drinking atmosphere. The psychiatrist often is a glorified snoop who may satisfy his curiosities about others while ostensibly relieving them of distress. This does not imply that one's motives should be pure in the pursuit of one's goals, since they never can be. However, we should be aware of these mixed motives if we intend to ferret out the whole truth about an individual's activity. Our behavior is the result of a mixture of motivations and we should be prepared to acknowledge that the mixture not only contains sublimations of instinctual needs, as Freud stressed, but also positive interests and desires.

We have seen that the neurotic is busy presenting his idealization and covering up his real self, and so it is clear that we have a more accurate picture of an individual when we know how he deals with himself as well as his public behavior. This does not excuse or relieve him of responsibility for his behavior, as we will note later on, but it emphasizes the notion that "to know thyself," and "to thine own self be true," is equally relevant in the question of morality as "Love thy neighbor as thyself."

This question raises the matter of the goals and purposes of psychoanalytic therapy. Is psychoanalysis designed to reform an individual, or to resolve conflicts by helping him adjust to the society in which he lives? Some societies promoted values (Hitler's Germany, Dobu culture) which we would consider inhuman. The question of adjustment then, raises many important issues about psychoanalysis being a tool or becoming an instrument to encourage conformity. Fromm feels that the goal of psychoanalysis is to produce a productive individual, a person who is relieved of his difficulties in his capacity to love and be loved which would enable him to be truly integrated, creative, and of good will. This does not involve the issue of adjustment to others as much as it implies the fulfilling of one's own potentialities. The notion of being of good will underwrites the humanistic ethic of Fromm, who feels that man is essentially good and interested in the welfare of others in a tender, loving way. Forces in society and in his own development thwart these attributes and capacities and result in destructive, uncooperative, and hateful activities. This, of course, is in sharp contrast to Freud's notion that man is essentially destructive and that society developed in order to constrain these instinctual forces. Goodness, for Fromm, represents constructive behavior, and the ethic develops out of this that whatever is constructive is good and that neurosis is ethically bad since it interferes with constructive behavior. This is the basis for Fromm's statement that "the neurotic symptom is an expression of a moral conflict."

The problem of good and evil introduces the problem of authority and ultimately the question of a supreme authority, or God. Fromm is interested in all these matters. However, it must be noted that he is attempting to construct a morality that is scientifically based, not deistically structured. Consequently, he recognizes two kinds of authority, the rational and the irrational. Irrational authority is based on power. In the face of the irrational authority man is busy trying to be approved of and thus obedience becomes a prime virtue. The rational authority Fromm calls the humanistic authority, whose sole interest is in man's welfare and not the welfare of the authority. Good, under this authority, implies fulfillment, affirmation, and the unfolding of one's potentialities. The distinction between the rational and irrational authority clarifies our thinking on the matter of conscience, guilt, and responsibility. The kind of conscience produced under a rational authority can be called a humanistic conscience and it is quite different from the conscience produced by an irrational authority. The authoritarian conscience is actually the voice of the external authority which has become internalized. This is identical to Freud's superego. Here conscience is determined by what the authority says is good or bad. What pleases the authority is good, and what displeases it is bad. Disobedience creates guilty feelings which stimulate concern about rejection and punishment. Rejection becomes a most potent form of punishment, since in the authoritarian framework the prime offense is disobedience or rebellion and the desire to be different. Guilty conscience means displeasing the authority, which often involves acts of creativity. Horney made some efforts to clarify the concept of guilt by distinguishing true guilt from pseudo or neurotic guilt. At the same time guilt needs to be distinguished as a theological problem from guilt as a psychological problem. Guilt refers to the affect or feeling that surrounds activities, thoughts, or phantasies which in the long run are defiant and hostile, or to rejecting attitudes toward the authority figure or toward one's own integrity. Guilt feelings may, however, be defensive devices which serve to emphasize the person's feelings of unworthiness and become the basis for demands on the environment. They are conscious and unconscious devices to diminish responsibility and punishment and do not encourage the individual to attempt to overcome the situation which produced it. Expressed guilt feelings are often exaggerated and recognized as insincere by the individual expressing them. These guilt feelings rarely ever lead to determined responsible activities designed to alleviate the problem. Instead, they produce more defensiveness and increased catering which enhances the feeling of subjection to the authority.

On the other hand, there are a variety of guilt feelings associated with responsible remorse over unproductive, unfulfilled living. These responses occur when one engages in activities that are unnecessarily or needlessly self-destructive, and they encourage one to attempt to resolve the cause of the guilt feelings. This might be called true guilt or guilt which arises in response to a rational authority or a humanistic conscience. The humanistic conscience is not an internalization of an external authority, but a check on one's own activities and functioning. Good feeling is a response to creative, productive functioning, while bad feeling or guilty feeling is in response to a failure in productive living. It is the essence of a real, ethical conscience because it is a response to one's own integrity and self interest.

Both types of guilt are felt as a source of distress to the individual. However, one is defensive, neurotic, and unproductive while the other has potentialities for self-improvement. The concept of guilt in theological terms often overlooks this distinction since it functions in an authoritative framework that is largely irrational. This distinction raises questions about responsibility, which has significance beyond the confines of psychology. Responsibility in Freud's deterministic and biological orientation often led to the assumption that the individual could not be held responsible for his neurotic behavior since it was the result of his inevitable libidinal heritage. How could a person be blamed for his aggressive or hostile feelings when they were biologically determined? This issue, coupled with the unconscious nature of one's wishes raised the question of determinism versus free will or choice as it related to the problem of responsibility. Fromm, like other neo-Freudian theorists, views neurosis as the result of a choice made in an effort to cope with conflicting tendencies and desires. The individual does make a choice, even though it is a greatly restricted one. He does decide what ultimately will be his goals, and in this sense has some responsibility for his neurosis and its ultimate fate. The existentialists make much of the notion that the individual must always make the ultimate choice as to whether he stands still or goes forward, and so he cannot avoid this decision.

It is clear that much happens to an individual that is beyond his personal responsibility. He does not choose his parents, nor can he determine or choose the atmosphere in which he will spend his early years. In this sense he has no choice or responsibility for the early developments in his life that are so crucial to the ultimate development of the neurosis. However, in spite of the forces that are outside of his control, there are many choices he does make in terms of how he will deal with these forces. If neurosis is entirely out of the individual's control, then it is a form of visitation and the neurotic can only be excused and not blamed for consequences of his behavior. The other view is that the neurotic is an individual whose living has become distorted by virtue of certain experiences and environmental conditions and the ways in which he has met them. One view assumes that the individual plays no role in the development of his illness while the other acknowledges the failure in his development as a result of his participation in a process which can be corrected with sufficient interest and concern. The issue of responsibility becomes a factor in the therapeutic process, since it is agreed by all psychoanalysts that unless the patient assumes some responsibility for his illness there is no possibility of change. The therapist must make a distinction between the individual's responsibility and where he is free of it. This allows him to distinguish between not accepting an individual's behavior while accepting him as a person. This becomes an integral part of therapy in which we reject the inadequacies or failures in living without condemning the person. Consequently, we must not deny the responsibility that an individual has for his own behavior. The issue is largely one of the degree of responsibility and the mitigating circumstances that surround his particular piece of behavior. When this issue involves the law, the problem is even further confused, since there are legal definitions for responsibility which are often at complete variance with our existing knowledge of psychology. The Durham decision has gone a long way to clarify the problem in the courts.[8]

In this connection we must recognize that responsibility is different from assigning fault. The determination of fault is generally outside the scope or interest of the psychoanalyst. It is of interest to the therapeutic situation only as a way of evading responsibility. Wherever the fault lies, and this can only rarely be determined, if at all, since every event is mutually determined or interpersonally produced, it is still the task of the patient to do something about altering it, rather than expecting the "other" to rectify the situation. This may be imposing an unfair demand on the patient, but it is assumed that when he comes for treatment he wishes to alter his unsatisfactory way of living rather than to reform the environment. When the patient says: "You can't blame me for this. After all, I am this way because my parents didn't love me," we must help him see that his present situation is his own responsibility. We do not focus on the ultimate responsibility for his present status. We suggest that while his complaints may have been true when he was a child, his mode of living at present is largely his own choice. But he then says: "Yes, but you're asking me to do something that my parents should have done. Why don't you get them to change their attitudes toward me?" To this response we can only say that it is the patient who is discontent and who is seeking help in re-organizing his living. The tactic of blaming it on the parents is similar to the broader tactic of blaming it on "others" and is a way of avoiding the necessity for personal change. The therapist's activity directs the focus from whose fault it was to "do you really want to alter your way of life?" Since we cannot force any change, we must encourage and assist the patient in the process of change. At times we lift the responsibility from the patient, not by assigning blame to anyone else, but by acknowledging that the patient may have been too small, weak, or dependent to have done anything about it in his early years. Although this mitigates the patient's guilt about his failure to do something at the time, it does not blame others.[9]

The question of responsibility and its relation to the therapeutic process has greatly interested the neo-Freudian theorists. In spite of the mechanistic, instinctivistic orientation of classic psychoanalysis, the issue of responsibility with its ultimate moral and ethical concerns crept into the therapeutic process. Although forces or energy have no ethics, the handling of problems in everyday practice inevitably draw up matters of judgment and morality. In recent years the psychoanalytic theorists have brought these questions into the open rather than permitting them to sneak in by the back door. The issue of responsibility can be seen in its totality by looking at the alcoholic as a social problem. The alcoholic is generally considered to be a neurotic whose difficulty affects his family as well as himself. When the psychiatrist examines the alcoholic, he decides that his drinking has been motivated by certain neurotic forces. At the same time he acknowledges the economic and social consequences on the family and on the community. This confuses the therapeutic issue with moral and social issues, since it is the legal responsibility of a husband to support his family. However, when a psychiatrist treats the alcoholic, he does not (if he wishes to be useful to him) say: "Look what you are doing to your family! You ought to stop your drinking!" He doesn't say this particularly since it will rarely, if ever, alter the drinking problem. The alcoholic does not drink to punish his wife or himself. He drinks for many reasons that are mostly unknown to him. The moral (or theological) view says "You are responsible. Your family is starving." The therapeutic view says: "You are a sick man. You are forced to drink because of problems and issues unknown to you, which are destructive to you and your family." The legal view says: "Whatever is wrong with you, you must support your family, so get out and work." In spite of all that has been said about the significance of responsibility in the neuroses, it is not unduly emphasized in the therapeutic process. To do this would certainly increase the patient's problem and his drinking. However, if the therapeutic process is to be effective, it must be an issue.

Because of his concern with the problems of morality and responsibility, Fromm has clarified the relationship of religion and psychiatry. Freud viewed religion from the standpoint of psychopathology, and diagnosed it as an obsessional neurosis. Fromm approaches it from the viewpoint of faith, and recognizes that faith is a universal requirement for human existence, and considers it to be a character trait. Faith is the ability to have some conviction about the worth of an idea, attitude, feeling, or belief, and is necessary for man's existence. Man must have faith in something. Faith, however, can be rational or irrational. Irrational faith is not a response to one's intellect, but is due to a pervasive uncertainty which produces a feeling of powerlessness and helplessness. It derives from the fact that man must have something to depend upon. This kind of faith has to do with power, and produces faith in an omnipotent authority figure. Rational faith is based on the

firm conviction of the productive, emotional, and intellectual qualities of the person in whom we have faith. It is a basic necessity
for human development and a requisite for the fulfillment of our
potentialities. Fromm's concepts of religion are based on this distinction. Fromm does not question whether man needs a religion.
It is clear to him that man must have a religion. The real question
is what kind of religion. For Fromm religion "is a system of
thought and action shared by a group of individuals, with a frame
of orientation, and an object of devotion." Religion is essential to
man because he requires something to deal with his feelings of
innate helplessness and dependency. Fromm contends that neurosis
is a form of religion, rather than religion being a form of neurosis.
It is a private type of religion which often interferes with organized
religions. The neurosis itself may take on religious aspects and
rituals which may resemble the traditional religious movements.

Fromm broadly categorizes religions into humanitarian and
authoritarian, and considers that a good religion is one which encourages man's fullllment. Consequently, religion should not be in
conflict with psychoanalysis, or any kind of therapy if its purpose
serves to enhance and fulfill man's potentialities. On the contrary,
he points out that psychotherapy is interested in the same goals as
religion is, in the sense of developing and encouraging man's
capacity for love. When this is the underlying theme in organized
religions, it is consonant with psychotherapeutic goals.

SUMMARY AND APPRAISAL

Erich Fromm, while developing no systematic theories about
personality development, has contributed greatly to the science of
psychology by his studies of the effects of the social, philosophical,
socio-economic and religious issues on personality development. His
major contributions lie in his elaboration of the way personality is
influenced by the interaction of the individual with his culture.
He has developed a scientific approach to the problem of morality
and ethics which will have a lasting influence on psychiatric therapy.
In emphasizing the limited role of instincts in human adaptation,
he has stressed the significance of learning and cultural indoctrina-
tion. The neurotic difficulties arise out of needs created by man's
existential dichotomies and the contradictions imposed on him by
his need to relate to a cultural setting. The separateness imposed
by his development out of animalness requires him to relate to

other humans in ways that are available to him. The most successful method is through love, which allows for the most productive
relationship. In his elaboration of the role of culture, he has made
important observations about the effects of authoritarianism and its
influence on character formation. Fromm's views are more descriptive of Western societies, and there are some questions as to the
validity of his views for other cultures at other times. He is criticized
for being too superficial and judgmental in his opinion of theory
and therapy, and that his contributions are of greater interest to
sociologists than to psychiatrists.

Although his views on theory have had an influence in extending
the scope of thinking of other theorists, particularly Horney and
Sullivan, his contributions to therapy have been practical and useful. He has clarified the goals of therapy as an unfolding of man's
potentialities rather than a process of adjustment. He does not feel
that therapy has been successful or completed until the patient has
enlarged his capacity for loving and being loved. He has tremendous
respect for the neurotic, as did Jung and Rank, and he stresses
the positive elements of the patient's potentialities as well as exploring his inadequacies. This aspect of Fromm's therapeutic skills
has brought new meaning to the process of therapy. It encourages
the patient to recognize that not all of the tendencies that are
disapproved of by the culture are necessarily neurotic. For example,
many patients are ashamed of their softness and tenderness. They
feel they should be strong, and that tenderness should be discarded.
Fromm would point out that though this attitude is disapproved
of, it is a worthwhile attribute that should be encouraged and
developed. He helps the patient to see that although the culture
does not value this trait, it has great virtue and desirability in
developing strength of character and purpose. The tendency to
focus on the patient's neurotic tendencies and overlook his positive
attitudes is an outcome of the classic, therapeutic method. Fromm
has helped to illuminate its deficiencies. By his research into the
authoritarian aspects of our culture and the distinction between the
rational and irrational authority, transference as a therapeutic tool
has been strengthened. It has become clear that the patient's reactions to the therapist can be based on realistic factors. At times
the therapist can be an irrational authority who makes unreasonable demands and expects exceptional privileges. Fromm considers
therapy to be at an end when the therapist no longer appears as

an irrational authority. Values and value judgment have become part of the therapeutic process.

Fromm has elaborated the theme of man's need to relate to others in order to find some meaning to his existence. He feels that man can relate in a tender, protective way, and thus achieve the fulfillment of his potentialities. Therapy which recognizes these essential needs can help overcome the obstacles which interfere with the full development of his capacity to love himself, and thus to love others.

NOTES

1. The problem of relatedness is central to Fromm's contributions. In *Man for Himself* he says: "The main difference in theory of character proposed here from that of Freud is that the fundamental basis of character is not seen in various types of libido organization but in specific kinds of a person's relatedness to the world." This problem has become a core issue in much of the current work in the psychoses as well as the neuroses. The emphasis of the existential psychoanalytic theorists on relation, participation, committment, and inter-action has also brought this issue into prominence. Loneliness, was only vaguely acknowledged as a factor in the production of the neuroses and psychoses in the earlier theories. In recent years it has occupied a prominent place. See:

Will, Otto A., Jr.: Human relatedness and the schizophrenic reaction. Psychiatry 22:205-223, 1959.

Fromm-Reichmann, Frieda: Psychoanalysis and Psychotherapy, Collected Papers. Chicago, University of Chicago Press, 1959.

Weigert, Edith: Existentialism and its relation to psychotherapy. Psychiatry 12:399-412, 1949.

Tillich, Paul: The Courage to Be. New Haven, Yale University Press, 1952.

Sullivan, H. S.: Interpersonal Theory of Psychiatry. New York, W. W. Norton & Co., 1953. "Loneliness as an experience is so terrible that it practically baffles clear recall."

2. The statement that the "masochist is someone who is kind to a sadist" expresses very neatly the symbiotic relationship based on the exchange of hostile attitudes which serves the neurotic needs of both partners.

3. "Character," he says in *Man for Himself*, "can be defined as the (relatively permanent) form in which human energy is canalized in the process of assimilation and socialization."

4. Their slogan is "Stolen fruits are sweetest." They also make the joke comprehensible in which an individual who never buys his own cigarettes is asked which brand he prefers. He answers, "The other person's brand."

5. This type of character structure is primarily a feature of the consumer-oriented socio-economic structure. It goes along with the emphasis on advertisement and selling without a real relation to product. The revival of existential philosophical movements in the U. S. and abroad is related to the depersonalization, meaningless and emptiness of man's current living. This has produced a new variety of neurotic disorders characterized by a search for identity and a meaning to one's existence. See:

Miller, Arthur: Death of a Salesman. New York, Viking Press, 1949.

Reisman, David: The Lonely Crowd. New Haven, Yale University Press, 1950 and Individualism Reconsidered, New York, Free Press, 1954.

Wheelis, Allan: Quest for Identity. New York, W. W. Norton, 1958.

Frankel, Charles: The Case for Modern Man. New York, Harper & Bros., 1955.

Kahler, Erich: The Tower and the Abyss. New York, Harper & Bros., 1957.

Frank, Waldo: The Rediscovery of Man. New York, George Braziller, 1958.

6. Fromm says that productiveness is an attitude every human being is capable of unless he is mentally and emotionally crippled.

7. Fromm distinguishes sharply between productive love and what is called "love." Love is a most ambiguous word and may denote everything short of hate from love for candy or a symphony to the most intense feelings of intimacy. Genuine love is rooted in productiveness and is related to a mother's love for her children or the adults' erotic love for one another. It must, however, have the basic elements of care, responsibility, respect, and knowledge,

8. The Durham Decision, Durham v. U. S. 2T4F2d, sets new standards for the determination of responsibility as it relates to mental disorder. It allows for testimony in terms of relationship to a mental defect in the individual or as a product of the mental defect rather than in terms of a knowledge of right and wrong or as the result of an irresistable impulse. This has had many notable effects and has allowed the psychiatrist, in the role of an expert witness, to present sufficient data regarding the individual's life history and character development to allow for the proper determination of responsibility by the jury. It has had a most salutary effect on the determination of legal responsibility taking the newest findings of psychiatry into account. It is unfortunate, however, that the punitive attitudes toward asocial and antisocial behavior has led many jurists and penologists as well as psychiatrists to overlook the distinction between mental illness that results in criminal behavior and requires psychiatric treatment and criminal behavior unrelated to mental disease.

9. Salzman, Leon: Masochism and psychopathy as adaptive behavior. J. of Individual Psychol. 16:182-188, 1960.

——: Guilt, responsibility and the unconscious. Comp. Psychiat. 2:179, 1961.

——: Discussion on the question of honesty. J. of Pastoral Care. 14:65-77, 1960.

——: Observations on Dr. Tillich's views on guilt, sin and reconciliation. J. Pastoral Care. 11:14-19, 1957.

——: The psychology of religious and ideological conversion. Psychiatry. 16:61-75, 1953.

Masserman, Jules, ed.: Psychoanalysis and Human Values, Vol. III. New York, Grune & Stratton, 1960.

V

Harry Stack Sullivan

THE THEORY of personality development as propounded by Harry Stack Sullivan is perhaps the clearest formulation of psychoanalytic theory in the framework of the most recent advances in science. His theory stays closest to concepts and hypotheses which are definable and operational and which permit the greatest degree of exploration of the validity of these concepts. His theoretical framework has greatly expanded the understanding of what transpires inside of people on the basis of what is transacted between them. The theory of personality that he developed is called an interpersonal theory. Sullivan saw the science of psychiatry as the study of interpersonal relations which concerned itself with the manifest and observable behavior of the individual. This conception puts stress on observing the individual in action and in relations to others. He felt that psychiatry could not concern itself with those human activities which are beyond observation and available only by inference. Consequently his findings are always capable of being tested directly through observation.

Sullivan arrived at his formulations through an intensive study of clinical material, particularly schizophrenia and the obsessional states. He considered psychiatry to be primarily the science of human development, while the psychopathology of human behavior was a secondary derivative of that science. Psychiatry, he thought, was not a study of mental illness, but the study of the processes and events which transpire between people. Essentially, these processes are manifest in the realm of communications, both overt and covert. This contrasts with Freud's conception of psychiatry as the study of the pathology of human behavior. If psychiatry is a study of the processes between people, the social and cultural aspects of human behavior are crucial elements in his theory. For this reason his theories are of the greatest interest to other social scientists.

He drew heavily from the social sciences and gave them much in return. Although Sullivan's views have permeated the social sciences, his influence has been limited by his style of writing, which alienates many readers. The editing of much of his work which is being done currently will undoubtedly solidify his role and influence.

Sullivan studied the process of human development by a detailed examination of the stages of growth that the individual undergoes as a result of his interpersonal contacts and experiences. In addition to this, he felt that the various stages of development are influenced by the special physiological requirements of the individual during these stages. For example, the infant is entirely dependent on the benevolence of his environment and is unable to formulate his needs verbally. Later, he can express his needs verbally, but he continues in an environment peopled almost exclusively by the immediate family figures until school terminates this phase. Although these epochs will be examined in detail, it should be noted that the stress will be placed upon the contacts the individual makes with other humans during the developmental periods, rather than the activity of instinctual forces. The focus will be placed on the capacities and opportunities for relating to other humans that become available at different periods of development.

Although it is almost universally accepted by all psychiatrists and psychoanalysts that anxiety is the primary source of all human pathology, Sullivan believed it to be the mainspring for all development, normal and abnormal. He postulated that anxiety was the major impetus towards development, which proceeded from the innate necessity to utilize one's biological apparatus as its separate functions matured. Sullivan insisted that the maturation of muscle groups, the sensory and other physiological functions by themselves produced the impetus for the utilization of these capacities. The infant utilizes his maturing apparatus not only to avoid anxiety, but to fully develop these functional units. This notion of Sullivan's avoided any metaphysical postulates about self-fulfillment, or fulfilling one's real self. It involved only physiological facts about the maturation of biological functions. This is essentially the physiological concomitant of the biological process of growth involving irritability and lability.

Since psychiatry is a study of interpersonal processes, it concerns itself exclusively with observable data. Sullivan felt that psychiatry should not become involved in the immutably private data that is rarely accessible and relates to the completely private reveries which have no relation to others in the outside world. This is an area of Sullivan's thinking about which he has been justifiably criticized by others. He maintained that a great deal of activity which occurs in human being in their secret heart of hearts is largely unavailable for study and consequently has no place in the field of psychiatry. He was more interested in those elements in human behavior that are shared, rather than those which are distinctly personal and private. He tried to make psychiatry a scientific tool, and while he never denied the significance of individuality (and emphasized it in all his writings), he felt psychiatry was not the science of the singular, or the strictly personal.

Sullivan explicitly emphasized that man is an animal, bio-logically bound, whose development is culturally directed. Man, he said, is utterly dependent on his environment until there is a sufficient maturation of his potentialities to allow him to exist in-dependently of this environment. More than any other animal, man spends a larger portion of his life in such dependencies. The inborn potentialities or biological capacities which mature are not instincts, since they are extremely variable and labile, and their fate depends largely on the cultural setting in which they mature. Sullivan believed, along with some ethologists, that possibly only two in-stincts can be documented in man. These are the finger to thumb apposition and the pelvic thrust. All other descriptions of instinct, such as the sexual instinct or the death instinct, are either confused ethological concepts, or metaphysical formulations which have little to do with the biology of instincts. He felt that psychiatry seeks to study all biologically and conditioned interpersonal processes which occur in interpersonal situations in which the psychiatrist is an observer. What is studied is behavior, although the Sullivanian conception of the origin of behavior is widely disparate from the Watsonian behaviorists.

Sullivan formulated four postulates which underlie his theorizing and hypothesizing. Although these are at times self evident, they are also profoundly meaningful.

1. His first postulate is called the biological postulate. It states that man is distinguished from other animals by his living in a culture which requires interchange. This cultural interchange is

different from the herd behavior of many animals or the forced family or clan behavior of others. In man, the exchange is in terms of a mutually creative process which is dictated by the tender regard of one for another.

2. The second postulate says that man is more simply human than otherwise. Sullivan emphasizes the great similarities in man, in spite of individual differences. This follows from his notion of the role of psychiatry, and he indicated that even the most strikingly diverse human performances are closer to the behavior of other human beings than to animals. This stresses the similarities in man rather than the differences and attempts to minimize all the previous theorizing based on analogies to animal instinct and animal behavior.

3. The third postulate is called the euphoria postulate, and it states that the expansive or comfortable feelings in an individual are dependent on the presence or absence of anxiety. It says that when tension is at a minimum, the individual is in a state of euphoria. Although absolute euphoria does not exist in reality, neither does absolute tension. Tensions are produced by needs, and the satisfactions of these needs will reduce the tension. Anxiety interrupts the satisfaction of these needs and interferes more or less with euphoric feelings.

4. The fourth postulate is called the tenderness postulate. This is a formulation which attempts a dynamic explanation of the presence of tenderness in humans without postulating a maternal instinct or some humanistic formulation about the essential good will of humans. It says that the activity of an infant which arises from the tension of his needs produces tension in the mothering person, which is felt by the mothering person as tenderness. This formulation implies that tenderness is the response of a mothering person to the tension of needs in the infant. It states that the mother's reaction is an interpersonal response to the needs of another human being who is dependent upon her. This is the prototype for the development of tender interests in adults in other than mothering situations. It is a most useful postulate which arises directly out of Sullivan's interpersonal theorizing. Sullivan does not attempt an explanation of why, under certain circumstances, tension is felt as tenderness. This may have to do with the dependency status, or the degree of involvement in the rela-

tionship. It might be noted that this is a weak link in Sullivan's theory, since he sees anxiety generally as a restraining and inhibiting force, except in this instance. Here he visualizes it as a most creative force. The postulate is a fine example of Sullivan's attempt to frame human behavior in operational terms.

Most theorists have postulated that tenderness towards the infant is a prime essential for survival. The distress and tension of the infant's needs would, under other circumstances, stimulate anxiety in the adult. In this special instance it produces tenderness, which decreases anxiety, and enhances the infant's euphoria. The need for tender, benevolent interest for human survival has been amply documented by the work of Margaret Ribble and Rene Spitz. The contributions of these two workers have been of the greatest influence in stimulating the development of culturalist theories about human development. These studies made it clear that the infant needs more than physiological or nutritional supplies to survive. Unless some fondling and tender handling are present, the adequacy of nutritional requirements would not be enough for survival. This fact has altered the emphasis from the instinctual needs of the infant and focused it on the cultural requirements. It had been thought that mothers give loving care to their children because of maternal instinct or the pressures of society. Sullivan stated that the impulsion to tenderness toward the infant is stirred up by the infant's need. It is an interpersonal situation, and it provides understanding about the many situations and occasions where the so-called maternal instinct seems to be absent, or where mothers have little interest in their children and even abandon them. It has clarified the understanding of why mothers experience less difficulty in letting their infants out for adoption if the mother has not seen her child after delivery. On the other hand, if she has had some dealing with the child after delivery, she has greater difficulty in giving it up. This observation has been responsible for many of the procedures in adoption agencies.

The infant experiences tenderness from the mother through a process called empathy. This postulate of Sullivan enables the social scientist to develop theories about certain human capacities and abilities without having to resort to metaphysical hypotheses or instinctual forces.

Sullivan described two ultimate goals in human behavior. These are called end states to which the organism aspires. One is called the pursuit of satisfaction. Activities of this type are designed to fulfill the biological needs of the individual for food, air, sex, etc. The second goal is the pursuit of security. These are activities designed to fulfill other than the biological needs, that is, the cultural needs of the individual. Needs of this type rarely occur in an isolated fashion except in the earliest years. These end states are generally intermingled and operate simultaneously. In the adult, the security needs almost always take precedence once the basic biological requirements are satisfied. Security needs revolve largely about the avoidance of anxiety and the search for esteem, status, and acceptance. This formulation forced Sullivan to deny the focal prominence of sex and sexual needs in the human organism, since he saw the notion of being acceptable as primary. The individual will often dissociate his sexual needs in order to achieve such acceptance. The activities designed to fulfill these end states are generally mixed, and often both needs are satisfied in a single activity.

In infancy the security needs are satisfied through a process called empathy. This describes the observed situation where the infant, prior to any capacity for verbalization, responds to the atmosphere in which it exists, and seems capable of distinguishing benevolence from malevolence, anxiety from euphoria.

The process of becoming a human being is essentially the process of acculturation, of meeting and adapting to the cultural requirements in which the individual happens to exist. Although the infant cannot conceptualize this process as well as the adult, it is operating nevertheless, even in the earliest stages of infancy.

In fulfilling the end states, the needs are manifested as tensions which must be overcome. The individual sets out to fulfill these needs by a series of activities which if successful, are described as integrating or conjunctive. If the needs are fulfilled, the situation is integrated. If the needs remain unfulfilled after activity to fulfill them has occurred, then the situation is described as disintegrated or disjunctive. The presence of tension indicates that there is a need to be satisfied, which sets into motion activities which will result in either an integrative or disintegrative situation.

When a situation is integrated and the need satisfied, then the issue is resolved and the tension terminates. If, however, the tension persists, then conflict has entered the situation and anxiety is produced. Consequently, anxiety is called a disjunctive force. It enters the situation when security needs rather than biological needs are at issue. The tension produced by the biological needs of hunger or thirst do not stimulate anxiety, but rather some somatic symptomatology or somatic distress. This particular observation of Sullivan's has contributed a fresh approach to psychosomatic theory. He has demonstrated that in fulfilling a biological need, there is a decrease in the tonus of the muscle, such as the gastric muscle, for example. However, in the process of satisfying a security need there is generally an increase in muscular tone. When the infant is hungry, he cries in order to announce his need. The gastric musculature will be in a state of tonus. If he is fed, the tonus will decrease. However, if the cry is for attention, and not for food, and the need is not satisfied, the infant may learn to restrain the cry, but the muscular tonicity will continue. This tonus, which originally derived from the biological need for food, may continue in response to the unsatisfied security need. Even after feeding has occurred, the tonus may remain, and may even be increased in the absence of the reduction of security needs. This appears to be the case in many psychosomatic problems, where the unnoticed, or unsatisfied security needs of an individual may keep an organ or portion of the musculature in a state of tonus. Where there is an apparent state of satisfaction or reduction in tension, muscular tonus may still be present. It is in the distinction of needs of satisfaction, or biological needs, as opposed to the security needs that we can comprehend the dilemma of continued states of tension when biological needs are fully satisfied.

When a situation is successfully integrated, euphoria results. This is a state of self-esteem and power. This feeling of power or self-esteem is cumulative, and enables the individual to face and deal with further experiences of anxiety. A sufficient self-esteem is the prerequisite for dealing with feelings of powerlessness and helplessness which man encounters in the state of anxiety.

The performance and activities appropriate to the fulfillment of a need, or the relief of tension are called dynamisms by Sullivan. The term avoids the word drive, which is too controversial. Instead, it draws upon the physical sciences for a label that carries none of the limitations and prejudices belonging to the concepts of instinct or innate forces. The dynamism is the constellation of activities that utilizes simple or complex movements to achieve the relief of tension or the fulfillment of a need. In the infant, the cry with its muscular accompaniments is the dynamism which is most energetically used. It involves the oral areas almost exclusively, and is largely successful in filling the infant's needs. A dynamism generally utilizes a particular bodily zone with which the individual interacts with the world in order to fulfill his needs. The lust dynamism, for example, utilizes the genital zones. This sound suspiciously like Freud's libidinal zones; namely, the oral, anal, and genital zones. Sullivan, however, does not conceive of these areas in this way at all. He recognizes that human biological needs must be satisfied through certain bodily apertures, and that the experience involved may take a special coloration from the particular zone of interaction. This is quite different from Freud's notion that the quality of the experience is determined by the nature of the aperture. Hunger is satisfied through the oral zone. Because the infant's cry may produce the magical presence of mother, we can expect that some humans may associate magic with the mouth, and the mouth in some cultures may have magical significance. Sullivan views the zone of interaction with the environment—ears, eyes, mouth, anus, urethra, and genitals, in terms of the interpersonal interaction of the zones with the environment.

For example, the mouth or oral area is the source of interpersonal contact for the infant during its feeding period. The infant requires the assistance of another person for feeding and thus the oral area is the source of interpersonal contact for the infant during its initial contact with the world. Since food intake requires another person until the individual is able to feed himself, it has interpersonal relevance. At another stage in human development the anal area has interpersonal relevance, since bladder and bowel evacuation requires some assistance from outside sources. It is therefore hardly surprising that the oral and anal areas participate actively in the process of acculturation, since there is constant contact with the infant through these areas. When we study the development of personality in detail, this fact will become more evident. The urethral area has only slight interpersonal relevance, except that it is joined in the male with the genital apparatus. As the human being develops, the oral and anal areas require less and less intervention from others. They are soon able to function entirely without outside assistance. However, the considerable participation of others in the functioning of these zones in the early years produces marked effects in the later years. The genital area is particularly interesting in this regard since in the earliest years no human interaction is required. After the maturation of the sexual apparatus, another person is always required for the total biological function to be carried out. Of course, masturbation and other self-sentient activities can be practiced, but another individual is always necessary for the biological performance of procreation. Although artificial insemination may obviate this, we might expect widespread personality effects if it were to become a more common occurrence than it is at present. Although Freud considered these zones important because of the libido concentrated there, Sullivan considered them important to the extent that they required or encouraged interpersonal contact.

Sullivan described experience as occurring in three modes that are dependent upon the physical and mental development of the individual. He called the earliest mode the prototaxic mode which characterizes the period of infancy. In this mode of experiencing the individual cannot establish any serial connection between events. Things happen, but they have no relation to other events, except through the immediate contact involved in the experience. Since there is no capacity for separating oneself from the world, there tend to be the cosmic identifications so characteristic of this stage of development. This type of experiencing is a common occurrence in some mental illnesses, particularly in schizophrenia, where the patient identifies himself with the whole cosmos and cannot recognize himself as distinct and separate from the world at large.

He called the second mode of experiencing the parataxic mode, which is the common way of perceiving the world for the normal as well as the mentally ill. In this mode events are related because of their serial connection rather than any logical relationship. Events which follow one another are thought to be related regardless of their true relationship. If the thunder occurs when the door is shut, then the closing of the door is experienced as having produced the thunder. Similarly, if people laugh when one enters a room, the laughing is experienced as being related to one's entry into the room. The serial relationship in the parataxic mode of thinking establishes the relationship, not the examination of the true connection between the events. This mode of experiencing is common in human behavior, and it characterizes the distorted experiencing of the paranoid state. Parataxic thinking and parataxic behavior, however, are not synonymous with paranoid thinking and behavior. Sullivan makes a distinction and emphasizes the notion that paranoid behavior is only one aspect of parataxic thinking. The establishment of serial connection or parataxic experiencing is a stage in the development of rational or syntaxic thinking and is not, in itself, a characteristic of mental illness. However, it becomes pathological when the serial connections always have some malice and malevolence involved in them. Autistic thinking, which is prevalent in many mental disorders, also occurs in the parataxic mode of thinking. Autistic thinking is highly personalized, and the associations, connections, and relevances are not necessarily shared by others. They involve purely private experiences in the partaxic mode, in which connections have occurred to this particular person through serial relationships which have occurred to him and to no one else. In these instances we must establish the meaning of these autistic reveries by a detailed study of the patient's life experiences. The use of universal symbols does not necessarily illuminate the autistic revery. It is in this area that some of the most mischievous nonsense passes for psychiatric brilliance. The therapist who interprets his patient's private autistic reveries through some brilliant symbolic formulations based on nothing but educated guesses often disenchants the serious scientist, or educated layman, instead of impressing them with the so-called artistic aspects of psychotherapeutic technique. In these instances a more detailed study of the individual's own experiences might reveal the meaning of the autism.

The third mode of experiencing was called by Sullivan the syntaxic mode, or the logical, rational, consensually validated mode of thinking. In this mode an experience is validated through logical reasoning, or through the consensual or group confirmations of the event. For example, the discussion as to whether the group is really laughing at one's entry into the room could be determined by getting a statement from the group to determine whether they were indeed laughing at this, or whether they were really laughing at a joke told the moment before one's entry. It is true that there might be a group conspiracy to humiliate the individual and consequently, the group's statement might be deceptive. The syntaxic mode also applies to the kind of thinking that establishes that thunder is the result of an electric storm, and not the slamming of a door.

These three modes of experiencing occur simultaneously in all individuals, although hopefully, most adults experience largely in the syntaxic mode. In the neuroses or psychoses, one type may predominate over another, but it is rare, if not impossible, to experience exclusively in one mode. The value of discriminating between these ways of experiencing the world is that it offers many valuable clues to the confused and peculiar thinking that is found in mental illnesses. Sullivan has demonstrated that the psychotic, and particularly the schizophrenic thinking is neither peculiar nor alien to human beings, but simply a stage in the development of his mental capacities.

Sullivan described the process of personality development as a series of attitudes, maneuvers, techniques, and devices for dealing with anxiety. This collection of processes which are involved in filling the satisfaction and security needs is called the self-system by Sullivan. He avoided the term ego because he felt that Freud's term had too many preconceived and rigid notions surrounding it.[1] In addition, he felt that the term, self, was more expressive of the large role that it plays in the personality, while Freud visualized the ego as a prisoner of the id. The self, or self-system, is a collection of these processes designed to avoid the anxiety that arises in the attempt to fulfill security needs. The self dynamism which is the personality in action attempts to secure approval or prevent disapproval to avoid anxiety. Characteristics which tend to gain approval are personified by the individual as the "good me," and those which gain disapproval as the "bad me." There is a small, but highly significant set of personifications which represent the most unacceptable aspects of oneself, which are characterized as the "not me." These personifications play a crucial role in the development of the psychoses.

The focal concern in personality development is the avoidance of anxiety. Anxiety is a very distressing and highly disruptive event. At the extreme, it can produce panic and the total disruption of the individual. In lesser degrees, it 1) interferes with awareness of what is transpiring since the presence of anxiety requires complete focus on the ways of avoiding it or dealing with it; 2) by interfering with awareness it prevents any understanding of the causes of the anxiety and thus interferes with the development of insight; and 3) if insight into one's behavior and the effects of such behavior are not grasped, then one cannot develop any foresight. Consequently, anxiety disrupts the entire learning process and leaves one defenseless and caught in a vicious circle, since the presence of anxiety increases one's helplessness, which then produces more anxiety. The self-system attempts to override this vicious circle and permits one to function in a world in which anxiety is always present and constantly impinges itself upon one. The self-system tends to be constricted, since it focuses on reducing anxiety by staying within established and recognized paths of action. Consequently, personality in the face of excessive amounts of anxiety becomes constricted and focussed almost exclusively on the techniques for avoiding anxiety. For Sullivan, anxiety lies at the center of personality development and of neuroses and psychoses.

Sullivan defined anxiety as the response to, or the feeling of disapproval by a significant adult. This simple, but meaningful definition is the crux of interpersonal theory, since anxiety can only occur in an interpersonal context. It arises only in relation to fulfillment of security needs which are related to the cultural requirements. The development of anxiety therefore, can only occur in relation to another human being. The other person however, need not be real, present, or defined. Most often the other person is not present and may exist only in phantasy, or be a personification of someone else, or be a completely eidetic or unreal, imagined individual. The feeling of disapproval which is communicated need not be visible or apparent, but simply felt. With infants, when there is no possibility of actually determining the relationship of mother's anger or distress to the infant's behavior, the process is called empathy. This is a phenomenon which is also present in the adult when a feeling about another person is felt, even though there is no manifest evidence for the development of the feeling. Disapproval is often communicated this way, even when there is no overt expression of it. In the prototaxic or parataxic mode, this experience can be extremely discomforting. The infant cannot distiguish mother's anger at her husband, or the butcher, from anger or disapproval of itself. Anxiety may result in the infant from causes having little to do with his behavior. In the parataxic mode we can also recognize the possibility of feeling anxiety only through a serial connection of events which may have little or no relation to the individuals involved.

Anxiety is regularly accompanied by a typical set of somatic symptoms, such as palpitation, sweating, increased pulse and heart rate, gastric distress, and so on, in addition to the fear of impending doom and disaster. It cannot be tolerated for long, and the individual must take active steps to deal with it in one fashion or another. Horney described four general ways of dealing with it: 1) avoiding it, 2) fighting it, 3) resigning oneself to it, and 4) denying it by using chemical agents like drugs or alcohol. These techniques do not deal with the causes of anxiety, but merely placate it. Since the presence of anxiety interferes with learning and discovering the causes of anxiety, it is imperative that the individual develop some patterns of behavior that will gain approval and avoid disapproval in order to forestall the development of anxiety.

One important device for preventing the development of anxiety develops early. This has to do with one's skill in observing the beginnings of possible disapproval through the recognition of the forbidding gesture. Under these circumstances, the full circle of disapproval is short circuited by one's ability to identify the signals indicating possible disapproval. It is an efficient and useful operation, unless it has become too widespread. Under such circumstances the individual may notice forbidding gestures everywhere, and be unable to act at all.

For the infant, the significant adult is the mothering person. In the course of development this significant adult may be a sister, brother, friend, colleague, teacher, compeer, or anyone upon whom one's security depends. This implies that the significant person must have some influence or power to give or withhold which would affect the individuals feelings of security. An individual who is in a weaker or less esteemed role may offer no threat to another persons security, and therefore may be incapable of arousing anxiety in the other person. In the neurotic however, we find that everybody has the power to stimulate anxiety, since the neurotic's need for security is so extensive and indiscriminate. There need not be actual disapproval to provoke anxiety. What is crucial is that the individual expects disapproval for some piece of behavior even though he may not actually be getting disapproval. This is a complex situation in which anxiety is produced whenever there is a feeling of lowering of esteem in the eyes of a significant other, whether it occurs in reality or not. In addition, the frequent occurrence of anxiety is found when experience occurs in a prototaxic or parataxic mode, and the individual experiences anxiety based entirely on a fallacious interpretation of the views or attitudes of others. This is common in infancy and childhood. In short, the feelings of disapproval may be experienced with a person who is not disapproving at all. The response of anxiety is always formulated by the one who experiences it in terms of being looked down upon, disapproved of, not being liked, or of being a failure. The notion of free floating anxiety, which Freud described, has little meaning in Sullivan's system, since anxiety always arises in connection with some interpersonal experience, even though it can not be easily identified at the time it occurs. An individual deals with anxiety in various ways, and those who have difficulty in dealing with it at all may experience it constantly in a so-called 'free state," meaning the raw, unmodified psychosomatic accompaniments of the anxiety. Free floating anxiety means that for the moment it is in a raw state and has not been dealt with by some specific defense technique.

Sullivan's definitions and his conception of anxiety is of great practical value in the therapeutic process, since the anxiety experience points to the areas of low esteem and the elements of the individual's personality that he feels will produce disapproval. By exploring the anxiety experiences, the therapist is able to pinpoint the neurotic defenses and to expose the patient's distortions which have become a source of low esteem in his living. Anxiety is a warning signal, both for the patient to avoid treading on dangerous ground and to the therapist by indicating that he is approaching dangerous ground.

The process of learning was of great interest to Sullivan, since he conceived of personality development as being intimately related to this process. He had familiarity with learning theory and contributed to it. He felt that learning occurred in order to minimize anxiety and that the reduction of the anxiety gradient permitted one to learn more effectively.[2] Strong doses of anxiety can seriously impair the learning process, while mild doses of anxiety are necessary to initiate it. Learning, he felt, occurred through trial and error, reward and punishment, human example, and the process of deduction or conceptualization. The learning process in infants is aided by a remarkable phenomenon which Sullivan called the self-sentient capacity of human beings. This is the capacity to enjoy what one is experiencing while being the agent of the experience. Thumb sucking and genital manipulation are excellent examples of this capacity. While the infant sucks on the breast, he apparently enjoys the effort as well as the rewards. However, he is dependent on another person for this source of satisfaction. In sucking his thumb, the infant, for the first time in his life, not only does the sucking, but also feels what is being sucked. There is a feeling in the thumb as well as in the lips, and it is something one does to oneself and for oneself. This type of activity becomes very important in later years in dealing with anxiety. The infant soon discovers that the nipple is not always available to him, and he develops alternate ways of dealing with the potential anxiety which might result in the process of being unable to get the nipple. Thumb sucking is the first of such maneuvers which quickly spreads to sucking everything that can be gotten into the mouth. This type of activity becomes associated with all sorts of exploratory activity with differing results in different cultures. In some societies it is proper for the infant to get its toes into its mouth and to suck its thumb. In other places, thumb sucking and explorations around the anus and genitals meets with strong disapproval. As far as the infant is concerned, all bodily areas are equal; none has special significance except that it might be more fun to explore some places than others. However, the adults may have strong objections to exploring and manipulating certain areas because of their own prejudices and masochistic attitudes. The adults unfortunately attribute cultural interpretations to the infant's explorations, and may consequently describe his activities as dirty or nasty. The infant can pull the lobe of his ear, but if he should reach across to his genitals, or behind to his anus, he is strongly disapproved of. The attitude regarding genital play in some cultures is disapproving and produces considerable distress in the infant. He cannot comprehend the adults' standards, and he doesn't recognize the sinfulness of his behavior. After repeated admonitions, hand slappings, and perhaps even hand binding, he may get the idea that such play is strongly held in disapproval. In the service of avoiding anxiety, the genital area may be totally disregarded, and this may result in what Sullivan calls the "primary genital phobia" which may produce lasting effects in the adult. The genital area is off bounds for some people, while for others it is under great restrait and inhibition, and one's attitude towards the genitals may be filled with a mixture of feelings of curiosity, awe, disgust, and prudishness. This produces a variety of sexual problems in the adult.

Personality Development

The development of personality is described in stages determined by the nature of the relationship the individual experiences during these stages. Sullivan describes human development in five stages: 1. Infancy—from birth to the beginning of language (one and a half to two); 2. Childhood—from beginnings of language to period of need for compeers (about five); 3. Juvenile—from period of need for compeers and the beginnings of formal education, to about eight to nine and a half, when there are the beginnings of the capacity to collaborate with others; 4. Pre-adolescent, from nine and a half to maturation of genital apparatus; and 5. Adolescent— from genital maturity to adulthood.

INFANCY

The human infant, unlike many other animals, arrives in the world wholly and totally dependent on the benevolence of the environment for its survival. It is completely helpless, and its cry is the only device it has for attracting attention to its needs. The cry has considerable power in an atmosphere of tenderness, while it can be irritating and infuriating when the environment is un- friendly. The infant has been said to exist in a state of omnipotent splendor in which all its needs are automatically fulfilled. Although this is possibly true, it overlooks the fact that the infant's existence is entirely precarious and uncertain. It has no power except its cry to influence the environment, and from the infant's point of view, the world may be a frightening and dangerous place rather than a nirvana.

This view of the infant's world can yield alternative theories regarding the joys and blessings of infancy. The picture of a help- less infant in an insecure world is posited by Horney and others as opposed to an omnipotent figure who rules the roost. This may be true even when the household is turned into a nursery and there is a predominant preoccupation with his needs. From the infant's point of view, he is constantly in want and cannot achieve his goals except by extensive activities and impatient waiting. He recognizes that he is always dependent upon the mothering person.

The infant's world centers around his mouth. It is the focus of feeding, feeling, touching, attracting attention, and pleasing mother. Freud described this phenomenon in terms of a concentration of libido. It can also be viewed in a relatively simple way, since there is no other possible way for an animal to survive except through ingestion, which takes place through its mouth. Conse- quently, the oral area is of crucial significance, and much of the early developments with regard to anxiety, the development of trust and tenderness, and the techniques for avoiding anxiety re- volve about this area. The mouth contacts the mother's nipple or the nursing bottle, and the infant can, through an empathic process, decide many things about the nature of the relationship with mother through his mouth, which may interfere or even interrupt the nursing process. It is at this time that anxiety makes its first appearance, and the infant has several ways of dealing with it. He may cry to force attention or go to sleep and wake up to a new situation. If the situation is very difficult, he may withdraw and even relapse, and go into a state of marasmus. The capacity to fall asleep in order to avoid anxiety situations remains a technique for many adults who, instead of becoming restless and uneasy when anxieties need to be faced, go to sleep easily and quickly. Sleep can be a life-saving procedure for the infant, for if the tension and anxiety were to increase and the crying were to continue, the infant would become dehydrated and eventually die. The cry is his most effective device for getting into motion the activities required to fill his needs. It is usually quite successful, and for that reason he clings to it for long periods of time. In some adults it continues to be a most potent technique for influencing the environment. The cry takes on magical significance in spite of the fact that in later infancy it may not work, or it may even produce the opposite effect. Its initial power is so great, and the human tendency to overlook instances of its failure so common, that the individual clings to the cry as a weapon for a long, long time in interpersonal relationships.

In infancy the beginnings of symbol formation and the recognition of signs are seen. The bottle, for example, becomes a signal for security and nourishment. The beginnings of the symbolization of the good and the bad parent take place at this time. Symbols enable the infant to recognize the forbidding gesture, which is a sign of impending disapproval. In this way he learns to alter his behavior in order to avoid anxiety. The skills that he develops in wooing and courting good will, and the endless number of devices that he becomes proficient at, speak for the extreme plasticity and versatility of the human organism. In spite of its biological immaturity, the infant is exceedingly skillful in learning the tricks that will please the adults, and he uses them extensively.

Although the infant discovers and learns devices to deal with the environment, it is not until the end of infancy that the infant is considered capable of being taught. Up to that time almost everything he wants is available, and only very few of his demands are denied. There are relatively slight limitations on his activities. However, when it is felt that the infant can comprehend the limitations of his environment, and ideally, when his muscular and neurological development is sufficiently advanced to enable it to deal with the cultural requirements, then the process of learning begins to take place. This involves the control of the sphincters, both anal and urethral, and these requirements become significant items in the infant's world. It is important to recognize that learning is possible only when the organs and the accompanying musculature has matured enough to be able to carry out the tasks imposed upon them. If training is attempted before such maturation has occurred, then we find a highly distressed infant who is being asked to perform tasks that he is biologically incapable of doing. A recent study by Dr. Harry F. Harlow of the University of Wisconsin with the rhesus monkey suggests that the intensive training of a rhesus at a task beyond its ability is not only futile, but may virtually immunize the animal against learning the skill later on. Dr. Harlow asserts that the same adverse effects may be observed in human beings.

The beginning of the development of self-esteem is recognizable in infancy. The self-system is a collection of attitudes and behavioral patterns that develop in order to reduce anxiety and maintain it at a low level. After a while it becomes loaded with techniques, dynamisms and tactics designed to keep the anxiety level at a minimum. The self-system begins to include an extensive set of personifications of oneself as well as others which are also devices to reduce anxiety. Certain aspects of oneself are personified as the "good me." These are portions of one's personality that seem to stimulate approval while other parts of the self are personified as the "bad me." These are the portions that generally stimulate disapproval and anxiety. If we agree that the self-system is designed to reduce anxiety, why should it retain "bad me" personifications which regularly produce anxiety? This is the crucial question in understanding the nature and purpose of the neurotic process. The "bad me" personifications are retained because they are frequently the lesser of two evils, and to eliminate them would be to give up something vital to the self. The individual is prepared to accept some anxiety in order to retain these personality patterns in spite of their capacity to evoke disapproval. This creates conflicts, and produces the neurotic patterns of behavior. If a child who has great interest in reading, or in other intellectual pursuits faces an atmosphere in which reading is disapproved of as being too sissyish, he may personify the intellectual aspects of his interests as the "bad me." Instead of abandoning this interest entirely, which he might do if the disapproval were extreme, he retains the "bad me" personification, since the rewards of reading are still too great to give it up entirely. In later years, anxiety and distress may occur when he attempts some intellectual activity, and if such anxieties are severe enough, he may abandon such pursuits entirely. In the process severe neurotic conflicts may ensue.

The third personification is known as the "not me." These are the aspects of one's living that have stirred up such anxiety in the past that the individual dissociates or represses these tendencies. They are often connected with experiences surrounding the genital or anal area, or are related to any "horror" provoking behavior for the adults. The "not me" experiences often accompany dreams and nightmares and are active participants in the schizophrenic process. They can result in denying or eliminating a part of the individual that has been highly disapproved of and that is essential to total living. In such circumstances the sexual behavior, for example, of these people often seem unrelated to their living and appears only in states of unawareness or seemingly divorced from their desires or interests.

Since the self-system is organized to minimize anxiety, it tends to be very restrictive towards new experiences, and limits them in the face of any forbidding gestures. It is responsive to slight anxiety, which serves as a warning against any further involvement. In this way the presence of much anxiety interferes with the broadening of personality and the limiting of one's development. The personifications which soon extend to phanatasied people and personified individuals may encourage faulty interpretations of another person's words or actions, and thus tend to induce further anxiety and restriction of movement. It becomes a vicious circle which narrows experiencing and acts to limit the learning experience, which is itself a bulwark against anxiety.

It is from this framework that Sullivan concluded that the "neurotic does not learn from experience," since he experiences only what will avoid anxiety, and therefore does not learn the tools and techniques for overcoming them. In addition, the neurotic can only see what his anxiety permits him to, and he becomes so preoccupied with activities designed to avoid anxiety that relatively few new observations are allowed to enter his sphere of awareness. The self functions in a way which will preserve its integrity, even when it is distorted. It achieves this through many processes, and particularly through selective innattention and dissociation. By selective inattention the individual focusses his attention on the main issues in his self-system and is largely inattentive to other events that are transpiring. He focuses on activities that are approved of or disapproved of or on those that produce anxiety and security. These are the main issues in his existence, and other events, experiences or activities will pass unnoticed. This limits the individual's development, although it serves the purpose of avoiding anxiety. In attending only to certain events, he becomes selective, and a great deal will go on around him which he will neither notice nor be aware of. When these events are drawn to his attention, he can recognize their presence, and the process of therapy is partly concerned with broadening the individual's awareness of these events. The increase in awareness helps to clarify the neurotic distortions. Dissociation occurs when the events or activities are too prominent to go unnoticed and too dangerous to be noticed. The whole motivational system needs to be dissociated, so that even if it were brought to the person's awareness, he could not recognize its existence until certain anxieties were first dealt with.

Consequently, the self is a limiting structure, and while it serves the purpose of reducing anxiety, it also reduces the creative activities of an individual. This is the essence of the neurotic process. The conception of neuroses of all kinds is dependent upon the particular technique the individual utilizes to restrict his experiences in order to reduce anxiety, which produces a distortion in his awareness. From Sullivan's point of view, it is only quantitatively different from the defenses utilized by the "normal" individual.

The self, if largely restricted in early years, inteferes with the further development and maturing of the individual. The direction and characteristics given to the self in infancy and childhood are maintained year after year at an extraordinary cost, so that most people in this culture, and presumably in other cultures, because of inadequate and unfortunate experiences in early life become inferior caricatures of what they "might have been." Only those feelings, phantasies, and thoughts which conform to the self will reach awareness. All others are dissociated or are selectively unattended.

Ultimately, the self is made up of "reflected appraisals." The evaluation of one's own worth and esteem is based on what significant others think of us. If others are respectful and tender, we develop a respectful attitude towards ourselves. If others are contemptuous or unfriendly, we see ourselves as degraded and unworthy. These attitudes may not necessarily reflect what others actually think of us, but rather what we think others think of us.

Fortunately, the self-system is not *entirely* restrictive, and does allow for some alteration and change. Subsequent contacts with people may alter some of the original "reflected appraisals," so that some warps can be corrected by later experiences. However, a very restricted self-system may not allow for subsequent clarification and may interfere with one's ability to satisfy one's needs in later life. This is what Sullivan means by mental illness.

CHILDHOOD

The period of infancy ends with the development of language and the beginnings of the process of acculturation, or educating the infant into the requirements of the culture in which he happens to be born. Depending upon the degree of anxiety and the restrictive rigidity of the self, which has begun its organization in infancy, the child will benefit or fail to benefit from the learning experiences in childhood. Since the self tends to avoid experiences that are not congruent to its current organization, it may have great difficulty in the era of childhood, where restraints, restrictions, and limitations begin to be imposed on the child. In the training process the factors of consistency and frequency are major elements in learning. The development of language and the value of words as tools are quickly grasped by the child.

The major burden in the childhood era is the necessity for learning the particular cultural patterns in which the individual lives. During this period his sphincters become capable of being controlled, and his muscles and nerves mature sufficiently to enable him to be trained in cleanliness. This is true regarding eating habits and dress, as well as toilet habits. This produces a rapid development of his self-system and the learning of new techniques to master the environment and to control anxiety. Since learning can only occur in the face of moderate amounts of anxiety, the process of acculturation is a difficult one at all times. There are rewards and statements of approval when the child trains easily. On the other hand, there is also considerable disapproval and punishment when he does not. In order to deal with certain impulses that repeatedly court disapproval and yet cannot be dissociated, the child begins to utilize a technique which comes to play a large role in his future living. This is the process of sublimation, in which certain unacceptable impulses are patterned in ways that are acceptable to the culture. The process of sublimation is highly successful, and permits one to retain many impulses which would otherwise need to be abandoned entirely by performing them in acceptable ways. At the same time, one begins to carry on a covert existence and to do many things which are actually a cover-up for something else. Covert activities are often looked upon as sneaky or nasty performances, but it is important to note that this is not necessarily true. Although there are many covert activities which go on outside of awareness and which may be detrimental to the individual, the sublimation processes perform very useful purposes. These are substitute devices which allow the individual to carry on some activities that may be culturally forbidden. The other alternative is to abandon the need, or, if this is not possible, to constantly run into disintegrative situations when one attempts to fill that need.

It is in childhood that there is the beginning of a new educative influence; namely, the experience of fear and anger. The experience of fear fosters learning through the fear of both physical pain and anxiety. The experience of anger develops the ability to combat authority and to deal with anxiety by getting angry at the person producing it. Later on, anger becomes one of the commonest responses to anxiety and is directed toward the person who is presumed to be responsible for it.

The problem of educating the child to the culture is made more difficult by the contradictory standards within the culture. The adult is often faced with the contradiction between what he does and what he wants the child to do. He is also faced with contradictions in communicating the standards of the culture to the child. For instance, it becomes rather complicated to teach a child that "honesty is the best policy," when at the same time we want him to know that there are times when he must not be absolutely honest. The child soon learns the contradictions of the culture and develops all sorts of rationalizations and verbalizations which are designed to cover up his failures and deficiencies. The verbalizations: "I'm sorry," or "excuse me," become favorite devices for getting out of tight spots. Because it proves highly successful, it becomes part of the skills and techniques which the child develops for manipulating the environment through proper verbalizations.

As the child encounters and absorbs all the educative forces that he must deal with, he experiences frequent failures as well as successes. For this reason, the need for tenderness and closeness is very great during this period. At times these needs are fulfilled by the parents. However, if they are frequently rebuffed, then the child begins to think of his tenderness needs as bad or undesireable. This is a particular problem for the male child, who is expected to be strong and manly and who mustn't run to mother for comforting. Out of a desire to make the child more manly, the father may derogate the child's need to be comforted. This may force the child to think of his need for tenderness as part of the "bad me." If this is carried to an extreme, it may produce a significant development which Sullivan called "the malevolent transformation." When this occurs, the child begins to consider himself bad, or unworthy when the tenderness need is felt and will rebuff it when it is offered him in order to be a "real man." In this way, he denies his tenderness needs because they produce anxiety. Tenderness, friendliness, or warmth are turned down, and the individual forces himself to live in an atmosphere devoid of concern or benevolent regard. This plays havoc with any possible success in interpersonal relationships and becomes the forerunner of paranoid developments which occur later in life. The rebuff also serves to antagonize the giver, so that on subsequent occasions it may no longer be offered. In this way, a person becomes surrounded by a sea of unfriendliness which he cannot overcome, because he is caught in a vicious circle.

Juvenile Era

The juvenile era begins when the child starts to manifest an interest in compeers and recognizes them as being like himself. In our Western culture, this is the beginning of the period of formal education. For the first time in his life, the child spends a regular part of the day outside the home in the presence of his compeers. Now he can see how other people live, and he shares with his compeers a common parental figure in the person of his teacher. If the school situation is good, and the child is not too warped, this can be a period of considerable correction. Sullivan emphasized the difficulties of benefiting from later periods of development if one enters these eras too full of anxiety. On the other hand, there is a great potentiality for correction through later experiencing provided the opportunities are present, and anxiety is not too great. In the school the child faces a quite different situation than he does at home. He must now share a parental figure upon whom he does not have exclusive call and from whom his formerly successful techniques may not get the same response. This may be sufficiently disconcerting so that he will refuse to go back to school, particularly if he has always been treated at home like a little prince. On the other hand, if he comes from a family where he has been pushed around and largely overlooked, he may find school a salvation. If his teacher is friendly and affectionate, she may be able to develop feelings of worthwhileness in the child. The child may discover that adults are quite human, with some better and some worse than one's own parents. In this period a great deal of the exaggerated and over-idealized notions of his parents may be corrected.

In presenting him with new authority figures with which he must deal, and with new social situations with which he must cope, the school does many other things for the child as well. The juvenile era is an energetic one, in which much emphasis is placed on being "in" with the other children and on establishing one's place and reputation. A great expansion of the self-system in social areas takes place, and the child begins to be self-critical and introspective. During this period massive generalizations about people are made which may be fleeting, or may become permanent. Stereotypes and prejudices begin to enter the life of the child, and the formation of an "in" and "out" group is a daily occurrence in the juvenile's play. The emphasis on belonging encourages the development of techniques of building oneself up by belonging, or tearing down those who don't belong. This unfortunate activity may persist in the later years.

The learning experiences which characterize this era are the three C's, cooperation, competition, and compromise. The development of the capacity for cooperation and compromise is fostered by the social activities which prevail in this era, and one must be prepared for it through some experience in sharing at an earlier stage. Competition is learned more easily, and quickly becomes a way of life with many complicating issues later on. The human necessities of competition, cooperation, and compromise are preludes to the stage of adulthood. Many of the juvenile preoccupations with competition continue throughout one's life, and are characteristic of the "chronically juvenile" neurotic. At the end of the juvenile era, it is presumed that the individual, through his experience with living, will begin to show a clear-cut personality. Certain characteristic ways of dealing with one's needs become apparent, and the individual begins to be a person in his own right. Although this is certainly true of the female, who matures earlier and more emphatically, it also begins to be noticeable in the male. When pre-adolescence is reached one is presumed to have learned the requirements of the culture and the techniques for dealing with other humans. So far, there has been very little experience with sex. Friendships have begun to develop in the juvenile era, but it is in pre-adolescence that the flowering of tenderness and true affection occurs.

Pre-Adolescence

The period from eight and a half to 12 years of age, sometimes earlier in girls, is notable for the development of the capacity to love and to collaborate with another human being. It is during this era that one develops a chum of the same sex with whom one can share feelings of closeness, loyalty, and dedication. It is with the chum that one first experiences feelings of love. For Sullivan, love is unrelated to lust or sex at this time, and it involves the notion that the "satisfactions and security of the loved one are as significant as one's own satisfactions and security." Relationships occur between people of the same sex because these are the easiest people to understand, and are most like oneself. The closest kinds of intimacy are formed, which are frequently very intense and without sexual elements. Such a relationship entails many hours spent together in discussing all aspects of life without fear of rebuff or humiliation. One begins to see the world through the eyes of someone else who is like oneself, and permits the appraisal of one's own values and ideals. This era allows for the greatest possibilities for favorable change, since the beginnings of tenderness and closeness are the soil upon which growth and maturation may be cultivated. The possibilities for removing warps at this time are most in evidence. The individual is open to a relationship based on mutual, tender regard without the complicating factors of lust. Freud described this era as the homosexual era through which every human must evolve in the course of his development. This description has had many unfortunate consequences, both in the understanding of this period and in the attitudes of parents and others toward these intimate relationships. In spite of the marked intimacy in the relationships which are established, it is unusual for homosexual actvity to occur during this period, since the sexual apparatus has not yet matured. When one friend matures earlier than the other, some homosexual explorations may occur, and in some particular circumstances, homosexuality may have its early roots in this period. By and large, the uneasiness about homosexuality is exaggerated, and the friendship is maligned and degraded by our concerns about the possibilities of homosexuality. A pre-adolescent who has been severly warped prior to this era may have great difficulty in relinquishing his chum and in attempting heterosexual activity. He may never abandon the intimacies of the pre-adolescent, and when his sexual gonads mature, may become a confirmed homosexual. It is not the pre-adolescent era which produces homosexuality, nor is homosexuality characteristic of this era. The severely warped person who is unable to move towards heterosexuality becomes fixed in this era, and never advances beyond pre-adolescent intimacies. Homosexuals almost invariably manifest love as it is encountered in pre-adolescence rather than in adulthood.

It is at this time too that intimate relationships increase, and one begins to have several chums and belong to larger groups. One soon develops interlocking friendships which are characteristic of adult society.

The real difficulty in this era develops as one approaches sexual maturity. Since there are varying rates of maturation, some partners mature earlier than others. Sexual needs develop in one and not the other and the partnership may begin to dissolve. The slower maturing partner may attempt some premature explorations with the opposite sex in order to keep up with his chum. He may be quite unsuccessful, pretend sexual experience and success, and actually be quite afraid. This may force him back into closer relations with the same sex, and even after maturation he may continue to be uneasy about heterosexual activities. The growing distance that frequently develops as adolescence approaches stirs up the problem of loneliness, which enters the scene of human activity very strongly at this time. This is accompanied by such overwhelming feelings of anxiety that one will do almost anything to overcome it. The experience is often so painful, that we quickly forget it once it's over, and get terribly busy and active in order to prevent it. It is loneliness that pushes the pre-adolescent into activities that he may be unprepared for, in order to retain his friendships. The other complicating issue during this period is the unequal rate of maturation between boys and girls. Since girls mature earlier, they are not particularly interested in the pre-adolescent boy who is just beginning to enter puberty. He is pushed aside for older boys. Much of the poor preparation for adolescence occurs at the later stages of pre-adolescence, when unequal maturing and pressure to avoid loneliness drives the individual into premature heterosexual socializing. Pre-adolescence ends at the maturation of the sexual apparatus.

ADOLESCENCE

This is the most stormy period in one's development, since the individual is faced with many new adjustments that have to be made. The most striking development is the maturing of the genital apparatus and the patterning of sexual behavior. To be fully clear about adolescence, one must again emphasize the distinction between lust and intimacy. In the pre-adolescent Sullivan described the great advances toward intimacy without lust. In the adolescent, lust begins to enter one's life, and intimacy now becomes complicated and enhanced by sex. Intimacy may frequently accompany the sex act or may exist without sex. Sexual relationships, on the other hand, do not necessarily imply any emotional intimacy, even though the word intimacy has come to mean the activity of sex. Intimacy can occur without sexual activity, and sexual activity can occur without intimacy.

Lust is a powerful need, and as such, it is a strong integrative force, pushing the individual to activities designed to fulfill the biological urge. However, sexual activity has the capacity to fill many needs. It satisfies the need for security as well as the need for satisfaction, and the need for intimacy in overcoming anxiety. Since it is capable of satisfying so many human needs in a single performance, it is extremely difficult to dissociate or to deny it. While this is done in certain religious and ascetic groups, it is accomplished with the greatest of difficulty. Even so, the physiological accompaniments, including the erections and wet dreams cannot be eliminated. Since it is a major dynamism operating in the adolescent and adult, it frequently collides with other dynamisms and produces many difficulties. In spite of its great pressures, it is questionable whether it is a prime motivating force. Its great capacity to fill so many human needs at one time makes it a very important item of human behavior. Sex is the one biological activity that requires another human being for its full expression. In its pressures for fulfillment, it has great potentialities for expressing and manifesting human and neurotic difficulties. It gets expressed in hateful as well as in loving situations, on occasions of great intimacy, or in the most fleeting encounters. There is also the tendency to separate lust and intimacy so that lust is considered bad and is practiced with people we despise. The tendency here is to reserve one's intimate relations for people one respects. This sets up a good-bad girl dichotomy, which produces endless complications inside and outside of marriage. When sexual contact is prevented for whatever reasons, masturbation is actively practiced, and while it may have had earlier beginnings in sexual explorations and later in sex play, in adolescence it is performed with the goal of producing ejaculation, or reaching a climax. While at first it may be a substitute for sex activity, it very quickly begins to serve the larger and more significant role of alleviating anxiety. At such times, masturbation becomes a way of dealing with anxiety and substituting for other psychological needs.

The adolescent faces the enormous problem of shifting from intimacy with the same sex to intimacy accompanied by lust toward persons of the opposite sex. This is a difficult task under the best of circumstances, but occurring at a period which contains so many other problems, it makes for a formidable task. The lust dynamism certainly eases the problem, since pressure for sex activity encourages the establishment of relationships with the opposite sex. However, unless there is adequate preparation in pre-adolescence, and a successful series of relationships during that time, the changeover may be highly complicated, and homosexuality, which has its roots in earlier periods of development, may become prominent. It is only when the sexual apparatus is mature that homosexuality can actually be considered to exist.

The reasons for homosexuality are manifold, and can only be understood as unique developments, arising out of the homosexual's background and experience. The primary genital phobia that is set up in infancy and childhood and is maintained throughout pre-adolescence plays a major role in its ultimate unfolding. When an individual grows up with loathing, disgust, or horror towards his genital apparatus, it is not surprising that he manifests avoidance tendencies towards the genitals of other people. The interesting feature is that the loathing of his own genitals prevents him from making adequate contacts with the genitals of the opposite sex. Thus it is the phobia towards one's own genitals that makes the heterosexual adjustment impossible. The homosexual is a person who fears, loathes, or avoids the genitals of the opposite sex. The pressure for integration of lust is so great that when one is unable to integrate with the opposite sex, the same sex is chosen as the easier way out. It is because intimacy and lust is impossible with the opposite sex that the homosexual establishes some modicum of sexual functioning with the same sex. Homosexuality can only be comprehended fully when it is appreciated that the problem is more extensive and complicated than a mere sexual aberration. It is a total personality problem that has as one of its symptoms the interest in the person and sexual apparatus of a person of the same sex. It is merely one expression of the difficulty in establishing secure and mature relationships with the opposite sex. This is the burden of adolescence, and when the genital phobias are severe enough, all sorts of sexual deviations in addition to homosexuality become manifest.

The problems of adolescence extend beyond the sexual apparatus, for the adolescent must also begin to separate himself from his family dependencies and become a human being in his own right. It is in the striving for independence and separation while he is still financially and emotionally dependent that a great many of the difficulties of the adolescent rest. While he is still a boy, he is struggling to become a man. There is much difficulty in his need to conform, to belong, and to avoid loneliness, and his need to rebel and to become independent. The lust dynamism assists this process in pressuring him to set up relationships that are independent of his family, and often in opposition to it. At the same time, the pressures for conformity are very great, and this produces so many of the bizarre minor rebellious movements in adolescence. While this is going on, the adolescent is also concerned with standards, values, and his future career. He is highly ethical and moral, and discontent with the sham and contradictory standards of his culture. He becomes engaged in the struggle of having to accept the adult's requirements and compromising his own high standards. For this reason, adolescence is a period of internal turmoil and self-searching. Religious interests and activities are greatest during this period, and religious conversions occur more frequently than at any other age. All in all, this period is characterized by turmoil, conflict, and much change. The adolescent often appears to be mentally ill, especially to the parents, but it is important to recognize that the unrest and confusion of the adolescent is part of the process of growing into adulthood.

It is expected that the adolescent will eventually grow into an adult. Unfortunately, this is not necessarily true. Some people remain involved in their adolescent struggles and searchings forever, and never settle on a permanent relationship with a member of the opposite sex. They are forever searching for the "ideal mate." These people are called the "chronically adolescent," and they constitute a large percentage of the patients seen by the psychiatrist. When an individual achieves the self-respect which makes him capable of meeting most situations with a capacity of intimacy that involves collaborative relationships and loving attitudes towards other people, one can assume that such a person is mature. It is a universally sought after goal which is, unfortunately, rarely achieved, though most of us arrive at some approximation of it.

SUMMARY AND APPRAISAL

Sullivan's interpersonal theory of personality has probably been the most fruitful contribution to psychiatric theory since Freud. Although he combined most of the contributions of Fromm, Horney, and other social scientists, he evolved a consistent, complete theory of personality which concerns itself largely with the adaptability of the individual to the culture and to other individuals. The security needs of the individual, which require him to overcome and deal effectively with anxiety, motivate his behavior and development. The methods which the individual adopts depend upon the maturation of his particular abilities. A detailed study of the actual experiences of the individual forms the matrix for his ultimate growth into manhood. This entails a successful passage through all the periods of development using the skills and knowledge gained at earlier periods of development. Sullivan has formulated workable hypotheses and theoretical statements about human development that can be tested and which have raised psychological theory into the beginnings of a true science.

Sullivan has been criticized for being too empirical and for not giving sufficient attention to the role of sex in human development. However, it is clear that in adolescence Sullivan does not minimize the role of sex in any respect. Certainly he has emphasized the role that non-sexual elements play in personality development. In this respect, he is in the same circle as the neo-Freudian psychologists who stress the role of the autonomous or non-sexual ego.

Sullivan's theories have advanced therapeutic techniques enormously. He was essentially a clinician who developed his theories out of his work with schizophrenics and obsessional. His contributions to therapy arise out of his conception of psychiatry as an interpersonal process which brings the therapist actively into the treatment process as a participant-observer whose presence can not be anonymous and who participates in the process in an active manner. Even when the therapist is viewed as detached, he inevitably participates by his presence, his verbalizations, his silence, his activity, or his passivity.

Sullivan developed a systematic, therapeutic approach through an intensive study of the process of therapy as a problem of interviewing. He felt that since the patient's distortions in living developed out of the necessity of dealing with anxiety it was necessary to explore these areas of anxiety.

The origins, sources, techniques, and consequences of the defenses against anxiety are examined in detail. Although Sullivan had a primary interest in the current life situation, he felt that a genetic understanding of the symptom helped to develop insight, and to convince the patient of the nature of his neurosis. He advocated a flexible attitude toward therapy and gave up many of the ritualistic practices such as lying on the couch, having the therapist sit behind the patient, or sessions of one hour duration, unless they had some empirical value that could be demonstrated. He interviewed actively and sharply, and at times produced shock effects on his patients by skillful use of satire and invective. His goal of therapy was to clarify the parataxic distortions in an individual's life and to arrive at some consensual validation of the individual's attitudes towards himself. He made specific contributions to the therapy of schizophrenia and the obsessional neurosis, with which he had great familiarity and skill. For example, Sullivan viewed the paranoid mechanism in a way that differed sharply from Freud's, and he dealt with it in a surprisingly different manner. While Freud considered the paranoid mechanism to be related to repressed homosexuality, Sullivan viewed it as an expectation and anticipation of derogatory appraisal related to the malevolent transformation of tender feelings. The paranoid individual expects a derogatory appraisal which arises out of his own critical attitude towards himself. Sullivan advocated the necessity for caution in offering the paranoid any tenderness except in the late phases of therapy, and suggested that the therapist adopt a straight-forward, direct attitude, in which annoyance and irritation would be communicated if it was felt by the therapist. Because the paranoid individual was sensitive to rebuff and anticipated it, he frequently precipitated it. Sullivan felt that the paranoid needed to discover this, along with the history of the development of his malevolent transformation. He did not think that homosexuality should be dealt with at all here unless it specifically played a role in the paranoid's life. He also felt that this was much less common than Freud described.

With regard to the obsessional neurosis, Sullivan saw this as a technique to avoid facing and recognizing a dissociated part of one's personality. The obsessional individual spends all his time hedging, talking around the issue, and using a variety of devices to avoid facing the areas of anxiety in his living. The obsessional feels helpless in the face of these dissociated impulses, and his major interest is in the development of power. In order to maintain this conviction of his powers to control and manipulate the world, he must avoid all areas of living which leave him helpless or powerless. Most of the symptoms of the obsessional state can be understood from this rubric. In therapy, Sullivan actively intervened with the obsessional to forestall his beating around the issue and using free association to divert attention from the main issue. Sullivan's skill in treating the obsessional demonstrated his grasp of the interpersonal processes in therapy and his profound knowledge of the techniques the human being develops to avoid anxiety.

NOTES

1. Sullivan coined many new words in developing his conceptions about personality. He tried to avoid the confusion which surrounded using old words which have established meanings. This tendency has encouraged many psychologists to accuse Sullivan of coining new words without altering any of the old ideas. Sullivan was a precise writer who had great difficulty in communicating his ideas because of a fear of being misunderstood. Consequently, he published very little during his lifetime and most of his work has been edited by the Washington School of Psychiatry for more comprehensive reading. However, the reader is left to decide whether the necessity for clarification justifies the additional burden for the student of using new terms.

2. The relationship of learning to neurosis and learning theory to psychotherapy was developed by Sullivan in all his writings. It was similar to the contribution of Alexander and French in their conception of the "corrective emotional experience." Sullivan's views were further amplified by O. H. Mowrer, C. Rogers, and other psychologists interested in psychotherapy. See:

Mowrer, O. H.: Learning Theory and Personality Dynamics. New York. Ronald Press, 1950.

Dollard, J. and Miller, N. E.: Personality and Psychotherapy. New York. McGraw-Hill, 1950.

Mowrer, O. H.: Learning theory and the neurotic paradox. Am. J. Orthopsychiat. 18:571-610, 1948.

Pavlov, I. P.: Conditioned Reflexes. London, Oxford University Press, 1927.

VI

Other Neo-Freudian Theories

ALTHOUGH THE THEORIES of personality development of Horney and Sullivan are complete systems of psychology, many psychiatrists and psychoanalysts have been making significant contributions to psychiatric theory in more restricted ways. It would be impossible to deal with all of them, and consequently I will touch on a few whose work appears to have the greatest ultimate significance in influencing the direction of psychological theory. One of the foremost of these investigators is Sandor Rado, who in addition to his career as a medical organizer and administrator at Columbia University, is a theoretician of considerable stature. He has developed a system of psychological theorizing based on the concept of adaptation. He has had an extensive background in classic psychoanalysis and until 1939 operated in the framework of the libido theory. At that time he abandoned the libido theory and reformulated his psychoanalytic conceptions in an adaptational psychodynamic framework. Although accepting the undisputed contributions of Freud, he has raised many significant questions about some of the doubtful areas in Freud's theorizing. In 1956 in a paper entitled "Adaptational Psychodynamics" he presented his revised approach to psychoanalytic theory. He not only took issue with the libido theory, but formulated a new approach to the unconscious and to the goals and techniques of therapy. His clarification of the sexual deviations arises from his recognition of the interrelated physiological-psychological aspects of human functioning. In his earlier paper on the "Paths of Natural Science,"[1] written in 1922, he expressed a viewpoint towards science and the scientific method which has characterized his productions ever since. He feels that psychoanalysis must go back to its attempts to answer the question: *How,* and must avoid metapsychology in framing the answers.

His concept of human behavior is based on the dynamic principle of motivation and adaptation. Adaptation of an organism is achieved through its interaction with the culture. Behavior is seen not just as a means to an end, or in terms of cause and effect, but also in its adaptive value, or its effect on the welfare of the organism. Adaptation involves improvements in the organism's patterns of interaction to increase survival possibilities and promote self-realization and perpetuation of its type. Rado has developed a conception regarding the development of mental disorder that is tied to the physiology of the organism. Although this places a significant emphasis on biology, it is quite different from the stress Freud placed on instinct. For Rado, the organism is the outcome of an evolutionary history, and is a self-regulating, biological system. The needs of the organism are the results of the interaction of inherent predispositions (genotypes) and the environment (phenotype). The environment becomes involved with the security needs of the individual. Integrative activity of the organism is dominated by what Rado calls the hedonic control mechanisms which are responsive to pleasure, pain, emotion, and reason. He visualizes this control in a hierarchal fashion, going from the most to the least primitive: 1) pleasure-pain, 2) emotional, 3) emotional thought, 4) unemotional thought. The type of control mechanism which is operating will determine the nature of the disorder. In the perpetual interaction of the organism with the environment there is the necessity for constant care and repair of the organism. Activities in this connection are designated as emergency behavior. These adjustments serve adaptational and survival needs of an organism.

At the hedonic level, the organism responds to pain by attempts to rid itself of the agency producing it. The next level of functioning is the emotional level that is actuated by brute rage or brute fear which produces emergency activities of flight or fight.

The next level of functioning is the emotional thought level, which is neither objective or rational, and tends to feed the emotions. The level of unemotional thought is the highest level of functioning, and is dominated by reason, logic, and common sense. Behavior is integrated at any, and often at four levels. The unit of the integrative apparatus is the action self. This is in many ways identical to the self-system of Sullivan's, and it is the dynamic unit in the development of the individual. This action self is derived from the interaction of self-awareness (proprioceptive activities of the infant) and the willed, or desired activities of the infant. At the outset, the action self has no boundaries or limitations. Ultimately, there is a necessity for acknowledging the limitation of the omnipotent powers of the infant and differentiating between the self as desired and the self as one really is.[1]

Conscience grows out of the necessity for establishing some restraints in our demands and enables the individual to function in a cooperative fashion in a social context. The mechanism of conscience are rational and emotional and originate in the child's relationship to its parent. It is under the necessity to gain parental approval that conscience develops. This process becomes the most effective and valuable mechanism of self-restraint. Pride develops out of the action self's capacity to produce pleasure for the organism. This is ultimately related to the organism's capacity for self-restraint and success in loving, being loved, and respected. The management of pride is a highly significant determinant of behavior. Thus, the personality expands through fulfilling the possibilities of the action self which produces the feelings of pride or ecstasy and triumph. Culture develops through a gradual subordination of hedonic self-regulation to emotional and unemotional thought. This picture of the development of personality is highly condensed, but it illustrates the stress Rado places on a continual interplay of psychology with physiology, omitting teleology as an explanatory concept.

The pathology of human behavior is determined by a process of miscarried repair as well as overproduction of the emergency controls which Rado calls the over-reactive disorders or discontrol disorders, such as phobias. The adaptational principle helps illuminate a great many aspects of neurotic behavior which have long remained inexplicable. Many activities of the neurotic are designed to overcome the faulty response patterns, but they miscarry and fail. This is apparent in the depressive disorders about which Rado has much to say. This notion of miscarried repair clarified the expiative and demanding behavior of the depressed individual as an attempt to overcome his desperate need for love. The concept of an over-production of emergency reactions is extremely useful in comprehending phobic disorders as well as the obsessional states. However, the application of these concepts to the problem of sex and the sexual deviations has produced its greatest rewards. Rado has made lasting contributions to the clarification of the role of sex in human behavior. In 1940 in a scholarly examination of the concept of bisexuality, he brought scientific methodology and clarity to the area of sexuality, the cornerstone of Freud's original contributions. Bisexuality was a concept borrowed from earlier sexologists and given to Freud by his friend Fliess. Freud never fully examined the validity of this concept for humans, yet he applied it generously. It became a crucial concept in his views on homosexuality, and an explanatory principle for the most varied of human disorders.[2] Rado examined this concept through a historical survey as well as a critical examination of its biological validity. He concluded that "there is no such thing as bisexuality either in man or in any other of the higher vertebrates. In the final shaping of the normal individual, the double embryological origin of the genital system does not result in any physiological duality of reproductive function."[3] The sex of an individual can be determined only by the character of the reproductive system as a whole, and the remnants of opposite sex are of embryological and developmental interest, producing no ultimate psychological influences. This paper is a classic for its organization and documentation of a psychological postulate of extreme significance in psychoanalysis. Through a logical and cogent survey of many such theories he demanded a reexamination of Freud's concepts which were accepted as fact when they only have had historical significance. As a result of these studies, Rado abandoned the libido theory and explained sexual deviations as a response to anxiety. Homosexuality was seen as a disorder of stimulation when anxiety inhibits the standard stimulation patterns. Reparative adjustments take place and produce the aberrant forms of stimulation. In 1949 he reclassified the sexual disorders. He stated that the male and female are adapted to specific roles in sex, but the patterns of performance are culturally varied and modified. In man, as opposed to animal, coition is determined by orgastic pleasure, not reproduction, and is often independent of it. Orgasm elicited by mechanisms other than pleasure seeking are experienced as novelties and surprises. Rado identifies a standard pattern of coitus, which is based on biology and physiology and not on custom or prejudice. This standard pattern involves penetration of the male organ into the female before ejaculation. It is a standard by which one studies the sex performance rather than a goal below which there is an element of abnormality. The cultural situation may assign superior roles to male or female, but biologically neither is more essential or valuable, since both are necessary. As a matter of fact, he points out that the male envies the female as frequently as the other way around. Orgastic maturity and reproductive, social and economic maturity occur at different chronological ages. This produces much difficulty in establishing an adequate sexual adjustment in the human.

Culture plays a major role in producing sexual deviations and distortions. Through threats and displays of disgust and displeasure regarding the genitals and the patterns of competition and co-operation in general, the individual develops distorted sexual patterns of behavior. Fears and guilty feelings (guilt fears or self-reproaches) make sex activity a threatening situation. This causes a distortion in the individual's sexual organization and interferes with the "standard coital performance." Reparative activity ensues which produces the modified patterns of behavior we call the sexual deviations. Rado has classified the modified form of behavior in three ways: a) situational, b) reparative, c) variational. The situational modifications are dependent on the availability of opportunities for sexual activity as well as the healthy, exploratory interest of the free, uninhibited individual. While they are significant only because the culture has categorized them as "abnormal," they are modifications which produce no basic alterations in the personality structure. The reparative patterns, however, arise out of the need to deal with fear and guilt (Sullivan's primary genital phobia) regarding the genitals. The reparative devices include: a) Organ displacement when persistent genital fear forces other bodily parts to replace the genitals. The choice of part is often dictated by earlier accidental experiences. b) Pain dependence—here pain is accepted as a prelude to pleasure in the process of repair. c) Contact avoidance—voyeur, exhibitionist, etc. Here, contact is avoided and only the arousal techniques are perpetuated. d) Solitary gratifications—fetishism, wet dream, masturbation, illusory self-fulfillment (day dream) transvestism, etc. Here, avoidance is produced by phantasy and play acting fulfillments. e) Homogeneous pairs—homosexuality, where partners are still looking for the opposite sex. Fear and resentment forbid them, but the male-female patterns of sex activity are still maintained in the activities of the homosexual. Variational modifications refer to the many ways of performing the sexual act.

Rado's conceptions of the pathology of sexual disorders has been translated to other mental disorders, with less significant success.

In schizophrenia he as attempted to demonstrate that the schizophrenic is largely an inherited defect of two kinds a) integrative pleasure deficiency, and b) proneness to disordered function of the proprioceptive system. The pleasure deficiency reduces the motivating power of the welfare emotions and allows for excessive rage. This undermines the individual's self-confidence and his capacity to enjoy life and the affectionate relationships in living. In addition it reduces the coherence of the action self. Three reparative processes are set into motion: a) in the security system, which emphasizes dependency; b) a technique of scarcity and limitation of activity as well as c) a reduction in pleasurable pursuits. This conception views the schizotypal disorders (as Rado calls them) as developmental stages of organization of the action self, and the symptoms derive from the breakdown of these mechanisms. Although this helps understand some of the symptomatology in schizophrenia, it remains mainly descriptive, and since Rado considers this disorder to be also entirely inherited and a defect in neuronal organization, he has little to add to the psychology of the disorder. However, when we come to the mood-cyclic disorders, we find that Rado has contributed a great deal to our understanding and treatment of depressions.

Prior to 1927 Rado had made some contributions to the problems of depressions which arose out of his work on the addictive disorders. He saw depression at that time as a problem of loss of self-esteem rather than one of hostility. He said that "they [the depressed individuals] are far from evincing [toward themselves] the attitude of humility and submission that alone would befit such worthless persons—on the contrary, they give a great deal of trouble, perpetually taking offense and behaving as if they had been treated with great injustice." Rado saw depressive behavior as expressing a "desperate cry for love," and he related it to the oral phase of development. Here, he indicated for the first time that the depressive reaction was an attempt at reparation of the ego's self-regard which was annihilated by the loss of love. Later, Rado expanded this concept and recognized the reaction to be an expiatory overreaction with the assumption of self-blame and punishment for the loss of love. The expiation is an attempt to reinstate oneself into the loving care of "mother." These attempts, however, are complicated by strong resentments which are turned on the beloved persons in order to force them to love him. This quickly becomes a vicious circle. Depression is thus an instance of mis-carried repair and the techniques in therapy arise directly out of this view. One must seek out the early processes of repair which are brought into play, which include excessive, inappropriate fears. The critical task is to bring the emergency emotions under control and to remove the inhibitions and generate the emotional matrix dominated by the welfare emotions (pride, love, etc.). The therapist must hold the patient to an adult level of cooperation and the child-like, parentifying behavior must be exposed.[4] Both aspects of the process, the need for love and the tendency towards resent-ments, must be met in a direct way and all the behavior must be viewed in terms of the opportunities and responsibilities for independent living. The therapist plays up the positive aspects of the patient's activities. The notion of disease being a result of miscarried repair has been applied very successfully to the prob-lems of the alcoholic and narcotics addict.

Rado has made a significant contribution in clarifying the con-cept of the unconscious by abandoning the topological view of mental organization and approaching it from an adaptational view-point. He views the mental apparatus in terms of its reporting and non-reporting activities. The reporting process is synonymous with awareness and with the process of inspection and introspection and constitutes consciousness. The non-reporting levels of the brain are the activities which are inferred and verified only through consciousness. This simple distinction avoids all the metaphysical speculations about the contents, dynamics, and special attributes of the unconscious, while retaining all the dynamic value of the areas of mental activity which are out of awareness. The non-reporting areas involve the functions of storage, automatization of patterns of behavior as well as attitudes and feelings which are under repression. In the non-reporting areas feelings may be discharged as dreams or somatic symptoms or in other rudimentary ways. In this area activity is stereotyped and consists also of abandoned adaptive patterns of behavior which may reappear under stress. The value of this concept lies in its ability to use the dynamic and explanatory value of the unconscious in a way that avoids its reification as a "place" or storehouse filled with primal instincts.[5]

As a natural outgrowth of Rado's thinking, he has formulated some novel and significant views on the treatment process. In 1939, when he began to feel that the libido theory was a handicap to therapy he stressed the "necessity for describing the actually observable dynamics in terms of integrative ego functioning." He recognized that the ego had a safety function which he called "emergency control" that acts by flight, fight, or the choice of the lesser evil. Anxiety produces these emergency responses. Neurosis is ego-functioning altered by faulty measures of emergency control. In 1955 he formulated further notions about the process of therapy which summarized his views. However, Rado's ideas are always in flux and he is always open to new developments. Presently, he believes that a) prolonged indiscriminate past history taking yields diminishing returns; b) developmental frame of reference (as opposed to adaptational frame) tends to concentrate all interest on the past and neglects the present; c) the modifying power of undoing a repressed impulse is very much overrated; and d) the transference situation as utilized by Freud encourages the development of an obedient child who is dependent. This allows the therapist's interpretation to be absorbed by the patient.

Rado divides therapy into a reconstructive and a reparative phase. The goals in therapy should always aim at reconstruction. In therapy, however, we must distinguish the treatment behavior from the actual life experiences of the patient. The patient's treatment behavior (as opposed to behavior elsewhere) may range from magic craving to self-reliance and aspiring which involves a positive motivation for change. The most typical kind of treatment behavior is the parentifying type that was described by Freud as transference. Although patients can be treated at all levels, the goals and techniques differ, and one must vary the procedures to stimulate the most aspiring type of cooperative behavior.

In the therapeutic process one must first recognize the organized types of behavior and identify the miscarried repair processes. These come into play early in the individual's life and include inappropriate fears, rages, and inhibitions. The task in therapy is to bring these areas of behavior under control, remove the inhibitions and generate a matrix of welfare emotions (Adler's notion of social behavior). The final task is to help the patient learn how to act on his liberated emotions and become a participant in living. To do this, it is imperative to keep the patient on an adult level of cooperation and discourage all child-like, magical cravings. Self-esteem must be bolstered on realistic grounds. The patient must learn to be self-reliant without making the analyst a scapegoat for his grievances. The therapeutic value of an interpretation rests on its ability to effect some emotional re-education.

In summary, Rado has attempted to establish psychoanalytic theory and practice on a rational basis, utilizing the insights of Freud. He has done this by foregoing all of Freud's metaphysical concepts and studying behavior as observable and verifiable by the sense organs. He has abandoned motivation for adaptation, believing that Freud's theories stressed development rather than adaptation. His theories have encouraged many new insights into man's behavior, particularly in the area of sex, depression, and therapy. His influence on psychoanalysis has been formidable, especially in his emphasis on the necessity for clear thinking and clarification of the methodology of psychoanalysis.

There are a great many psychoanalysts who have made contributions that would entitle them to be included in any collection of contemporary psychoanalytic theorists. However, space permits only the mention of a few of them. William V. Silverberg of New York has developed a most interesting concept which he calls *effective aggression.* His thesis is that mental illness originates as responses to traumatic experiences occurring in the early years of life. The organism has needs that are essential to survival, and wishes that are not necessary but greatly desired, such as sexual, aesthetic and social gratification. The degree of success in fulfilling one's wishes and needs, Silverberg calls effective aggression. This represents ego success and is initiated by the ego, not the libido. The notion of effective aggression involves ego activity not only in defense, but also for positive achievement. This differs from Sullivan and Horney although Silverberg has attempted the synthesis between Freud and Sullivan. This concept of ego is broader and more closely approximates the observed activities of the ego. Effective aggression has quantitative as well as qualitative factors, and self-esteem is built up by a continuing effective aggression.[6]

Self-esteem has two sources: a) inner-effective aggression and b) the outer opinion of others. This raises Sullivan's formula of self-esteem as "reflected appraisals" to a slightly higher dimension. Danger to self-esteem lies in the failure of effective aggression and the disapproval of the parental figures.

Franz Alexander, the dean of American psychoanalysts, although remaining more closely identified with the classic theoretical framework, has contributed greatly to therapy and to some of the tradtional concepts such as transference. Much of his work in the psychosomatic disorders has been the source and stimulus for the great advances toward a more holistic or field view of these disorders. He is a prodigious researcher whose open minded approach has enhanced the esteem of the psychoanalyst in the scientific community. In collaboration with Thomas French, Alexander formulated new insights into the process of therapy. Their innovations in the treatment process have been empirical and capable of verification. Rather than a routine that is applied indiscriminately to all patients, they have demonstrated the value of a flexible technique and the validity of varying the treatment hours per week or the total time in therapy as well as the setting up of a treatment program after formulating the dynamics of the patient's problem. Alexander's major contribution to therapy lies in his emphasis on the necessity for a "corrective emotional experience" for the ultimate resolution of a neurotic disorder. His work can be studied in detail in a number of technical and philosophical books he has written.[7]

Clara Thompson's major contribution derives from her therapeutic skill and her contributions regarding female psychology. These views were opposed to Freud's notions and were a potent force in undermining his theories on female psychology. She demonstrated that the female was not only beset by biological problems but was limited and constrained by cultural pressures. She felt that the myths concerning feminine deficiencies were largely male originated and propagated. She highlighted the inevitable conflicts that would ensue in the liberation of the female in view of the special problems that beset her in pregnancy and child care. Primarily her leadership of an eclectic school of psychiatry encouraged adventurous leaps into psychoanalytic research. She viewed psychoanalysis not as a completed science with infalliable principles, but as a new, immature collection of ideas that are tentative but extraordinarily useful.[8]

Frieda Fromm-Reichmann made her greatest contributions in the theory and therapy of the psychotic disorders, particularly schizophrenia. Although well grounded in traditional theory under the teaching of Freud, Kurt Goldstien and Georg Groddeck, the work that identifies her was influenced largely by Harry S. Sullivan. The center of her technique was essentially the communication of understanding to the schizophrenic and the recognition that the schizophrenic is capable of intense attachments which can be used to therapeutic advantage. Her great warmth, devotion and humanity served to alleviate their intense anxieties and permitted the exploration and comprehension of the schizophrenic's defenses against closeness and intrusion from a hostile world. Her patience with the catatonic and paranoid individuals not only produced striking results, but also advanced immeasureably our understanding of schizophrenia. The clarification of the significance of counter-transference phenomena predated the current interest in this area of therapy and she recognized the importance of separating the realistic from the unrealistic responses of both patient and therapist towards each other. She emphasized the therapist's inclination to escape into defensive counter-transference maneuvers whenever the patient's onslaughts became too intense. While personally performing astonishing feats with withdrawn patients, she brought the analysts' work down to a sound, practical, and comprehensible attack on the patient's major defensive systems. In her later years, she stressed the role of loneliness in the development of psychic disorders, particularly the psychoses. She contributed extensively to psychoanalytic literature, but made wide use of the term "intensive psychotherapy." This was not necessarily to distinguish it from psychoanalysis, but to indicate the identity of psychotherapy and psychoanalysis. She introduced many parameters and innovations into the treatment situation and preferred to call her work intensive psychotherapy even while she was using the traditional theories and concepts in her practice.[9]

Bernard Robbins has made some interesting and potentially significant contributions to the problem of consciousness and therapy. Because he has written very little and his work is unobtainable elsewhere, I will present it at some length.[10] His major emphasis is on a clarification of the role and function of the unconscious in our mental economy. He has raised some disturbing questions about Freud's concepts of repression and questions about latency which have thrown new light on the role of consciousness in mental disorders. Dr. Robbins believed that neuroses are disturbances in consciousness, not diseases of the emotions. The emotion which is presented at any given time is always consistent and appropriate to the prevailing state of consciousness and is not a re-emergence of "dormancy" or coming out of the unconscious. He particularly emphasized the fallacy of dealing with the unconscious as an area in which time has no meaning and where ideas, attitudes, or impulses remain encapsulated and outside the influence of time or change. He felt that psychiatry is the study of the process of dealing with change. "Consciousness is the total process of living which reflects the objective world which is in constant change and development."[10] It not only reflects life, but acts upon it. The patient's reactions and emotions are part of his conscious existence and always appropriate even when they seem to be utterly inappropriate to the state of his consciousness at that particular time. They are always an accurate reflection on how the individual is viewing the world at that moment. The presence of anger, or affection, etc., in therapy is a reflection of an altered state of consciousness, not a "return of repressed feelings." What happens in the unconscious is of interest, yet we must ultimately deal with the conscious ego. Our concern in psychiatry should be with consciousness, not the unconscious, since it produces a false view of the world and may produce feelings appropriate to this false view. The therapist's task, therefore, is to help achieve an accurate reflection of reality. Some of Robbins' views eliminate the necessity of postulating an unconscious.

Irrational activity is not motivated by infantile emotion but is a reflection of consciousness. Robbins took issue with the historical and developmental approach to psychiatry and felt that while the child is father to the man, the current situation cannot be regarded as qualitatively identical with any recalled episode. Although the concept of repression has been most effective in understanding changes in behavior associated with childhood training, it is not the only possible way of undertanding it. Trauma may not produce repression, but a change in consciousness and the attitudes and values with regard to the individual's way of viewing the world. In this way our living may be fundamentally altered by such traumatic events. Irrational activity is determined by an irrational consciousness so that the paranoid consciousness sees no separation of self from the world and no nexus between cause and effect, thus, he sees no connection between his objectives and the tasks needed to achieve them. Much of the paranoid symtomatology may be understood from this viewpoint. In this framework we could also understand the schizophrenic's consciousness. Robbins felt that schizophrenia is a disease of conscious existence characterized by feelings of transcendence and mysticism. This feeling of personal autonomy and independence of natural law is accompanied by modes of thought that rely on illuminations which transcend ordinary powers of understanding. This feeling of invulnerability and omnipotence is generally an aggressive attack on reality. The schizophrenic panic is the terror involved in the possibility of change at the advent of a new life situation. Faced with a threat to his transcendent and invulnerable existence and a necessity to face the real challenge of living with a commitment to rational and realistic goals, he responds with increased feelings of transcendence and misconceives the environment. The threat of dissolution on such occasions produces activity to preserve the transcendence rather than to change it.

He has presented some valuable ideas on the therapeutic process and has emphasized the difference between insight and change. The difference lies in activity which effects the movement from insight to change. There is great reluctance in classic therapy to encourage activity and to recognize that psychoanalysis is a social practice which emphasizes the connection between activity and change. The old view of intellectual and emotional insights is dependent upon the use that is made of insight. The quality of insight changes when it is put into practice and what really matters is whether it is put into practice or merely discussed as an intellectual exercise. The laws governing psychotherapy are identical with the laws governing growth. This does not involve adjustment or the recognition of problems, but the actual utilization and acting on these insights. The process of cure depends upon the recognition that mental activity is strictly determined and that the factors that distort our perceptions are largely out of awareness. Freedom and cure are interchangeable concepts which involve the necessity of submitting to social standards but not through the relinquishing of individual freedom. Ferenczi, Rank and Freud proposed a freedom at the expense of society; that is, that health constituted freedom at the expense of the society regardless of its form. Robbins, however, considers cure and freedom to be a recognition of all necessities, internal and external, personal and social, and the interdependence of the two. In therapy, the technique of free association should mean the association of relevant material relating to the issues involved, and not a freedom to maneuver so as not to advance the treatment. The therapist must not only note the symptom, but help erase it. Interpretations are used to elicit the cooperation of the patient to alter and change his personality and life and to achieve a freedom to act in accordance with the real necessities in his life. Transference attitudes are real attitudes determined by the here and now relationships and distorted attitudes refer to the distorted consciousness of the patient.

The patient must be analyzed in toto and in action, not as ego or superego or id, but as a total individual. Change occurs when there is an enlargement of the horizon of correct awareness in a social context. The nature of the relationships with others is the ultimate test of cure and the therapist sides with the patient who "is to become" rather than the patient "who is." Activity is essential on the part of the therapist as well as the patient, and the patient must be forced through various devices to cooperate in the endeavor. Robbins' theories and formulations are the deepest penetration into an ego psychology without entirely abandoning the concept of the unconscious. There is a clear recognition of Freud's essential contribution, but Robbins took issue with some of the underlying assumptions. He disagrees strongly with Freud's mechanical conception of the impact of society on the individual which did not fully acknowledge it as a mutual interaction. Man as consciousness is the product of this interaction. It is not only man's physiological equipment that determines the nature of the interaction and the kind of individual that evolves. Instead, it is the fluctuating changes in the external environment and the social structure that determines this interaction. Humans are not merely physiological machines, but thinking, conscious animals whose existence is occupied with correct or incorrect perception and conception. To the extent that he misperceives, he behaves inappropriately.

In summary—although trained in the classic psychoanalytic theories, Robbins developed his conceptions outside of the libido theory framework. He has made a forceful attack on the concept of the unconscious and he developed some views about the neurotic process as a distortion of consciousness. In the area of therapy, he has clarified the forces involved in healing, particularly with regard to the necessity for activity and change after insights have been achieved.

Much work has been done by other contemporary theorists on the expansion of the role of ego which has placed greater emphasis on the conscious processes, thereby minimizing the unconscious elements in the mental economy. These studies range from the emphasis on the ego as a perceptual organ (Melanie Klein, Lawrence Kubie, Ernest Shachtel) to the ego as the integrative organ (Thomas French) in the psychological functioning of the individual. The ego is variously described as the autonomous ego, integrative ego, or creative ego. Some work has been done on the problems of creativity in which the role of conscious mentation is stressed as opposed to the unconscious elements in the creative process (Kubie, Schachtel).

Existential Analysis

In recent years there has been a development in Europe that has attracted considerable interest in the United States. It is the extension of existentialist philosophy into psychiatry with the development of systems of existential analysis. In some ways it is a reaction against the classic theories of Freud which were too mechanical and put undue emphasis on the biological elements in man's behavior. In other respects it is a development in ego psychology which parallels the developments in ego psychology in the United States, except that they move in different directions. The ego psychological developments in the United States are moving into a more operational and rational approach to human behavior with emphasis on the conscious and the "here and now." The existential analysts are also concerned with consciousness almost exclusively, but from an irrational, unsystematic, and pragmatic point of view.

Existentialism is a unifying philosophy and stimulates the view of man as an holistic animal, not mind and body or mind or body, but a being that exists as a whole in spite of the fact that he is made up of parts. In this sense the existential philosophers encourage the practitioners of science towards a goal that Whitehead has called "the organismic view of man." This goal is to see man in his totality if we are to truly understand him. Existential philosophy also underlines the notion, so highly developed by the neo-Freudian psychologists like Horney, Fromm, Sullivan, et al., that experiencing is the only authentic theme of psychology. By raising some highly meaningful questions about relatedness, isolation, death, and dealing with the individual as "being-in-the-world," it has forced the psychologist to expand and re-explore the concepts of love, the meaning of intimacy and loneliness, and the effect of the knowledge of our ultimate death on our daily living.[11]

Existential philosophy concerns itself with existence or consciousness as valid fields for objective study in spite of the fact that terms like "being" or "perceiving" have no logical or definable value. It is an approach to the study of man which sees man as a biological being who is concerned with ultimate values, who, while self-subsistent, is dependent on others and, while he exists as an individual, requires the fellowship, community and relatedness of other humans.

The existential philosophers who had something to say directly to psychiatry and psychoanalysis have been few in number. However, they raised questions which were largely similar to those social scientists who felt Freud's theories to be too biologically centered. They 1) stress man as an experiencing animal who "lives in a world," which must be reckoned with and not merely a focus for man's activities; 2) they emphasize the elements of participation in human experiencing and focus our attention on the issues of death, finiteness, loneliness and isolation, and 3) they recognize that man's creativity and productiveness comes from a decision and responsibility that man takes on himself as the true goal of his living.

Søren Kierkegaard, the father of existentialism, produced profound insights regarding the role of anxiety in human behavior. This was prior to Freud. Karl Jaspers aimes at a scientific method in developing his philisophy. He is the exponent of an idealistic, humanistic view of existence and a belief in reason as a method of studyng existence. He examined the attitudes and decisions involved in meeting the inescapable situations in life such as death, conflict and change. In addition, he recognizes the limitations of a scientific methodology to thoroughly understand man since he felt that ethics, morality, existential conflicts and an abiding search for truth also motivates man's behavior. Martin Heidegger views man as being concerned with his own being in his everyday existence of "being-in-the-world" with others. Anxiety for him is a fundamental feeling, since it results from a necessity to confront the world. To live in the world means to participate in it and not to retreat from it. He has also broadened our grasp of how man faces the knowledge of his own death. He says that it is impossible to experience death in perceiving the death of others, since death is not like going to the end of a road, but is an emptiness, a nothingness, a non-being which permeates man's existence from its inception. Man's ability to confront the possibility of death, frees him from petty projects, and gives him the freedom to negate as well as to produce. Man for him is always projected towards the future and thus has some real problems in a psychological sense in dealing with time. Martin Buber, Hans Trub, and Paul Tillich, who are primarily theologians, have also contributed to psychoanalytic theory. Buber has emphasized man's need to be accepted by his fellow-man and to become meaningful to the other person's existence. Trub has stressed man's need to affirm himself by encountering and responding to the other person. Paul Tillich has emphasized the significance of participation in the world in order to be accepted in spite of one's deficiencies and inadequacies. Jean Paul Sartre, who was greatly influenced by Heidegger, has stressed the issues of freedom and choice which involves man's ability to reconcile the impossible task of being sure and certain and accepting the fact he is a being who never can be, but who is always about-to-be. Man is always projected into the future with the open possibility for becoming what he is. The ambiguity of being part of a world (in-itself) and yet separated from it produces despair and forlorness and a yearning to reunite with the world (for-itself-in-itself). Sartre's ethics involve freedom as an absolute value, being not only man's duty, but his natural condition. Being one's self is the aim of wholesome living, and bad faith or insecurity (mauvais fois) is being what one is not. Thus, one can see how the philosophy of existentialism has direct relevance to some of our theoretical developments in psychoanalytic theory in recent years. To this extent it has been fruitful. However, existential philosophy has also been the basis for several elaborate psychiatric theories with their own methodology and therapeutic techniques. While some of these existential analysts (Medard Boss, Ludwig Binswanger, Viktor Frankel, etc.) have contributed some useful insights, they have gotten bogged down in establishing a "system," and the holistic attitude implicit in the philosophy gets lost in the search for the phenomenon of "existence" which often overlooks man's biological origins. A philosophy should perform the task of directing or producing a Weltanschauung, and should not itself become a scientific method or research tool. It should determine the nature of the hypothesis, and not necessarily the techniques for exploring or validating the hypothesis. When a philosophy becomes translated into a technique of research like Marxism, for example, it becomes doctrinaire, restrictive, and too one-sided.

Some of the work of the existential analysts has contributed to recent developments in theory which are close to the formulations of the neo-Freudian theorists.

Ludwig Binswanger, a psychiatrist who studied with Heidegger, has attempted to explore the problems of love by distinguishing the two modes of existence, love and care. Care is characterized by "taking someone by something," thus fulfilling the material needs of another person, while love is a togetherness, a participation without force, control, or pressure. Love is not a sentiment, or a feeling, or a sublimation, but a total mode of existing. This mode of existing embraces all possibilities and is a true union of the "you and me" into the "we," and thus the we is always female-male, and each partner is female-male, receptive as well as active. In love the difference between male and female disappears (as opposed to Freud's notion of the biological innate nature of sexual psychological differences) and each partner loves as well as being loved. This notion has put new light on the fixed roles of male and female and the difference between love as intimacy as the sado-masochist symbiosis that is so often called intimacy. However, when Binswanger and his followers developed their own psychotherapeutic theories and methodology, called logotherapy, it becomes confused by detailed material and minute analyses of patient, phrases, idioms, drawings, etc. The idea is to get into the patient's world and visualize it from within. This has expanded our knowledge of the feelings and attitudes of these patients. To do this we need to encourages the development of trust and allow the patient to escort us into his distorted world. We cannot force our way in by false assurances or elaborate pretenses. Some therapists have distorted this most meaningful concept by trying to enter the psychotic world by artificially assuming a role in this world. The therapist pretends to be a figure, generally the significant one in the patient's distortions. While this may produce astonishing results it does not appear to produce the high recovery rates claimed by these therapists. The technique is a naive but bold oversimplification of the delusional process and deals frivolously with patients' enormous problems of loneliness and despair. The forced intrusion into the psychotic's world may enable the play to continue on some reality-unreality basis for a little while, but it does not become truly involved in the mechanics of the patient's disease and the needs satisfied by his symptoms. The patient soon distinguishes this insincere, frivolous and disrespectful play acting. Other therapists using this viewpoint think that by an incautious and free use of symbolic language one can enter a patient's unconscious world and share it with him. Sharing the patient's world can not involve identifying with him and accepting his distortion as being real. While this may produce some relief from loneliness or despair, it becomes a *folie-a-deux* rather than a return to sound living. These distortions of the logotherapy techniques do not minimize the valid benefit derived from a voyage with the patient into his distorted world through a detailed study of all his productions.

Karl Jaspers, in his book on psychopathology, has emphasized the existential elements in the phenomena of anxiety of responsibility. However, he too has developed a technique and methodology called phenomenologic analysis which attempts to describe the essence of an experience; not the objects but the forms of consciousness of the object. The phenomenological study of personality attempts to see and experience the patient's personality rather than to find out about the patient in terms of his needs or desires or goals. Medard Boss,[12] an outstanding practitioner of Dasein Analysis, has made a study of the sexual perversions from the existential point of view and has added new meaning to the pathology of sexual behavior. He sees the perversions not as a disturbance in sexuality or libidinal development, but as the lack of development and maturity for all the possibilities of love. They are produced by a neurotic incapacity to love in a total sense. It is a problem involving man's capacity to express his love in all ways, particularly in the area of sexuality.

A cursory survey of the theories some of the existential psychiatrists suggests that they are approaching man in a total sense, visualizing him not only as a biological entity but also as a creature who lives in a world that creates problems that he must deal with. The existential analytic development has stimulated us to review and revise some of our notions regarding the issues of love, death, and time. It has suggested therapeutic maneuvers and techniques which are extremely close to the attitudes of the neo-Freudians, particularly Horney, Fromm and Sullivan. In insisting that the therapeutic process should involve the issues of participation and acceptance, they emphasize that aloofness or objectivity are obstacles to the process. The petty issues of lying down versus sitting up or three or four visits a week as well as the more meaningful issues of the importance of current versus past experience become side issues when the major emphasis is participation. It has also placed great interest in values since it esteems self-affirmation and self-fulfillment as positive, healthy, and worthwhile. When existential philosophy is translated into a theoretical and therapeutic framework, however, its significance and value is lost. It develops its own language and methodology and its influence on psychoanalytic theory and practice becomes minimized.

NOTES

1. Rado's organization of human development is related to his concepts of adaptation. This emphasis has recently re-entered psychological theorizing which has been dominated by motivational conceptualizations for some time. The biological aspects of personality are explored from a more sophisticated level than the study of instincts. This emphasis tends to focus on the medical aspects of psychoanalytic therapy and to develop theoretical conceptions which are more closely bound to the medical disciplines.

All references are to *Psychoanalysis of Behavior*. New York, Grune and Stratton, 1956.

2. It must be noted that in Freud's interpretation of bisexuality we find a particularly masculine bias. This is related to his notion that "libido could always be called 'masculine' no matter whether it appears in man or in woman, in the sense that as an instinct it is always active, even if directed towards a passive aim." (Three Contributions to the Theory of Sex.)

3. Rado, S.: A critical examination of the concept of bisexuality. This paper is included in his collected papers, Psychoanalysis of Behavior, New York, Grune & Stratton, Inc., 1956, p. 139.

4. The therapeutic implications which arise out of this formulation are profoundly useful. They are more fully developed in the chapter on therapy, but in essence they recognize the multiple levels of adaptation which require varying technical maneuvers. This is true about many of Rado's conceptions. They are developed in such a fashion that the technical and therapeutic consequences flow directly out of his observations. It is clear that his ideas are the result of extensive experience in therapy as well as a rich philosophical and scientific heritage. See also his paper on Depression, Problem of Melancholia, pp. 47-63, Psychodynamics of Depression, pp. 235-242.

5. This particular contribution was developed further by the author of this book in a paper called: Guilt, responsibility and the unconscious. Comp. Psychiat. 2:179-187, 1960.

6. In his book, Childhood Experience and Personal Destiny, New York, Springer Publishing Co., 1952, he said: "The task demands that the ego be given a theoretic basis for its functioning; in other words to postulate for it a specific kind of drive or energy which has survival of the total organism as its chief goal and which operates by the medium of effective aggression. An advantage of the latter concept is that it permits us to see the ego as concerned with matters not accounted for it we regard it as activated solely, or even mainly by motivations of defense. It is an operational concept, which accounts for the ego's efforts in the direction of achievement as well as of defense."

7. See bibliography for titles of a small portion of his writings.

8. In her paper: Cultural pressures in the psychology of women. Psychiat. 5:331-339, 1942, she pointed out that every single trait attributed by Freud to a biologically determined development of the libido (penis envy, repression of aggressiveness, passivity, masochism, weak super-ego, rigidity, narcissism) can be explained in terms of the cultural influences on the character structure.

9. Although her writings were limited to one book, *Principles of Intensive Psychotherapy*, and a collection of papers called *Psychoanalysis and Psychotherapy* (see Bibliography), her influence is widespread in the treatment of the neuroses as well as the psychoses.

10. His published works consists of several papers in a now discontinued magazine called *Psychotherapy* published by the Robbins Institute, several others in various journals and some still in manuscript form.

11. This has resulted in a considerable body of writing both in Europe and the U. S. A book by Rollo May, Existence, New York, Basic Books, 1958, which has had a wide sale attests to the interest in these developments. Other psychiatrists have also contributed useful articles on therapy from an existential viewpoint. See:

Strauss, E.: On Obession. New York, Nervous & Mental Disease Monograph, Colm, Hanna: Healing and participation. Psychiat. 16:99-111, 1953.

Weigert, Edith: Existentialism and its relation to psychotherapy. Psychiat. 12:399-412, 1949.

Harold Kelman, Leslie Farber and the Journal of the American Ontoanalytic Association.

Kierkegaard, Søren: Either-Or, Concept of Dread. Oxford University Press. 1944.

Jaspers, Karl: Allegemeine Psychopathologie. Berlin, Springer Verlag, 1948.

Sartre, Jean P.: Existential Analysis. New York, Philosophical Library, 1953.

Marcuse, Herbert: Philosophy and Phenomenological Research, vol. 8, No. 3, 1948.

12. Boss, M.: Meaning and Content of Sexual Perversions. New York, Grune & Stratton, Inc., 1949.

VII

Sex

IN THE TWENTIETH CENTURY sex and sexual behavior were pushed boldly into the forefront of the psychology of man by the monumental work of Sigmund Freud. Yet, it is only in comparatively recent years that sex has been assigned any special significance in its effect on human motivation and behavior. In the earliest recorded literature the fundamental motivation for human behavior was usually ascribed to love or hate, or the feelings of friendship and companionship. It was love for one's family, clan, friend or nation, or the hatred for one's enemy and the foreigner which provided the main themes for these early legends and epics. Power drives, struggles for domination, status, wealth and authority, were the issues in these adventures and epic struggles. Although sexual activity was no less in evidence, it was dealt with in matter-of-fact terms and did not seem to occupy a position of greater prominence or privilege than any other physiological activity which was accompanied by pleasure. Some of the *Canterbury Tales* are delightful stories of how sex was viewed in lusty and unrestrained terms. The point is that sex has not always been the object of special or peculiar interest, even though it was as much a source of pleasure then as it is today. Banquets, orgies, and minor and major ceremonials in all civilizations and at all times were as heavily involved with eating and drinking as they were with sex. As a matter of fact, while sex played a minor role in most, and a central role in some, eating and drinking were almost always central to these ceremonials. This was not due to any particular moral or conventional injunction with regard to sex since all physiological functions had few restraints imposed upon their performance. A history of manners and social amenities during that period would deal largely with proprieties of dress and table behavior rather than with sexual concerns. The advent of Christianity with its ascetic and proscriptive attitudes towards sex produced a marked change in the attitude toward sexual activity. Sex was considered to be satanic in origin and necessary only to preserve the species. In some Christian sects, as in the priesthood, it was entirely forbidden. Sex was sinful, dirty, and a source of pleasure that distracted the individual from the contemplation of the divine. Consequently, sex was placed in a most ambiguous position; enjoyed and practiced by almost everyone, yet considered unholy and subhuman. While husband and wife might be actively engaged in it, it was not considered a proper subject for open discussion between them. Pornographic art and literature grew up, and were designed to fill a need which was not allowed expression in more appropriate ways. In this atmosphere, Victorian prudery, which was the climax of sexual restraint and inhibition, placed an even greater burden on sexual performance. Sex was not a fitting concern for proper people, as well as being outside of medical interest. The genitals, the sexual apparatus, and certainly sexual behavior were concerns only of dirty minded people or scientists, who for some ill-fated reason found it an area of curiosity and interest. Freud began his medical career in this atmosphere.

When he and Breuer discovered that their patients had notable sexual difficulties, they became convinced of the relationship of sexual behavior to certain abnormal mental states. Because of this turn in their research, Breuer abandoned the project. Thus, Freud's observations of sex as it manifested itself in profound inhibitions, distortions, and repressions, was characteristic of the era in which he lived, aside from any factors implicit in the sexual instinct. His recognition of the profound influence it played in the social milieu as well as in the patients he saw may have been a reflection of the extreme emphasis placed on its denial and restraint. In this sense, its role in personality development may have been exaggerated by the era rather than any inherent element in sex itself. It is a tribute to Freud's genius and integrity that he noted the influence of an aspect of human behavior that was available for all to see, if they would dare to. Only prejudice, fear, and the inevitable contamination of scientific doctrine by existing conventions and moral attitudes permitted the physicians prior to Freud to avoid recognizing the crucial role that sexual activity played in health and disease. Freud broke through these bonds to a certain extent and acknowledged and investigated sexual behavior. However, while overcoming this prejudice, he retained many other social and scientific prejudices which were current during his working life. To speak of psychoanalysis as pan-sexual because it focuses so sharply on sex is to consider engineering one-track minded because it deals with machines and mechanical designs. Freud neither introduced sex nor discovered it. He exposed what was available to all scientists and physicians, if they could put aside the restrictions of their cultural prejudices. He brought sex out of the bedchamber and into the arena of scientific scrutiny. The fact that he considered sex to be the mainspring of human motivation and activities such as art, religion, etc., to be mere sublimations of sex may be an error in his theorizing, but it is not evidence that he was preoccupied with sex either personally or professionally. As a matter of fact, Freud, according to his biographer, Ernest Jones, was a rather restrained and somewhat prudish man who was prepared to abandon sexual activity himself at an early point in his career.

In a letter to Fliess, Freud said: "Also sexual excitation is of no more use to a person like me."[1]

Erich Fromm speculates that Freud's theories are proof of his inhibited sexuality. He said that Freud, the great spokesman for sex, was altogether a typical puritan. To him, the aim of life for a civilized person was to suppress his emotional and sexual impulses and at the expense of the suppression, to lead a civilized life. Freud's sexual inhibitedness may sound like a contradiction to the fact that in his theories, he gave such a central place to the sexual drive. But this contradiction is more apparent than real. Many thinkers write about what they lack, and what they strive to achieve for themselves, or for others. Furthermore, Freud, a man of puritan attitude, would hardly have been able to write so frankly about sex had he not been so sure of his own "goodness" in this respect."[2]

Psychoanalysis has dealt extensively with sexual development as long as its theories revolved around sex as a focal influence in personality development. As alternative hypotheses have been presented, less emphasis has been placed on sex. This is not because Freud was pan-sexual and the current theorists are not. It is largely due to a revision of some *of the basic hypotheses* regarding personality.

Freud dealt with sex in terms of the prevailing scientific atmosphere of the late 1900's. He examined it as an instinct and isolated the components of the instinct. Thus, the sexual activity of the human was examined in the mechanical framework of an energy theory called the libido theory which was described in earlier chapters. Sex was not viewed simply as a physiological function but was considered to have special significance in motivating the development of the human animal. However, the psychology of man has developed around various fundamental needs, some biological and physiological while others are psychological; for example, avoidance of loneliness, which necessitates human exchange and relationship. Some systems of personality development overemphasize the biological aspect (Freud), while others minimize the biological (Existential analytic theories).

It should be noted that some physiological activities of the human are entirely personal and neither require nor desire other humans in their performance. The activities of the autonomic system as well as the cardiac, the respiratory, the digestive and the excretory systems fall into this category, in spite of the well-known fact that tension or anxiety may affect their functioning. Other physiological activities do not require, but generally desire the presence of other humans. This particularly applies to ingestion or eating. Eating has become a highly socialized physiological function where not only the company of other humans is sought, but free, unimpeded sharing is allowed and encouraged. Eating thus becomes a physiological activity that enables man to fulfill many of his needs while satisfying his hunger. Sex, however, absolutely requires another person for its total biological fulfillment and under circumstances of the greatest physical intimacy, where there is potentially the maximum amount of give and take. Thus, some physiological mechanisms are most intimately involved in man's psychology, while others are only distantly interrelated. Sex appears to be most heavily loaded with psychological overtones to the extent that it is more frequently practiced to fulfill some psychological needs rather than the procreative or biological (physiological) needs. This helps us to understand its pre-eminent role in human behavior.

The striking significance of sexual activity was not fully recognized until Freud removed it from the false morality of the Victorian era into the light of scientific scrutiny. He assumed that it not only had a prominent role, but a basicly determining one. It was apparent to Freud that sexual activity was singularly suited to influence and to elucidate man's psychology. While some of the reasons have already been touched upon, the capacity of man to postpone the sexual act remains the greatest single source of its influence on his psychology. The ability to postpone the act to almost indefinite lengths, unlike any other physiological activity of man, permits phantasy to enter into its performance as well as allowing time for its influence to be felt on another human being. Phantasy may even replace the sex act itself, and in a theory of personality development like Freud's, where imagination plays a crucial role, the sex function would be of greatest interest since it allows for the maximum play of the imaginative faculties. Not only can its performance be postponed the longest, but it is capable of almost infinite variations in its performance, and thus the possibilities for its distortion become unlimited. In addition, it is the physiological function that requires the greatest physical and often emotional intimacy, and is most subject to cultural control and restraint. For all these reasons it plays a greater role in man's psychology than any other of man's needs. Whether it plays a determining and motivating role is a different matter. Although some theorists see it as the force that motivates all human activity by its instinctual pressures, others see it as a physiological function which by virtue of its interpersonal necessities plays a major part in the human drama.

Sex plays this primary role by virtue of its unusual capacity to fulfill major psychological needs (such as avoidance of loneliness, satisfaction of loving needs, etc.) while performing its biological function. Sex activity, as was pointed out before, is the only biological activity that requires another person in order to carry out its full biological function of procreation.[3]

In the hierarchy of physiological functions extending from the autonomic system which is entirely intrapersonal and which operates independently of outside sources of stimulation to those functions which are impinged upon by the outside, sex is in the extreme position. It not only requires some outside stimulation, but can only be performed with another person, in the flesh or in phantasy. Thus, by necessity it has interpersonal relevance.

As a result, it is most intimately associated with all the aspects of interrelatedness, both constructive and destructive, pleasurable and painful. It encompasses all the elements of interpersonal relationship, such as conflict, struggle, and every maneuver, technique, and dynamism of human behavior. Thus, it is the royal road to understanding character structure as the dream was the via regia for Freud for understanding the unconscious.

In our awareness of the role of others in character formation, we would expect that those functions which are influenced by others play a greater part in character development than those which develop independently of outside sources. Thus, eating, which absolutely requires another person for a prolonged period of time, in the early years, occupies a major area of interaction with the culture and plays a crucial role in character development. In the oral period the presence of a mothering person is essential. Defecation and urination in the anal period require less cooperation and intervention, except in the earliest years. However, these undergo great cultural control in terms of cleanliness and propriety and thus become an area of interaction in terms of conforming to the cultural requirements. With other physiological functions, such as breathing, heart action or sweating, the effect of the culture has only indirect influence, such as prejudices regarding body odor, and so on. Sex, however, from its inception to its extinction, always requires another, and thus inevitably plays a major role in character formation. Sexual maturity occurs at a period in the individual's history when the bulk of his patterns, attitudes, and relationships with other people are already largely formed. Thus, a biological function which requires another person arrives on the scene already heavily loaded with complicating factors. Its pressure for performance, however, is so great that it overcomes many obstacles and becomes established more or less satisfactorily in most individuals. Its unusual capacity to alleviate or dissipate anxiety makes it a most useful instrument in interpersonal situations. However, biologically it presses for fulfillment with no greater urgency than hunger, thirst, or other basic physiological needs. It can, as a matter of fact, be more easily abandoned than any other physiological need. This is demonstrated in the life of the ascetic or in religious movements. In circumstances of deprivation, as in prisoner of war camps, it is easily abandoned. Under these circumstances the focus is almost exclusively upon food, rather than sex. In addition, most individuals will cling tenaciously to certain ideals or values relinquishing sexual satisfactions for long periods of time if necessary. Only in extremely distorted states do we find individuals seeking sexual satisfaction at the cost of other values or standards.

INFANTILE SEXUALITY

Freud's description of sexual behavior in children was confirmation of the libido theory. This theory permitted the extensive use of symbolism and allowed for sexual interpretations of behavior of all kinds.[4] There is considerable evidence that supports the notion of sexual activity in infants and children in the sense of genital interest. One can observe the child's manipulation of his genitals and his curiosity about the genitals of the opposite sex. Many questions about sex, conception, and childbirth are raised, and as one approaches adolescence, there is a growing preoccupation and concentration on one's appearance as an object of sexual interest. However, these and other pieces of such evidence are not sufficient to support the contention of infantile sexuality. It rests mainly on the application of the libido theory which presumes that the sexual energy or the libido invests certain zonal regions at certain periods of development. With this assumption we then interpret aspects of the zonal behavior as being libidinal (sexual). At the same time, we interpret some aspects of behavior as sexual simply by analogy. Thus, sucking behavior is considered to have a libidinal basis because in the adult sucking plays a role in the sex activity of both the male and the female. Because retention or release of the rectal and bladder contents is sometimes associated with pleasure and excitement, it is analogized to the pleasure in delaying and expelling the seminal fluid. Such analogies are meaningful only when the initial premise of the presence of libido at these areas is already accepted as a fact. The appearance of contentment and bliss which is followed by sleeping after infant feeding is likened to the contented sleep which follows sexual gratification. Such observations are capable of a variety of interpretations which depend upon one's initial assumptions. They do not necessarily establish the true meaning of the experience. They only confirm the initial assumption and are not conclusions drawn from an independent examination of the behavioral sequence. This is an example of circular reasoning which finds evidence to support a theory which is the basis for discovering the evidence. Freud attempted to distinguish libidinal from sexual and infantile from adult sexuality. Libido was a broader term than sexuality viewed as adult intercourse, and while he was constantly warning about this confusion, some of his concepts are derived from this very confusion. The child is assumed to have adult notions of seduction and parental intercourse in order to give meaning to the Oedipus complex. Castration, penis envy, etc., would have little effect on the child unless the penis was visualized in adult terms as an organ of significance in terms of pleasure. Yet, the concept of infantile sexuality rests almost entirely on the necessity to distinguish it from adult sexuality. The libido theory suggests that many activities are sexual in terms of being libidinally organized yet not identical to adult sexuality, in spite of the fact that the phantasies and symbolic interpretations are always made in terms of adult sexual activity. When we observe a child playing with his genitals, we interpret it as sexual only when we conceive of its similarity to the adult genital play called masturbation or activity preparatory to intercourse. Otherwise, it does not have greater significance than playing with the ear, umbilicus, or a big stick. This situation is not made more believable by pointing out that the child seems to have a dreamy orgastic-like expression as if he were experiencing an orgasm to prove the identity of purpose in genital manipulation in the two year old and the twenty year old. It is only another reflection of our interpreting by an analogy that rests on a previously decided point of view.

The genital activities prior to the maturation of gonads are prime examples of the manifold functions of the sexual apparatus. Since the biological function of sex is necessarily absent prior to maturation, the genitals become sources of curiosity and comparison and are utilized in the attempts to conform or rebel just as any other organ is. The genitals may be the basis for mutual exploration and chumship, competitive play, and the establishment of likenesses in seeking compeers. This is true of all the physiological structures, yet the genitals may become more significant if cultural prejudices and pressures encourage it.[5] However, for the child, it is conceivable that the genitals are not viewed as specially significant or in a separate category from other physiological structures. Unless the culture dictates this significance, comparisons of genital size or difference, for example, may stir up many questions, but apparently fewer than are stimulated by comparisons of manual dexterity or organic defects. The problem of who and what one is, and being better or lesser than other children, are prominent issues for the growing child, and the genitals are included in this appraisal as is everything else. However, as far as we know, the child is incapable of visualizing the genital apparatus in its adult procreative capacity. Since this is a matter of learning and experience, it is impossible for the child to recognize the special value of the genitals as sexual tools. Freud was fully aware of this, yet many of Freud's major hypotheses, particularly the Oedipus complex, assumes some unconscious knowledge of adult sexuality in order to account for its formation. Since we know that the Oedipus situation occurs very frequently in precisely the terms which Freud described it, we may need to search for explanations other than sexual ones to account for its appearance. Many of the neo-Freudian theorists have done this. The cardinal importance of curiosity and the energetic exploratory activities of infants and children in personality development has not been given sufficient attention except in some recent personality theories (Piaget, Sullivan, Schachtel). It is this fact that attracted Freud's attention regarding the genitals. Yet, even if this were the complete story, it is apparent that manipulation of the genitals produces a qualitatively different kind of satisfaction which seems to surpass the manipulation of almost any other part of the body. The ear seems to have some special significance in this regard, but this appears to be short-lived. It is similar in many ways to the automatic response to sweets which produces a special kind of pleasure in children. Once the genitals are discovered and manual manipulation occurs, it becomes actively sought after. Whether we call it masturbation, which generally implies sexual overtones, or manual manipulation, which has some of the connotations of non-sexual activity, it becomes a favored activity, particularly at times of tension and stress. One must distinguish between genital manipulation and masturbation, the line being drawn at genital handling to produce ejaculation which is called masturbation, while all other contacts should be called manipulation. Although the distinction may be unnecessary after adolescence, prior to this it would avoid the tendency to label a phenomenon which looks like something else but which may be different from it. One can account for the phenomena of genital handling in many ways without postulating the adult equivalent of masturbation. The genital area is clearly endowed with nerve endings which can produce pleasant sensory experiences. Prior to ejaculation, which has a sensory quality of pleasure all its own, the pleasure of genital manipulation is related to the number of nerve endings concentrated in the genital area as well as its easy accessibility.

In addition to the above distinction, genital must be distinguished from sexual. Genital refers only to the external representative and the executing instrument through which sexual activity can occur. This applies equally to the penis as well as the vagina. Sexual, on the other hand, refers to the total organ complex of the genital function with the gonadal organs, vesicular fluid in the male and

its accompanying tubular channels and muscular apparatus iner-
vated by nerves that have a spinal and cerebral connection. In the
female, it involves the gonadal apparatus with its tubular structure
and connections with the uterus, vagina, clitoris, and lubricating
organs. Although manipulation of parts of the sexual apparatus such
as the penis or clitoris may initiate a total sexual response, the act
may be initiated and produced in a variety of ways. To imply, however, that one part of the total function (the penis) is equivalent
to the whole (sexuality only) is to assume that the penis deals
only with sex. This is misleading. Thus, it is conceivable that many
uses can be made of the genitals, as in the male for whom the penis
serves as a passageway for urine as well as for seminal contacts.
Erections may result from a full bladder and at such times could
not be used for sexual purposes. In this way we could also recognize
the distinction between genital in the male before it can deliver
the seminal fluid, and after gonadal maturity when it is capable
of delivering seminal fluid.[6]

At any rate, infantile genital activity, whether we consider it as
mere exploratory activity or as arising out of pre-genital drives,
is generally practiced solo and in secret. Except for some mutual
play in late childhood and pre-adolescence, the manipulation of the
genitals is carried out in secrecy and is accompanied by considerable
guilt. Because of cultural taboos and prejudices regarding sex and
the genitals, the genital area comes in for considerable attention
and ultimately this has some effect on the sexual function. Sullivan
referred to this as the "primary genital phobia," and emphasized
the extreme effects of parental disapproval of genital touching and
exploring. It is difficult to determine whether the child either
literally or symbolically fears a loss of his genitals (castration fears).
The infant, all agree, cannot conceptualize the genitals in its adult
biological form and, consequently, measures designed to prevent
genital manipulation produce a total aversion or massive phobic
avoidance for reasons totally unknown to the infant. As the child
develops, however, some conceptualization is possible and the possible dangers to the genitals may be visualized in many ways. The
value of the penis as a procreative organ or as a source of great
pleasure is not yet clearly defined. Still, the parental threats and
prohibitions may be severe enough to stir up the fear of the loss
of the genital, but usually they are mild enough only to produce
continuing feelings of guilt concerning them. These guilt feelings

arise not only out of the failure to conform to the parental demands but also largely out of the inability of the individual to carry out his own resolutions to discontinue the practice. The guilt feelings of worthlessness, weakness, evilness, etc., are ultimately great sources of self-derogation for the emerging adolescent and the adult, since masturbation is continued throughout life for most people. It may be only an occasional occurrence or a continuing pattern, but wherever it occurs, it revives the old feelings of weakness and immaturity.

How do we account for these pervasive guilt feelings associated with genital manipulation? On the surface, the answer appears obvious since it is an act which disobeys the parental and cultural requirements. Yet, this cannot be the whole answer, since it is clear that even in those situations in which the parents take no position whatsoever regarding genital manipulation or masturbation or it is entirely secret, guilt feelings develop. It remains an intriguing question as to why some children feel guilty and fear some form of punishment when there has never been any overt threat of punishment or statement of disapproval. It could be that this is a truly biological fear hereditarily transmitted. This is too Lamarckian and otherwise quite unlikely. An alternative explanation would be to recognize the role of isolation in producing guilt feelings in the human. Since genital manipulation and ultimately masturbation is practiced alone, the isolation and lack of participation (except in mutual play and masturbation) with other humans becomes a major source of guilt. In mutual masturbation we must deal with a different problem, that is, the guilt which arises out of the fear of possible homosexuality, which is also sharply condemned in most cultures. However, it is often most apparent that the strongest self-accusations and denunciations revolve about the effect of masturbation in permitting and encouraging separation from other humans and the avoidance of intimacy, both sexual and otherwise. In children, the same problem exists since beyond the age of five, solo play is avoided and companionship is always sought after, whether it be real or eidetic. Certain activities which are sneaked or done secretly, such as eating the cookie or candy, as well as genital manipulation, may be accompanied by guilt, not only because they are disobedient activities, but also because of the solo, secret nature of the activity.

The presence of sexual activity in the infant and child prior to the maturation of the gonads is highly questionable, when we define sexuality either in adult terms or in terms of the broad meaning of the word *libido*. If we can accept the libido theory formulation and agree with Freud that all physiological activity, such as eating, defecating, and so on, are ultimately involved with libidinal energy which controls their performance, then, of course, we can observe evidence of this libidinal energy throughout the earliest years. Under this formulation eating becomes an activity designed to nourish the organism but is maintained by virtue of the libidinal satisfaction of the oral zone, or more simply, we enjoy eating because of its sexual (libidinal) connections. This becomes a hedonistic physiology which links physiological functions with pleasure in order to explain their functions. On the other hand, if we view the infant and the child prior to gonadal maturity as an animal whose physiological functions are all equally necessary to his survival and motivated by the need to adapt to his environment, we would find few evidences of sexuality as such, prior to genital maturity. Certainly, we would see a great deal of genital exploration and play with some greater emphasis on the genital areas than other areas. We might also note special phobic attitudes towards the genital areas in some cultures. These activities play a crucial role in personality development as do all other activities of the early developing human in shaping its future, but there is a serious question as to whether this sexual interest is the major motivating force in this development. The attempt to distinguish libido from sexuality in the adult procreative sense has not been entirely successful since while the difference may be defined in practice, it is frequently confused. Although Freud cautioned against mistaking libido for adult sexuality, he spoke of the Oedipus situation as involving phantasies of sexual seduction and jealousy with the danger of castration, which is an adult conception of sex. The presence and acceptance of infantile sexuality as Freud elaborated it is not necessary for a science of personality.

SEX AND PLEASURE

One of the main supports for the notion of the predominance of the role of sex in human behavior rests on the teleological notion that the sexual act is accompanied by great pleasure which provides a strong impetus for its performance. Under normal circumstances, the sex act is associated with varying degrees of pleasure. However, this is also true of many other physiological activities such as eating, defecating, and urinating. The degree and quality of pleasure in the sex act, however, is distinctly different from the satisfaction in other physiological performances. Yet, it is a highly doubtful thesis that a physiological function is performed or even motivated solely by the expected pleasure involved. Although Freud's pleasure principle implies that human activities are directed to the goal of producing pleasure and avoiding pain, we must take notice that this applies only to those physiological functions in which we have a choice and not in the automatic functions which are entirely out of voluntary control.[7] It is clear, however, that some physiological functions are accompanied by pleasure and others are not, and that their performance is not dictated by the expected pleasure. We shall see that the most vital functions are those which are entirely automatic and not associated with any noticeable pleasure in their performance. These functions are continuous, imperatively essential, and beyond any conscious control. They can neither be delayed nor postponed for any length of time. They are part of the basic machinery for operating the organism and have no social, cultural or interpersonal relevance. They include the cardiac, respiratory, and the other intricate but essential biochemical activities that are occurring all the time. On a slightly higher (or should we say lower level) of physiological functioning we find those activities which are also essential to the survival of the individual but which can be delayed for varying periods of time. They are accompanied by some degree of pleasure and involve social and cultural factors in their performance. These functions include digestion and excretion and although their physiological function is biologically organized, the patterns for eating and defecating vary in accordance with certain cultural patterns. At a third level of physiological functioning we have the sex function, which although crucial for the survival of the species, is entirely dispensable for personal survival. This function begins comparatively late in life and is capable of being delayed and postponed for varying lengths of time and even permanently abandoned. Under these circumstances, masturbation or nocturnal emissions will occur to deal with the physiological tensions which accumulate. However, the sex function is also stimulated by the actual or phantasied presence of other human beings as well as being the result of totally intrapersonal and biochemical stimulation.

Thus, pleasure in human activity seems to be associated not with the most vital functions, but with those that are under some degree of control by the individual and involved in an interpersonal context. In addition, physiological performances vary in their pleasurable capacity to the extent that they have interpersonal relevance. This is implied in the theories of Horney and Sullivan, although not elaborated precisely in this fashion. The recent developments in psychoanalytic theory have raised considerable controversy regarding Freud's pleasure principle.

To explore the relationship of pleasure with sex we must first clarify our usage of the terms pleasure, satisfaction, and happiness. Pleasure, for Freud, was visualized as the absence of pain, and was thus a negative concept. This could be visualized as the satisfaction or relief of discomfort which accompanies the emptying of a distended organ. This feeling, however, is qualitatively different and distinguishable from the pleasure which accompanies the productive use of our skills, or the success in some interpersonal venture. Schachtel refers to it as the "joyful encounter with reality in which the child enjoys both its own motor activity and the encounter with the various stimuli of the environment." Such activities are not in response to a need or tension of a need, but are exploratory, relation seeking activities that include "the positive joyful expansion of relatedness to the new and rapidly changing environment."[8] We can also define pleasure as an agreeable feeling that is opposite to pain. Thus, pleasure can result from relief of tension in a negative sense, or as a positive fulfillment of activity which involves the expansive, creative use of man's potentialities.

Happiness, on the other hand, is a state of contentment and satisfaction with one's whole being and person. Happiness would, then, refer to those satisfactions which follow a productive use of our physiological and psychological functioning, while pleasure would be a more limited and specific kind of satisfaction. A physiological function in itself from this point of view has no intrinsic, pleasurable potentialities. The satisfaction which accompanies it depends on the presence of nerve endings which yield pleasure, or may be the result of activity which may produce a euphoric or pleasurable feeling. The act of thinking in itself has no pleasurable physiological accompaniments. For most of us, it is even somewhat uncomfortable or unpleasurable. This is particularly noticeable when we experience pleasure from the relief of tension, where the tension initiates the activity, such as in hunger or a full bladder. However, useful, creative or productive thinking may be a great source of pleasure and happiness. In many activities, such as sports, or contemplation, and particularly in sex, tension is not necessarily the instigator of the activity, but the impulse to utilize our physiological and psychological heritage to the utmost. Physiological hedonism, a concept that is not shared by many psychologists, presumes that the pursuit of pleasure is what motivates the physiological performance. This is an unnecessary etiological assumption that is never made in regard to cardiac action or eating or defecating, but is frequently suggested with regard to sex. It has been a favorite notion that sex is pleasurable in order to guarantee the perpetuation of the species. This assumption also need not be made if we agree that instinctual behavior guarantees the sex activity. In humans, this same notion should apply. If we have a sex instinct, then we do not need the added ingredient of pleasure to insure sexual activity.

What is the pleasure in the sex act and where does it come from? Is it the same in the male and the female? It is apparent that any interference with a physiological function is accompanied by much displeasure and discomfort that is immediately relieved by the performance of the physiological activity. This is particularly noticeable in the autonomic functions such as cardiac and respiratory action. Here, the pleasure is clearly due to the relief of tension. At the level of ingestion and elimination, the pleasure due to relief of tension is also apparent since there is the possibility of building up some tension through delay or deliberate withholding. However, pleasure due to relief of tension in sex is the least significant although it certainly occurs. Masturbation or nocturnal emission which occur as a result of increased vesicular tension produce only negligible amounts of pleasure in comparison with other kinds of sexual activity. In addition, delay or inactivity by design or accident, rather than enhancing the pleasure in sex, may frequently reduce it. After a certain point of sexual abstinence, even the passion or desire for sexual contact may diminish and may even be permanently abandoned. Thus, the tension aspect of the sex function is probably the least important element in the pleasure derived from the sex act.

Many physiological activities are accompanied by more pleasure than can be comprehended as simply relief of tension.[9] Eating, drinking, participation in sports, sexual activity, etc., are highly pleasurable and far in excess of the pleasure due to relief of pain. Although eating, with its infinite variety of palate provoking possibilities, remains a major source of enjoyment for humans, sexual activity is undoubtedly capable of producing the maximum amount of pleasure. However, this is achieved as the result of both physical and psychological intimacy and, consequently, there are enormous obstacles and difficulties in accomplishing this goal. The maximum of pleasure is reached by relatively few people and then only occasionally. Eating is less burdened by interpersonal threats and complications and so may be a more consistent source of pleasure for many people even though its potentialities are not as great as in sexual activity. Eating demands some detachment, so that even eating alone can be an enjoyable experience. This has great relevance to the problem of obesity.

Thus, even the pleasure of eating is enhanced and brightened by the presence of other people with whom we have tender attachments. Food tastes better and digests more easily when the atmosphere or the setting is congenial. "I write these precepts for immortal Greece/That round a table delicately spread/Of three or four may sit in choice repast,/Of five at most. Who otherwise shall dine/Are like a troop marauding for their prey."[10] This excerpt is from a fragment of a poem by Archestratus called "Gastronomy."

Sex, since it demands great intimacy, has integrative potentialities for the maximum degree of satisfaction in its performance. What then is the source of this added pleasure over and above the relief of tension? It must have something to do with the satisfaction of other than the physiological functions and must be related to those peculiarly human needs, such as relationship, intimacy, and participation, activities which are related exclusively to the cultural needs of the human beings. Sexual behavior, once it becomes established, is always completely dependent on another human being for its complete biological patterning.[11] Sex can have such great capacities for pleasure not only because of the relief of tension and the preponderance of nerve endings in the genital areas, but because it is an activity that involves man in his most intimate relationship with another human. This seems to be the relevant variable since the pleasure can vary even when the tension and nerve endings are constants.[12]

The description thus far can be summarized by a table showing the hierarchy of physiological functions in terms of interpersonal relevance with the varying possibilities of pleasure associated with it:

| Lowest pleasure associated with relief of tension but highest in possibilities of satisfaction | sex
ingestion
elimination |
| Highest pleasure associated with relief of tension but lowest in possibilities of satisfaction | cardiac action, etc.
(autonomic functions) |

Whatever needs are being satisfied in sex, whether it be an expression of the total functioning of a healthy organism (lust) or the expansive feelings which accompany such intimate fellowship, whether it is involved with the feeling of power or control over another human being or the ultimate victory in a chase with its accompanying status; or whether it be the expression of hatred and contempt for another human being, it is a vehicle for playing out the elements in human involvements and as such has capacities for pleasure over and above the biological substrate. In this sense, we might say that the biological procreative function of the sex function has no greater potentialities for pleasure (except for the profusion of nerve endings) than other physiological functions like walking, breathing or defecating. It implies that any physiological function becomes more highly desired as a source of satisfaction as its interpersonal necessity increases. Certainly, the pleasure of sex varies considerably in the same person where the urge is consistent and the nerve supply constant. Not only the other person and all our feelings with regard to her or him are highly important, but even the time and the place. Certain occasions (in addition to the time in the menstrual cycle) hold great promise for greater pleasure. Our capacities with some people are enormous, while inadequate with others. This becomes a real issue in the understanding of the deviations and distortions of sexual behavior. It is unnecessary to belabor this point since it is a most familiar notion with most people that the quality of the sexual pleasure varies with the circumstances around which it occurs as well as the persons involved.[13]

Pleasure in sex activity also appears to be related to the extent of sophistication, intellectualization and education with regard to sexual matters. These factors often lead to prolongation of the fore-play as well as the act of sex itself. This type of behavior which enhances the pleasure in sex is not necessarily biologically useful. If sexual activity were motivated solely for procreative purposes, a minimum of fore-play with early orgasm would be of greater value as it is among all animals. Kinsey, in his study of male sexual behavior, mistakenly considers this behavior more potent and masculine and finds it very common in the less educated segments of the population. Since sexual behavior is certainly motivated for reasons other than procreation, we find that the goal is to prolong the sex act in all its phases. In addition to the heightened pleasure due to prolongation of tension and anticipation, the extended intimacy and tenderness which occurs under these circumstances creates an understandable desire to prolong it as much as possible. While the goal is ultimately the orgasm, the preliminary endearments are maintained until it is physiologically impossible to restrain it. Early ejaculation may be resented by the woman and often viewed as evidence of lack of love.

The postulation of a pleasure-pain principle regarding human behavior involves a philosophy of physiological hedonism and is useful only to the extent that it helps us understand some of the grosser physiological functions. At higher levels of performance there are needs and values other than the pursuit of pleasure that motivate human behavior. The pleasure principle describes activity which is opposed to the reality principle in the sense that it disregards the cultural requirements. This is the behavior of the anxiety ridden individual who must fill his needs immediately without regard to consequences because of the overpowering discomforts of anxiety. It does not necessarily describe the behavior as neurotic, since some biological functions can or cannot be delayed according to the imperiousness of their physiological demands. The ability to postpone gratification was the cardinal principle distinguishing the pleasure principle from the reality principle. However, some functions can be delayed and others cannot. In some people all their needs, even those capable of being delayed must be immediately gratified. This we recognize as neurotic and it arises out of the need to assuage, distract or appease some anxiety in the individual. Sexual activity is one human performance which can be postponed or delayed and as such cannot be entirely comprehended under the rubric of the pleasure principle. It is the biological activity that is under the least pressure for fulfillment in the sense that it is not essential to the survival of the individual, even though it has such overwhelming force in activating the human being. It is most capable of being delayed until suitable conditions are available, and by far the greatest amount of sexual activity is in response to other than procreative demands. Thus, the pleasure principle as enunciated by Freud needs to be expanded beyond a biological basis and must include some principle of tenderness or other factors which initiate its performance. The capacity to postpone the act of sex in spite of all its pleasureable potentialities is more intimately related to education, fear of intimacy (other than sexual) and a variety of other mechanisms rather than to maturity. In contrast to the definition of maturity which is linked to sexual maturity (Freud) we would need to include factors of intimacy and tenderness as well as responsibility and intelligence. The techniques or skills involved in prolongation of the sex act or the achievement of mutual orgasms, or the like, would only be partial ingredients.[14]

Sexual Deviations

The description of the sexual variations and deviations occupies a special place in the field of psychiatry. They are classified and described in great detail and until very recently were considered to be separate and distinct mental aberrations. No other physiological activity has merited such extensive classification, and while this can be understood historically, it is no longer a constructive process.

Nosology, or the science of classification, plays a vital role in the early development of any science and is a necessary first step in the organization of information in that science. In the absence of data regarding causality, the earliest classifications are usually descriptive and reflect the prevailing philosophical and scientific attitudes toward the phenomenon studied. As information accumulates, it becomes necessary to re-examine and revise the original classification. There is often considerable resistance to altering a long established view, which is related to the general stickiness in clinging to known concepts and familiar classification schemes. This is often complicated by the overriding authority of the original genius who made the classification. Since nosological schemes not only reflect the state of a science but can foster or impede it, the necessity for periodic reappraisals based on solid advances in the field is clear. The history of science is replete with instances of outmoded theories and fallacious formulations which retarded the development of the science because of the supreme authority of the master. Although our understanding of the dynamics and history of mental disorders have outpaced our classifications, we still retain to a great extent a descriptive type of classification of mental disorders. This is particularly true in the classification of the sexual disorders. Magnus Hirschfield, and particularly Krafft-Ebbing, who catalogued and described the varieties of sexual behavior and labeled them perversions or deviations according to the prevailing views of science, sex and morality, were the pioneers of classification in this field. Their classifications, however, were largely encyclopedic descriptions containing no great understanding of the dynamics. At best, the causal explanations are almost entirely unacceptable today. The first real effort to catalogue the sexual disorders in motivational terms was made by Freud in his "Three Contributions to the Theory of Sex." In this paper, sexual activity was examined within the framework of his instinct theory and variations were described in terms of the aim, object and impetus of the sexual instinct. A sexual disorder could be understood either as a fixation of libidinal development, or some distortion of the developmental process. Although it was a great advance over the purely descriptive classifications, it rested on certain assumptions; namely, the concept of sexual behavior as an instinct and other related hypotheses, such as the libido theory and the theory of bisexuality. This classification, which had many advantages over previous ones, tended to view sexual distortions as disease entities and described every variation in sexual behavior under a separate category, which resulted in an extensive classification implying a separate etiology for each category.

Recent advances in our knowledge of sexual behavior and its deformations suggest alternative classifications. Some are inclined to eliminate them entirely and see them only as symptoms of character disorders and not as separate entities. There is much to be said in favor of this view of the sexual deviations, since the work of Horney, Sullivan, Rado, and some existential analysts, particularly Medard Boss, suggest that the variations in sexual behavior are not primarily derived from the disturbances in the sphere of sex, but are manifestations of anxiety and other problems arising elsewhere in the personality.[15] If we accept the biological basis of the instinct theory, than Freud's classification remains largely intact and useful in spite of the changes he and his students have made in the views on perversions and homosexuality. When sex patterning and sex behavior is largely dependent on cultural patterning and the problems of relatedness, then we find the familiar categories of voyeur, exhibitionist, sexual deviate, fetishist, and so on, purely descriptive of a piece of sexual behavior without any reference to the dynamics involved. Sandor Rado's views on the sexual distortions are related to the adaptive value of these alterations. He indicated that threats, fears and phobias regarding the genitals interfere with the standard coital pattern which produces reparative activities in order to adapt to the new situation. These reparative devices produce modifications of sex behavior which have previously been subsumed under the categories of sexual deviations or disorders. These modifications are in response to anxieties and he makes the important distinction between modifications which are situational and occur under circumstances in which opportunities are unavailable, and those which are variational and part of the exploratory interests of the healthy energetic human. The reparative patterns are those which produce alterations which, hertofore, have been called deviations. His views have the advantages of comprehending some of the dynamics involved in the deviation and, consequently, is operationally more useful than the older classifications.

Medard Boss, a Swiss existential analyst, has further broadened our understanding of the sexual deviations by emphasizing the subjective elements in the deviate's behavior, rather than focusing on the manifest aspects of his behavior. In this way, he explains perversions and deviations as the lack of development and maturity for all the possibilities of love and as produced by the neurotic incapacity to love in a total sense. It is not a problem of mechanical causes or incomplete fusion of instincts or deterioration or displacement of those instincts. He refutes Freud's views in general in terms of his partial conceptions of human existence, i.e., body impulses, love objects, psyche, mind, etc. Deviations involve man's incapacities to deal with love as a realistic issue in his living. Consequently, there is no need for special categories of sexual behavior, but merely an understanding of how a particular person, because of his failure to develop a capacity for loving relationships performs his sexual activity in unsatisfactory ways depending upon the nature of this incapacity.

In view of the aspects of interpersonal intimacy involved in sex, it becomes clear that the sexual deviations are largely involved in processes which are not related to biological defects or faults, but rather to interpersonal deficiencies. There are occasions when sex serves no procreative purpose, as in childless couples (through no design on their part), for whom sex can be the most intimate expression of their companionship and love. This is equally true in the extensive sexual activity which occurs with no biological goals in mind. In these instances it serves not only as an expression of intimacy, but can also be used in the service of the neurotic needs of both partners. In sex deviants of all sorts we find that they are almost always (except in the rare endocrine disorders) capable of functioning biologically and can impregnate and conceive. However, they avoid the sexual apparatus of the opposite sex for a variety of reasons, other than through instinctual or biological deformation.

The deviate always has problems in his interpersonal functioning, such as intimacy, closeness, the capacity to love and trust, and so on. Although they prefer methods other than genital intercourse, rarely is such contact permanently interfered with. Their procreative funtions are intact even though their preference reduces the possibility. It is very common to find deviates of all kinds being married and having children. Their deviations are frequently expressions of other than sexual needs. No two deviates are ever precisely alike either in their personality make-up or method of expressing the deviation. The deviation is specific to their own personality make-up even though it can be categorized under broad headings.

If sex occupies no special role in the development of personality as so many current theorists suggest, why the great concern with the manifest varieties of its expression? The Kinsey report was notable in discovering the amazing capacities for variations which are possible in the sex act. Do we describe or identify the varieties of ways that people eat, defecate or sleep? Do we dignify them by special classifications or describe them under special syndromes unless they have some relevance to a particular disease entity? But sexual activity is different and does occupy a special role in our culture. For this reason sex is singled out for special notice. But we must not allow cultural prejudices and enthusiasms to color our scientific appraisal of the phenomena. Our notions of sexual deviations need to be refined in view of the current developments in psychoanalysis. Mere collections or descriptions of the variations of sexual performance have only a limited value in any science of sexology. The variations and deviations are related not only to constitutional differences but to the character structure of the individuals involved. Sexual deviations should ultimately be integrated into our classification of character disorders. This may minimize the medico-legal problems and be an impetus for improved therapeutic techniques in their treatment. They will then be considered symptoms and not syndromes, and a more rational approach to their treatment may be forthcoming.

Premature Ejaculation

The question of the biological basis for sexual deviations versus the cultural view can be examined more clearly by studying in some detail a rather common sexual difficulty. Premature ejaculation is a condition which highlights the elements of participation in the sex act and thus illuminates the role culture plays in sexual activity.

Except for rare instances, there must be a maximum of participation for the sex act to proceed to climax, and each participant must perform the role dictated by his sexual organs. Consequently, both male and female are indispensable, and neither has any special or preferred status in the performance. In humans, however, the responsibility for pleasure and orgasm in the female has been assigned to the male. This appears to be the case only in recent years, particularly in Western cultures. It is this responsibility which creates the necessity for a category of deviation called premature ejaculation which would not exist if the duration of intercourse were not an issue in producing orgasm in the female.

Premature ejaculation is the sexual deviation that has no counterpart in the female. Although frigidity is often considered to be the female counterpart of premature ejaculation, operationally impotence is the masculine counterpart. Frigidity involves the inability to achieve a sexual climax, while premature ejaculation involves the exaggerated ability to do so. Premature orgasm in the female is the counterpart of premature ejaculation in the male, while impotence in the male is related to frigidity in the female. Early orgasm in the female is never considered premature, since whenever it occurs it does not necessarily terminate intercourse. It is not equivalent to premature ejaculation, either in its dynamics or ultimate effects. Unlike premature ejaculation, it is often highly valued by the female and is flattering to the male. It is regarded as a desirable feminine trait as opposed to premature ejaculation, which is considered to be evidence of inadequate masculinity.

What characterizes premature ejaculation? Is it the rapidity of ejaculation or too early ejaculation in particular instances with particular people? When is it premature ejaculation as opposed to delayed orgasm in the female? The prevailing definitions are not helpful in this regard since they vary from ejaculation prior to penetration to any ejaculation which precedes orgasm in the female, whatever the duration of intercourse. This involves determining the usual, or normal duration of intercourse, and then calling premature ejaculation that which occurs prior to the minimum time. Such a definition, which depends upon orgasm in the female, becomes meaningless, since it attempts to define a situation in terms of one factor when there are many other relevant factors involved. Thus, it could be premature ejaculation without orgasm in the female, and not be premature ejaculation after a few strokes if orgasm did occur in the female. The syndrome depends not only upon one's concept of the function of the male in providing orgasm for the female, but also upon the question of usual duration of intercourse. At what point in time does the problem of orgasm become the responsibility of the female?

If we limit the concept of premature ejaculation to ejaculation prior to entrance, we have a clearly defined syndrome of considerable significance. When it invariably occurs, we have a biological impediment, and intercourse is permanently interfered with. It is equivalent to a masturbatory experience and eliminates any possibility of sexual satisfaction for the female except in deviant ways. However, its invariable and inevitable occurrence is a rarity, although it must occur at some time in the life of every male. We are interested here in the type of premature ejaculation which is an extremely common occurrence and is present in the normal as well as in the neurotic and psychotic. In these instances, ejaculation occurs prior to orgasm in the female, and it comes to the attention of the psychiatrist either because the male feels inadequate and concerned about not satisfying his wife sexually, or the wife presses the husband to investigate his inability to be a more competent male. In either case the pressure comes from the female and is not related to the duration of intercourse as much as to whether or not she achieves orgasm. If the female achieves an orgasm after one or two strokes, with ejaculation in the male, it may never be regarded as pathological. An operational definition of premature ejaculation is required to clarify these confusions. It might refer to ejaculation occurring immediately upon penetration or after a few strokes, offering no possibility of producing orgasm in the female. It is assumed that some contact and friction is ordinarily required for orgasm to occur in the female. This definition avoids rigid time boundaries or an evaluation of the normal duration of intercourse. It is flexible enough to include those situations where ejaculation occurs so quickly after penetration that no reasonable amount of contact and stimulation occurs to the female. It is not defined in terms of a number of strokes, but by the interpretation of the partners and their attitudes towards each other's performance. Ejaculation prior to insertion is certainly premature and is an extreme form of this syndrome.

The question of prematurity in the male requires a clarification of what constitutes the orgasm in the female. This whole question is shrouded in mystery and was solved by simply asking a woman if she had one. If she said yes, then it was established that she did. This was the entire basis for our information and knowledge about orgasm in spite of Freud's distinction between the vaginal and clitoral orgasm. This method would be entirely feasible if we could assume that a woman always knew when she had an orgasm as the man does.[16] However, as our experience has repeatedly shown, the woman is often entirely unaware as to what constitutes an orgasm. Often, orgasm in the female seems to consist of a gradual heightening of tension in the perineal area accompanied by an increasing tumescence and sensitivity of the clitoris which is relieved by a sudden orgastic experience accompanied by a gradual detumescence and relaxation of the muscle tones in the perineum and elsewhere. This can be identified by most women and reported as orgasm. This does not relieve us of the problem of objectively identifying the orgasm by some manifest signs. Some clinicians claim that there is a discharge analagous to the ejaculation of semen, but this finding is not generally accepted as a positive indication of orgasm. At present we can only count on subjective impressions, but some guide lines must be drawn in order to arrive at some useful formulations. We must avoid those frequent situations where an orgasm is not acknowledged because the woman expects some rapturous experiences that are impossible to achieve or the other extreme where orgasm is claimed whenever some pleasureable feeling is felt in the perineal area.

What makes an ejaculation premature? Is it premature for the male, or for the female? The name implies that it is premature for the female, since it provides orgasm for the male. It is premature for the female, since it terminates intercourse and prevents orgasm in the female. The presumption is made that the male orgasm should be timed to fit the female, and that simultaneous orgasm is considered to be the most desirable and mutual type of intercourse. Its possibility is considered to be a function of the male. It has been noted by many writers that orgasm in the female is more slowly attained than in the male. Although it is frequently possible for the ejaculation to coincide with the orgasm in the female, it is not necessarily a function of the male's potency or capacity. The simultaneity of orgasm is not the exclusive responsibility of the male. It is the result of a variety of accidental, constitutional factors, and mutually satisfactory responses in both partners. Although it is a highly desirable outcome, it is largely dependent upon the partners' capacity to lengthen and shorten the sex act.

When did premature ejaculation become an issue in male and female psychology? Is it possible that this syndrome did not exist prior to the emancipation and enlightenment of the female? It is only when society becomes polarized towards the female and the possibilities of insisting upon satisfaction from sexual activity that the symptom becomes prominent on the scene of human behavior. Although orgasm may have been lacking in the female, it did not become an issue for the male until her pressure, insistence, and complaints made it so. It may even have been a source of distress for the female, but until it became an area for discussion, it was not brought to the attention of the male, and, consequently, it did not come to the physician. Kraft-Ebbing, in his classic work, *Psychopathia Sexualis*,[17] does not even speak of premature ejaculation, but describes a syndrome of "abnormally easy ejaculation." This syndrome has no implication of prematurity, since it is described in terms of the male only. According to Kraft-Ebbing, abnormally easy ejaculation is due to "excessive psychical excitement or irritable weakness of the ejaculation center." Forel, in his book, *The Sexual Question*,[18] does not even mention this problem. I have had great difficulty in finding any article on this subject prior to 1900, and Dr. Ernest Jones, in a personal communcation, says that: "My impression is that hardly anything was written on that subject."

When sex became a subject available for discussion to male and female, it encouraged women to make some demands in terms of their sexual needs. This varied with the social and intellectual level of the female, and this situation prevails today with regard to the problem of premature ejaculation. Thus, dependng upon the social, intellectual, and cultural role of the female, the issue of the duration of intercourse becomes more or less pronounced. It is only in those segments of the population where the female can and does express her rights that the symptom arises and requires therapeutic intervention. This was indicated in Kinsey's study on timing in intercourse. He noted that early orgasm in some segments of the population, particularly laborers, was not considered to be premature by either male or female.

The coincidence of the orgasm is not the responsibility of the male alone, but the result of an accumulation of mutually satisfactory responses in both partners. The attitude of the partners have towards each other plays a vital role, and the duration of intercourse depends upon many factors, among which is the potency of the male. The capacity for prolongation of intercourse has to do with physical vigor, drugs (especially alcohol), the interval since the last intercourse, the novelty of the occasion, etc. It is possible for many men to prolong the sex act and thus to frequently produce orgasm in the female. This involves the capacity of the individual to put off immediate satisfaction in terms of future reward, which is involved in producing the greater satisfaction in one's partner. Potency seems to be of minor relevance in this regard, since it involves the total problem of maturity, the consideration of the needs of another person, and the willingness to accommodate and satisfy these needs. This may require education, training, and the ability to limit one's own needs. The discrepancy between sexual behavior in animal and man is highlighted in this regard, since in the animal kingdom the fast and energetic performance is usually more highly regarded biologically. However, in sexual terms in the human it is often the slow and less intense individual who may also be the less amorous and potent individual, who is rewarded.

It is surprising that one does not associate ease of erection or intensity of lustful excitement with consequent rapid ejaculation to either high potency in the male or extreme desirability of the female. It is easily conceivable that the attractive, sensuous, exciting female quickly arouses one's lustful feelings with intensity of desire and performance, and, consequently, early ejaculation. What might be flattering to the female in every regard prior to actual intercourse, becomes evidence of selfish disinterest as soon as intercourse occurs. The male is asked to be excited, amorous, and enthusiastic until he gets to bed and then suddenly to take it easy, control his activity so as to prolong the sex act. Kinsey says in this connection: "It would be difficult to find another situation in which an individual is quick and intent in his responses and who is labeled anything but superior; but in most instances it is exactly what the rapidly ejaculating male probably is, however inconvenient and unfortunate his qualifications may be from the standpoint of his wife in the relationship." The capacity to lengthen or shorten the sex act in the male does depend upon the individual and can reflect both conscious and unconscious attitudes towards the partner. In many cases, it is neither an index of potency, nor a measure of interpersonal relationships of the partners. As a matter of fact, excessive prolongation of intercourse or ejaculatio tarda may be symptomatic of the homosexual or the male with a minimum of interest in the female.

Premature ejaculation is an extremely common symptom and seems to be intimately related to the obsessive-compulsive dynamism, and to subserve the operation of power.

The symptom occurs only in relation to a specific person and in specific situations. Unlike other mental phenomena, it cannot occur in the absence of the sexual object. This is the reason why premature ejaculators masturbate without ejaculating prematurely. It occurs only with real people as opposed to phantasied partners. It probably occurs on some occasions in all people, since it is essentially a response to anxiety. Although premature ejaculation can occur in fatigue states, hyperactive drug states, prolonged abstention or excessive excitement, etc., it is primarily an anxiety-provoked phenomenon which occurs in relation to a conflict situation in which the individual is involved. The symptom results from this conflict, but does not solve it. It produces, instead, further anxiety, since the sexual performance does not improve while the conflict continues. The brief case history which follows will illustrate some of the points discussed above.

Patient A had an active and successful sex life during the first year of his marriage. During the second year some difficulties arose, and although the relationship appeared to be working out, he began to notice that he was ejaculating prematurely. The ejaculation would occur after a few strokes and under very special circumstances. It occured only when intercourse was stimulated and precipitated by his wife, who was an aggressive, domineering individual. During the first year of marriage the patient was active and energetic in his marital affairs. As he slowly relinquished this role to his wife, quarrels became more frequent, and the patient always felt subdued by his wife. Premature ejaculation invariably occurred when he was angry with her. In this way he punished her, and indicated his indispensable role in the marriage. Although there was some guilt about his supposed inadequacy, there was at the same time a secret satisfaction and a lack of real impetus to eliminate the difficulty. He did not recognize any problem, and it was his wife who had pushed him into treatment. The symptom was a relatively minor problem in a severe obsessional character structure. The occasions for premature ejaculation became less frequent as the tug of war and power struggles lessened in the patient's living.

What transpires in the man who suffers the discomforts of premature ejaculation? The situation is approximately the following: from the outset of his sex life or during the course of it, he has the distressing experience of either ejaculating before penetration or after a few strokes. He is left anxious and ashamed and behaves as though he were a disgraced male. Consequently, at the next attempt, he is very anxious lest he again ejaculate prematurely. He senses the woman's anxiety and concern, and in his earnest desire to perform well, tends to exaggerate the effect he is producing on the female. At this point, he becomes caught in the sociological and cultural attitudes towards the male, such as the equation of prolonged intercourse with potency, and conceives of his partner in the sex act as being dissatisfied, distraught, tense, and angry. He must eliminate the prematurity, and in this tense atmosphere, it either gets worse, or continues unabated. With increasing concern and anxiety, it becomes less and less possible to overcome it. After a short while, his partner complains, threatens, and possibly denies him any contact. He is miserable, and thinks of himself as a failure, unmanly, impotent, weak. What goes on covertly is quite different. As the wife becomes more angry, she also begins to recognize the importance of her husband in his potential capacity to afford her some gratification. He has become more essential to her existence and through his inadequate performance, has managed to control her pleasure and effect her living. She becomes more tender, concerned, and interested, and the husband temporarily feels victorious; his anxiety diminishes, and premature ejaculation may disappear. If it continues, his partner may become more vitally concerned, and encourage him to see a psychiatrist. If it is only temporary, we may see recurring episodes, for as his orgasm improves, his partner demonstrates less interest and concern and tolerance for him. Premature ejaculation returns and the cycle begins over again. This is perhaps an oversimplified version of the involved and complicated interchange that occurs, but it does demonstrate some aspects of the power struggle involved in this symptom. The problem is often initiated in marriages where the partners are prudish, uninformed, and uncommunicative in sexual matters. They may have secret expectations with regard to their sexual activity and hesitate to voice their disappointments. Although they appear resigned to unsatisfactory sexual relationships, they covertly resent and demand more from it. This often produces premature ejaculation in the male and increases the tension in the relationship. In these instances, the problem, which may originally have been due somewhat to ignorance or prudery, now becomes a matter of demand, control, and manipulation of the partners.

In this symptom we can notice most clearly the element of power as utilized by the sexual function. The very presence of the symptom serves to put the male in the role of the generous, giving person who, in his generosity may or may not give pleasure to the female. The variations and fluctuations in the appearance of the symptom coincides most clearly with this element in the relationship between man and woman. It provides a most sensitive weapon for vindictively punishing or graciously satisfying the woman. The patient's problems may involve fear of feminine aggressiveness, unconscious jealously, injured feelings, expressions of contempt, fear of women's genitals, concern over conception, etc., but operationally it is used as an instrument of power and manipulation in interpersonal relations.

This helps us understand those instances where premature ejaculation may occur with one's wife but not with other women or with prostitutes. The power struggle which may be producing it in the wife is absent with the prostitute or the other woman. There is no dependent relationship with the prostitute, and one's ability to dominate, control, and manipulate the situation is amply satisfied. The seduction and winning of the girl other than one's wife often satisfies the power element and since there are few ties and tensions and the struggles are minimal, prolonged intercourse can occur. Although the individual may have many obvious problems with regard to women, the prostitute or paramour does not stir them up, and so there is no premature ejaculation, although other sexual deviations may be present, reflecting these other problems.

This symptom is often seen in homosexuals who are capable of some heterosexual contact. In these cases one can clearly see the role power, control, and manipulation play in the symptom. It does not represent the feminine component in the personality—quite the contrary. It represents the attempts at more masculine expression of the aggressive need. The homosexual who is capable of heterosexual contact frequently suffers from ejaculatio tarda. It has been noted also that in heterosexual marriages, the homosexual partner has had premature ejaculation, which serves the purpose of shortening the contact, disappointing his wife, and "showing her who's boss!"

Premature ejaculation is probably present much of the time in the obsessional dynamism, where there are elements of obscure power operations directed at maintenance of control over everything that happens.

Premature ejaculation is an even more powerful element in interpersonal relationships than impotence, since impotence offers no possibilities of satisfaction, and there can be no expectations from or disappointment in the male. One knows what to expect from the impotent male. In this sense, impotency services a different function in interpersonal relationships, namely, a resigned indifference to the demands of the female.

Many questions still remain to be solved in this problem. For example, is the significance of premature ejaculation different when it occurs in the neurotic, psychotic, or so-called "normal" individual? Is it different when it occurs only transiently than when it is a persistent accompaniment of the sex act? How do we understand its variations with the same woman on different occasions, and with repeated performances on the same night? Why does it occur with some women and not with others? Why do we see it in "potent" males, and find it absent in homosexuals? Is it always abnormal? Why does it not occur during masturbation in individuals who always ejaculate prematurely during intercourse? Most of these questions can be answered when we view the symptoms as an outgrowth of interpersonal struggles. From this framework, it becomes a technique in interpersonal transactions and a weapon of power. It appears to be present only in an interpersonal context where the participants are engaged in some form of struggle, whether for status, prestige, or dominance. It is used as an active instrument to push, force, and coerce, although the users often appear to be passive individuals. When we examine an aspect of sexual behavior in this symptom, we note that it has more relevance to the extra-procreative function of the sex act and is intimately involved in the dynamic process of dealing with anxiety in interpersonal relationships. It is a result of anxiety, and not a cause of it. The symptom then becomes an operational maneuver in an interpersonal context, unconsciously serving the needs of the ego to establish or reaffirm some self-esteem. As such, it represents what we would commonly call an "aggressive" or maculine trait, and is an active operation in the service of the maintenance of personality integration. The symptom provides us with an opportunity to re-examine other sexual deviations from this frame of reference. It may then be possible to see the dynamic, operational function of the deviations, and in understanding the interpersonal relevance, to provide therapeutic tools for their control.

Summary

Biological sexual activity has interested the natural scientist for a long time. The extra-procreative aspects of the sex function, however, has been shrouded in secrecy until Freud emphasized its roles in personality development and its relationship to love, tenderness, and maturity. In a monograph published in 1938 called, "Modern Sexual Morality and Modern Nervousness," Freud said: "Broad vistas open up for us when we bear in mind the fact that man's sexual instinct is not at all primarily meant to serve purposes of reproduction but is intended to furnish certain forms of gratification." Freud pursued the biological impact of sex on personality. Recent personality theorists have stressed the psychological aspects of the sex function, emphasizing its significance in all matters of human exchange and relationship, and recognizing its capacity to fill the purely human needs of the human animal, namely, companionship, love, and the avoidance of loneliness. Consequently, cultural factors play a major role in the issues of courting, mating, and the determination of normality and abnormality in sex behavior. These cultural factors become involved in the sexual function in the same way that cooking and the use of utensils have altered the physiological function of ingestion. They do not alter the essential mechanics of the function, although they may dress it up in various ways. This dressing, however, plays a crucial role in man's psychology.

Although large numbers of animals, particularly mammals, maintain close relationships in family units, the arrangement is designed, as far as we know, for biological convenience rather than on the basis of tender regard for one another. In addition, the close, at times monogamous relationships in the animal kingdom are entirely instinctive in origin and designed for procreative purposes. In the human, however, the close association of the sexes, and the consequent family units serves purposes far beyond procreation, so that at times homosexual or heterosexual unions occur without any goal of procreation. Man's needs are served in these relationships— avoidance of loneliness, companionships and mutual tender exchange. These are instances in which sexual intimacy serves other than biological purposes. In those instances where procreation is also the goal it is often very difficult to determine whether in a specific relationship procreation or the alleviation of anxiety and loneliness or the need to prove one's power or manliness is the major objective. Because so much of the human drama is enacted in our sexual performances, they often present the most illuminating facets about an individual's personality.

The relation of sexuality to love and tenderness is a problem of great concern to the neo-Freudian theorists. For Freud, the matter was relatively simple in his notion that love was mature sexuality and all forms of creative enterprise were sublimations of the sex instinct. It is becoming clearer through the work of Horney, Fromm, Sullivan, Suttie, and the existentialist analysts, that sexual maturity is only indirectly related to love, and that creativity is a much more complicated process than mere sublimation. Biological sexual maturity is a purely physiological development which occurs in all animal species unless there is some hormonal impediment. Love, however, as far as we know, is a "human" development, based on many achievements in addition to sexuality. The capacity to enjoy sex to the fullest is proportional to the amount of intimate, tender regard one has for one's partner. Maturity in a biological sense is not synonymous with competence or the capacity to utilize matured functions. Competence and the potentialities for pleasure, particularly in sex activity, is dependent upon one's capacity to love and be loved by another person. This is the reverse of Freud's formula that sexual maturity is love. Loving relationships permit the maxi-

mum security from anxiety, loneliness, and the maximum performance of sex with its attendant pleasures.

Creativity was always a dilemma for Freud. He once said that
psychonalysis can do nothing towards elucidating the nature of the
artistic gift, nor can it explain the means by which the artist works.
This was certainly true as long as we viewed it merely as a
sublimation of the sexual instinct. Creative activity arises out of
the fullness and expansiveness of Man's potentialities and is dependent upon many factors, in addition to the psychological ones.
The concept of sublimation was meaningful in explaining the
development of the plastic arts, but fell far short when it attempted
to explain Man's interest in philosophy, religion, and other ethical
systems.

Creativity is a unique, human achievement, expressing all of
man's capacities, ideals and goals. It arises out of the fullness of
his physiological and psychological potentialities. The act of creation, however small or great, must involve some mature investment
and tender regard for some human being, however anti-human
the production may be. It presupposes a minimum of human contact and intercourse, and implies either a tender relationship or a
craving for one. It seems to have no direct relationship or only an
indirect relationship to Man's sexual activities or development.
Attempts to correlate creativity with sexual difficulties as Freud did
with da Vinci, are exercises in the literary application of psychoanalytic theory. One could endlessly document instances of the
creative process in individuals who had numerous sexual problems
as well as those whose productivity was enhanced by an active,
healthy sex life. However, it is doubtful if any instances of creativity
could be found in circumstances which did not express a need to
communicate or participate with another human being in the fellowship of living. Creativity may frequently be a substitute for real
living, but it involves more than mere sexual fulfillment. Creative
experiences can serve purposes such as overcoming man's emptiness
and despair by means of the exhilaration induced by the manifold
pleasures implicit in creative activities.

NOTES

1. Bonaparte, M., Freud, A., and Kris, E., eds.: Origin of Psycho-Analysis.
New York, Basic Books, 1954; Letter to Fleiss, 3/10/97, p. 227.
The description of Freud's personal life in his biography by Ernest Jones and

the reminiscences of Hans Sachs and others bear out this impression of Freud as a somewhat shy and modest individual who rarely displayed any tender feelings publicly. Erich Fromm, in his book, *Sigmund Freud's Mission* (see Bibliography), states that only a man whose sexual life was beyond criticism and completely without blemish could undertake the scrutiny of the sexual functions in man. Yet, in many respects, his investigations of sex were mechanical and impersonal in the same way that he referred to relationships between people as object relationships.

2. Erich Fromm: *Sigmund Freud's Mission*, p. 31-33. This interesting volume attempts the difficult task of relating Freud's theory to his own personality. It is illuminating in many regards, but it also suffers from the psychoanalytic fallacy of reducing all ideas and attitudes to early developmental issues without sufficient recognition of the variety of influences which are brought to bear on the development of ideas.

3. It is conceivable that this situation may be strikingly altered with the widespread usage of artificial insemination. At that time, the foregoing thesis may need to be radically altered, except that sexual activity will still be most enjoyable when another individual, particularly someone of the opposite sex, is involved. Consequently, even when procreation is fulfilled by artificial insemination, sex may still play a paramount role in fulfilling the multiple needs of man. When the practice of artificial insemination becomes widespread, however, child rearing practices and family life will be severely altered and a dehumanizing process will be an inevitable result. One by-product of this development may be to elevate the ingestatory function to the role previously enjoyed by the sexual function.

4. The undisciplined use of symbolism for the sexual organs as well as sexual activities has led one critic to remark that the penis will soon be called a sex symbol. By implication, inference, and analogy all forms of behavior, particularly in infancy, can be called sexual. This is most regrettable when extrapolations from adult behavior, as in fellatio, are analogized to thumb-sucking and thus considered sexual. When cigar smokers are considered to be practicing a sublimated form of fellatio we must recognize that such verbal games have serious consequences, both in our understanding of the phenomena in question and in alienating our more precise scientific colleagues. It is necessary to distinguish between symbols that result from our theoretical prejudices, such as that all pointed, lengthened objects represent the penis, and symbols which are the direct outgrowths of an individual's experiencing.

5. H. S. Sullivan observed that genital touching in all ages is related to the easy availability and access of the genital area. He pointed out that the arms, when placed in a state of rest, either in a standing or lying position, will fall on the genital area.

6. Thus, genital, particularly in the male, should refer to the penis, which serves a multiple function before and after puberty. It also serves to deliver urine as well as seminal contents. Sexual should refer only to the function complex which includes penis, seminal vesicles, gonads, and endocrine system which functions over all. Penis play would not automatically be called sex play, particularly when the individual may only be freeing the penis from tight trousers, etc.

7. It should also be noted that the pleasure principle probably applies only under extremely limited circumstances, such as in the foetus, or in very early infancy, or during sleep. Schachtel, in *Metamorphosis* (see Bibliography), makes the point very clear when he demonstrates that Freud's pleasure principle probably applies only where there is an embededness relationship as opposed to an activity relationship. See also T. Szasz: *Pain and Pleasure* (see Bibliography).

8. Schachtel, E. *Metamorphosis,* p. 64.

9. With regard to other sensory pleasures in seeing, smelling, touching, and tasting, we could also develop the thesis that a part of the satisfaction arises from other than physiological sources. A significant part of the sensory pleasure in seeing and smelling is associated with the recall or associative reference to odors or sights that have previously been pleasurable due to some significant event or person. Who cannot recall the pleasure in tasting a dish which reminds us of home and mother? This is particularly apt in the olfactory area where certain smells may revive whole congeries of pleasurable feeling. Unpleasant sensations can be accounted for in a similar fashion. It is apparent that most sensory experiences that have a pleasurable connotation are heightened by associative factors generally relating to previous experiences or to persons in connection with such experiences. The sex act may, at times, be initiated and enhanced by olfactory, visual, auditory, and other sensory experiences.

10. M. F. K. Fisher, in her delightful book on the art of eating, says: "Too few of us perhaps feel that the breaking of bread, the sharing of salt, the common dipping into one bowl, mean more than the satisfaction of a need. We make sure such primal things as casual as tunes heard over a radio, forgetting the mystery and strength in both." Art of Eating, New York, World Publishing Co., 1937, p. 42.

11. Whenever I speak of the total dependency of sex, I am not unaware of the onanistic and other perverse ways of achieving some sexual satisfaction alone. However, such activities will never produce offspring and so cannot be considered as a complete, biological pattern. I am referring only to the physiological function of sex, which is reproduction.

12. Alan Watts suggests that maximum sexual pleasure is related to the on-going relationship involved, and not in the relief of tension. A. N. Watts: Nature, Man and Woman. New York, Panther Press, 1958.

13. Joseph Nuttin, in his book: Psychoanalysis and Personality, New York, Sheed and Ward, 1953, points out that the pleasure in sex may be involved with the fulfillment of interpersonal needs over and above the physiological rewards. He says: "It is however necessary to examine one special form of this need for contact on the psycho-physiological level of human existence, the need for sexual contact. Besides the physiologcial conditions and function which when experienced psychically impel the organism to seek food, air, other biological conditions drive it to make specific kinds of total contact with the actual bodies of its fellow creatures. The biological organism is not only a "mouth" open to certain elements in the biological sphere. It is also an appeal for total contact with certain bodily forms in the social sphere (i.e., one's fellow creatures). Here too special physiological chemical and physical factors condition the sexual need: nevertheless as psychically experienced and as manifested in

behavior, the sexual need is one aspect of the need to enter into contact with others. It is this need which spontaneously impels the individual to physical intimacy and to total contacts with others which are as varied as are the chemical exchanges in the biological sphere."

Paul Tillich, in his book: Love, Power and Justice, New York, Oxford University Press, 1954, says that: "Man strives to reunite himself with that to which he belongs and from which he is separated. And this is true not only of Man, but of all living beings. They desire food, movement, growth, participation, in a group, sexual union, etc. The fulfillment of these desires is accompanied by pleasure. But it is not the pleasure as such which is desired, but the union with that which fulfills the desire. Certainly fulfilled desire is pleasure and unfulfilled desire is pain. But it is a distortion of the actual processes of life if one derives from these facts the pain-pleasure principle in the sense that life essentially consists of fleeing from pain and striving for pleasure. Whenever this happens life is corrupted. Only a perverted life follows the pain-pleasure principle. Unperverted life strives for that which it is, it strives for the union with that which is separated from it, though it belongs to it. This analysis should remove the prejudice toward libido, and it can give criteria for the partial acceptance, partial rejection of Freud's libido theory. In so far as Freud describes libido as the desire of the individual to get rid of his tensions, he has described the perverted form of libido. And he has acknowledged this implicitly (though not intentionally) by deriving the death instinct from the infinite never fulfilled libido. Freud describes Man's libido in its perverted self-estranged stage. But his description in which he joins many Puritans (old and new ones who would be embarrassed by this alliance) misses the meaning of libido as the normal drive towards vital self-fulfillment."

14. E. Schachtel, in his book *Metamorphosis* (see Bibliography), deals with the deficiencies of Freud's pleasure principle in a most comprehensive fashion. In developing his thesis regarding the difference between the embeddedness affects which consists of diffuse discharges of tension versus the activity affects which are directed, sustained and activity sustaining tension, he has clearly distinguished between pleasure as a relief of tension and pleasure which is the effect of the positive, active utilization of man's skills and potentialities which may sustain tension and avoid relief of tension. Such pleasure is often far more desirable than the pleasure from relief of tension. This thesis, which is well-documented philosophically as well as clinically, clearly defines the validity of the pleasure principle as applying only to the embeddedness affects and therefore refers to humans for a very limited period of their existence. It seems to apply to infants for a few weeks of their life, to sleep and possibly old age during early convalescence from severe illnesses. For most human activity otherwise is involved in stimulation and activity where there is a desire and enjoyment of activity rather than a wish to eliminate it.

He gives some excellent examples distinguishing the pleasure in eating when one is in a state of deprivation and distinguishes this from the eating of the gourmet. He points out that: "In extreme hunger or thirst the specific quality of the food does not matter, it is hardly noticed; the hungry person eats so hastily . . . he does not notice or pay attention to the taste unless it is unpleasant. The discriminating enjoyment of food is the specifically human quality in eating and drinking while Man has in common with animals the negative pleasure of the relief from hunger. The gourmet wants to keep the mild tension of his appetite, stay with the taste of the food, the activity of eating becomes his goal rather than the state of satiation, the return to quiescence" (p. 64). With regard to sexual pleasure, his view emphasizes what I have suggesed. He says: "The analysis of sexual pleasure is particularly difficult because in Man it is practically always inseparably tied up with other emotions, such as, love, power, return to child-like embededness, anger, search for approval or recognition, destructive sadistic impulses, etc. These emotions play a large role in determining whether sexual pleasure has more the character of relief from tension (embededness affect) or of the positive pleasure in the process of relatedness. In Freud's thinking, sexual pleasure originally consisted entirely in the satisfaction due to the sudden decrease of tension. He explained the pleasurable character of sexual excitement, doubtless a state of increased tension, by minimizing it as a mere fore-pleasure and contrasting it with the orgastic end pleasure which he saw entirely as discharge gratification. Later he began to doubt this position, but his doubt did not lead him to a reformulation of his theory of sexual pleasure. If discharge of tension were the only source of sexual pleasure it would neither be understandable why the sexual pleasure in intercourse is preferred by most people to pleasure in masturbation, nor why variations of the sexual act are a source of pleasure. Both the range in the subtle varieties of sexual behavior and the openness towards and temporary staying with the caresses and contacts preceding orgasm are the typically human elements which distinguish Man's sexual pleasure from the sexual satisfaction of animals. Their significance parallels what has been said about the specifically human aspects of the positive enjoyment of food. Not the mere discharge of tension, but the enjoyment of the ongoing process of encounter is the decisive factor. In sexual pleasure this factor is heightened if there is genuine mutuality in which the giving of pleasure is enjoyed together with the receptivitiy towards pleasure" (pp. 67-68).

15. See Bibliography for titles of the works dealing with sexual disorders.

16. In certain pathological states the male may also be unaware of an orgasm and the ejaculation does not follow spasmodic contractions in the urethral musculature.

17. R. von Krafft-Ebing: Psychopathia Sexualis. New York, F. A. Davis Co., 1901. This was an encyclopaedic collection of sexual perversions with vivid descriptions of the symptomatology and an elaborate classification. However, very little information was supplied as to cause or treatment.

18. A. Forel: The Sexual Question. New York, Physicians and Surgeons Book Co., 1922. This was an extremely popular book for young people in the early 1900's. It was the source of sex education for most enlightened individuals and the absence of any reference to premature ejaculation is significant. This might imply its rarity in the population or else that it was a subject still barred from public discussion.

VIII

Female Psychology

OUR KNOWLEDGE of the psychology of the female has been limited and hampered by the male-centered orientation towards all psychological phenomena. It is only in comparatively recent years that the female has been considered an object worthy of scientific concern. Freud not only described female development in terms of the male but implied that the female was a "second-rate male." Freud's postulates about female psychology were often so extreme and antifeminist that his views on this subject betrayed his sociological bias.[1]

Freud believed that the female suffers a severe biological trauma at birth in not having a penis. The female thus has an inevitable and immutable envy of the male and an unceasing desire to possess a penis. The Oedipal situation of the female can never be fully resolved and she is required to make substitute solutions for her real desires. The search for the penis is finally consummated with marriage and birth of a child who symbolically replaces the penis. In spite of this solution, the woman is left permanently dissatisfied, and this fact is responsible for a great many of her neurotic incapacities. Freud formulated his theories concerning the female on the masculine inspired assumption which had its roots in the Old Testament that while bisexuality was the common fate of mankind, the male sex was the primal, original sex from which the female was a secondary outgrowth. The bisexual theory was the prevailing view of sexual development until recently when it has been challenged. This theory implied that in the course of development of the sexual apparatus the sexual potentialities of both sexes are present. As development proceeds, one sex takes precedence and the biological rudiments of the opposite sex remains. In addition to the embryological remnants there are also psychological concomitants of both sexes which then play a crucial role in personality development.

Freud assumed that the early psychological development of the male and female were entirely similar and were determined by oral, anal and genital influences.

At the start of the phallic stage however, the girl is simply another "boy," centering on her clitoris as the boy does on his penis. Since she has not fully "discovered" her vagina she has a more complex adjustment to make in transfering her area of sexual gratification from the clitoris to the vagina. In addition, she must shift her first attachment from the mother to the father and must go through an Oedipal stage which in the girl is called the Electra complex. This shift occurs when the girl realizes that she lacks a penis and is "wounded in her self-love by the unfavorable comparison with the boy." The absence of the penis is blamed on the mother. From this discovery she "feels castrated" and develops penis envy and strives to regain a penis from the male.

Penis envy leaves permanent scars in the female which markedly affects her personality. Feelings of inferiority and vanity are expressions of the feelings of this lack and represent her efforts to compensate for this lack. Practically all her drives and ambitions are attributable to her hopes of retrieving the lost penis. The evidence that Freud presented for such attitudes were rather flimsy and were based on the statements of young girls who often express a wish for a penis and on the symbolic evidence in dreams and phantasies of adult women. His theory of female development rests on such evidence. These formulations regarding the female are essentially sociologically directed and limited by the philosophical and cultural prejudice of the nineteenth century. Freud, in discussing John Stuart Mill's views, considered Mill to be a man who was free of the conventional prejudices of his age except in the matter of female emancipation and the woman question. He said of Mill:

This is altogether a point with Mill where one simply cannot find him human ... It is really a stillborn thought to send women into the struggle for existence exactly as men. If, for instance, I imagined my gentle, sweet girl as a competitor, it would only end in my telling her, as I did seventeen months ago, that I am fond of her and that I implore her to withdraw from the strife into the calm, uncompetitive activity of my home. I believe that all reforming in law and education would break down in front of the fact that, long before the age at which a man can earn a position in society, nature has determined woman's destiny through beauty, charm and sweetness. Law and custom have much to give women that has been withheld from them, but the position of women will surely be what it is in youth, an adored darling, and in mature years a loved wife.[2]

Erich Fromm, in his book on Sigmund Freud's mission, says:

> Freud's views on the subject of emancipating women are certainly not different from the views held by the average man in Europe in the '80's. His attitude, as expressed in the letter to Martha, about John Stuart Mill shows how intense was Freud's need to put women in an inferior role. That his theoretical views mirrored this attitude is obvious. To look on women as castrated men, with no genuine sexuality of their own, always jealous of men, with a weakly developed superego, vain and unreliable, all this is an only slightly rationalized version of the patriarchial prejudice of his times.

Most classical psychoanalysts accepted Freud's views on the female in toto. However, many of his students attempted to clarify and develop some of his concepts and relate them both to hormonal factors and the cultural problems of the female.

Helene Deutsch, who has been particularly interested in this problem, emphasized the innate passivity of the female child in the earliest years rather than as beginning in the phallic era of development. Although this did not contradict Freud's views, it raised questions about the essential similarity of the early years of development and suggested that a process of sexual identification begins quite early. Her theories supported many of Freud's contentions and indicated that the masochistic wish to be violated and humiliated physically and mentally are the clues to feminine psychology. Thus, intercourse was for the woman a passive act of being overpowered. However, she has more recently restated her views and indicated that adolescence in the female may be strongly motivated by ego drives toward self reliance and independence.[3] Although superficially it appears to be related to sexual interests, actually it is a primary factor and is related to some impulses toward growth. Her views on motherhood at times differ from Freud's and she has emphasized the closeness of the mother's attitudes and behavior as a reflection of her own girlhood.

Therese Benedek has also made some crucial innovations in the theories of female sexuality by noting that the innate femaleness of the girl directs her development through identification with her mother. This notion puts more emphasis on the superego and takes the emphasis away from castration and penis envy. She casts some doubt on the universality of the hypothesis of pregnancy as a fulfillment of the wish to incorporate and retain the penis. She has presented data to indicate that other infantile phantasies as well as cultural factors determine the desire for pregnancy. The fetus may not only represent the missing penis, but may also be a symbol of another woman's pregnancy or her heightened beauty during pregnancy. It may also represent feces or other regressive phantasies.

Her studies of the hormonal relationships of the sexual function suggests that many female characteristics may be innate and controlled by hormonal factors rather than the psychological issues of castration or penis envy.

Donald W. Winnicott, in his concept of *primary maternal preoccupation,* has likewise raised the issue of hormonal elements in the maternal relationship to the child. Benedek feels that the male model of the reproductive organization is inadequate to explain the female reproductive function.

In 1927 Karen Horney, in a paper called "Flight from Womanhood," took issue with some of the classic views on female psychology. At that time she was still working under the libido theory framework but was dissatisfied with the notion of penis envy. She wondered whether the concept of "penis envy" was biologically rooted and whether the female is seriously interested in becoming a male since there was sufficient evidence to document a concept of "envy of the female" by the male.[4] In her views on female psychology, she noted that the symptoms attributable to penis envy, like the tendencies to berate, derogate and replace the male, are present in the male as well as the female and are often understood more comprehensively on grounds other than penis envy. In addition, the symbolic evidence in dreams are often misread or interpreted literally to conform to some preconceived notions about the existence of penis envy. This results in the common fallacy of having a theory that slants observations which then confirms the theory. There are many reasons why women prefer the interpretation of penis envy rather than a full recognition of their tendencies to derogate and compete with their husbands. It is easier to blame one's neurotic problems on being born a female than to recognize superiority of others based on their innate needs and willingness to work. Most significantly, however, she recognized that cultural factors more adequately explained the particular problems of the female and also permitted a broader view of their psychology. Women, for centuries, were divorced from the political, economic and socio-economic problems of the day. Their activities were limited to special areas of influence; the home, and particularly the kitchen and the bedchamber. In these restricted areas, women focused their needs exclusively in relation to the male and consequently they elevated love and loving relationships to an exaggerated extent. In addition, the woman was forced, through the economics and politics of family life to be exclusively dependent on the male. The attempt of Freud to show some relationship between masochism and femininity was based on this set of observations. Horney attempted to show that masochism does not have any feminine biological roots, but is rooted in the cultural problems of the female. Classical theory postulates a feminine masochism which attributes many characterological traits to the fact of being female. Women are presumed to be dependent and submissive and to desire to be pushed about while they play the martyr's role. The problem, as Horney saw it, was not one of masochism, since she felt that masochism was not primarily a sexual problem but a cultural one. The so-called masochistic behavior of the female, she believed, represented her attempts to gain control over others through a demonstration of weakness and incapacity. Historical factors have not only fostered masochistic attitudes in the women, but by virtue of the success of these attitudes, women frequently fight the possibility of altering or improving their status. The dependency on the male, as well as the contrast of her physical capacity, have at various times, particularly where physical requirements are essential, forced the woman to lean heavily on the man. Being dependent on the man has forced the woman to be a source of gratification to the man in order to maintain and sustain his love and interest. This behavior is rooted in cultural uncertainty, not in the biologically excessive need for love. This factor is largely responsible for the emphasis on beauty care and maintaining erotic attractiveness for the male under whatever standards are fashionable.

Although Freud's views were essentially anti-feminine and rooted in biology, he was also an astute observer who recognized the influence of cultural factors, even though they played an insignificant role in his theoretical formulations. He said: "But we must take care not to underestimate the influence of social convention which also force women into passive situations. The whole thing is still very obscure."[5] However, Freud's views are at times shockingly reactionary and naive in the light of the twentieth century.

Clara Thompson interested herself particularly in this aspect of psychoanalytic theory. She amplified many of the criticisms of Freud's views on female psychology and documented them with her own findings. She indicated that in a patriarchal culture women are under the control and prejudice of the male and must fill the standards and requirements of the male culture. They must accept the economic inequalities and legal handicaps that the culture supports. This tends to produce many of the problems and characteristics attributable to the female. After a while the woman herself begins to accept the situation as given and comes to consider herself inferior and second class. In the past 100 years the role of women has been undergoing marked changes which are reflected in the present confused situation. Prior to the industrial revolution, the woman's life was focused on the kitchen, where she played a large role in the family economy. However, with the growth of industry and the factory which forced the man out of the home, the role of the woman became narrower and her interests more restricted. They no longer shared in the family employment and the household unit was destroyed. Prior to the 1900's a successful life for a woman was to achieve marriage and raise children. After the First World War, when women began to enter industry, they began to make more demands on society and themselves, and the whole pattern of life was altered in many significant ways. Nowadays, Clara Thompson said, women make three types of adjustment.[6] Some marry and their interests are limited to being homemakers, some women make a career and never marry, and some work, but also marry. The first group seems to have the least distressing problems and often manages a full and satisfactory existence in the home. The second group, on the other hand, while achieving some kind of economic freedom and independence, is nevertheless frustrated and lacking in emotional freedom. This is undoubtedly the group that Freud had in mind in his description of penis envy. The third group have the greatest problems and are caught in endless conflicts. Their values are in flux and they not only have to rear children but also compete with the male in the ordinary course of maintaining their professional life.

Many of the limitations that still plague women arise out of the continuing patriarchal prejudices. Dr. Thompson emphasized the unequal opportunities for economic, educational and political development for the woman. The woman's inferiority has been forced upon her and accepted as a fact by both sexes. The woman more often strongly resists any alteration in her status than the male. This is understandable on the basis of the long history of second class citizenhip and domination in a patriarchal culture, which makes the woman's position very uncertain if any radical changes occur in the social structure. Although Freud saw penis envy as the central fact in the neurosis of the female, Thompson visualized penis envy in a symbolic way. She said that it is not the penis that the woman desires, but the cultural privileges which accrue to the penis as a symbol of the male.[7] The particular personality traits that Freud said were intrinsic to the female have greater relevance to the cultural situation than to biological inferiority. Their dependent status is frequently determined by their economic insecurity, particularly under conditions of child bearing and child rearing. Thus, they are forced to focus their living on a relationship with the male and center all their affectionate interest in this relationship. Freud described this aspect as a "greater need to be loved," than the male, while Thompson saw it simply as a necessity under certain cultural conditions. The tendency to conform and accept the male's values and standards is a way of adjusting to this necessity, and is not due to a weak superego. The lack of flexibility and tendencies towards stubborness and rigidity is related to the lack of opportunities for further development for the woman after she reaches the thirties. The cute, charming, cosmetic activities of the female are the techniques for maintaining control over the male.

Currently the role of the female is in great flux, and while her status has changed and greater opportunities are open to her, her conflicts have increased. Opportunities are not entirely equal and prejudices still remain. There is still a great confusion in the notion of freedom of the sexes and often it is defeated through an exaggerated mockery of what constitutes her freedom. Freedom for the female does not mean her being able to equal the physical prowess of the male in order to work in the mines or on railroad construction, although this is already occurring in some eastern countries. The issues here are not entirely cultural, since there are biological differences in muscular capacity, and here freedom must be distinguished from equality in opportunities.

Bernard Robbins has clarified the problem of the sexual and non-sexual differences between the male and the female. He felt that the female's psychology is qualitatively different and that her Weltanschaung and technique for handling problems differ from the male. Neurotic compliancy and passivity is not the exclusive possession of the female and envy in the female is not directly related to the penis. Although he stressed the similarity between male and female, he pointed out that man's exploitation of woman has produced character changes which reflect this social structure. Arrogance, aggression, or passivity are essentially neurotic and dehumanizing in the male *and* the female. Yet the culture and social roles do produce essential differences. Childbearing and motherhood are social roles limited to the female, and it is the nature of this social and biological role and the physiology underlying it that determines the special differences of the female.[8] Freud assumed that all the differences were physiological and were related exclusively to the presence or absence of the favored organ. Although sex in humans plays a significant role in their activity. it has become more than a physiological activity. The female has learned to use the activity of sex to serve many purposes and goals. Freud never quite understood that the female does not resent motherhood, the absence of a penis, etc., but the subservient social role imposed on the mother. He was vaguely aware that the female, in addition to her penis envy, needed to be viewed as a person in her own right.

Freud's conception of the psychology of the female was his weakest theoretical achievement. He was limited by the prejudices of the nineteenth century and his own patriarchal tendencies and heritage. In addition, the framework of the libido theory which was adequate and explanatory for the male was not as successful in defining the characterological developments in the female. To apply this theory to the female required drastic reformulations and so many additional postulates that the hypothesis regarding the female frequently disobeyed Occam's principle of scientific parsimony. Most of all, he attempted to explain all psychological differences in biological terms and overlooked the obvious effects that the culture imposed on both sexes. Freud saw the possibilities for the female in most pessimistic terms. Either they accepted their inevitable role and substituted a baby for the penis, or else they would develop a neurosis. Whatever their choice, unless they passively conformed to the male-centered culture, they were involved in "masculine protest" and penis envy. There are many female classical analysts of considerable stature in psychoanalytic circles who underwrite Freud's views on the female. However, as the cultural situation has in recent years clarified many of our supposed facts about the female, the classical analysts' views are being revised and the notion of inferiority is beginning to have only a limited meaning in the male-female conflict. Although in earliest vertebrate and invertebrate animals, it is possible to assign the name of male to the prominent member and trace the female from him, it is no longer possible in the primates, particularly man. On the contrary, it is conceivable that the "Y" chromosome in the male XY designation of sex chromosome is a degenerated X chromosome. This suggests that rather than being superior, the male is in a sense a degenerated female. At any rate, it seems utterly meaningless to attempt a hierarchy in sexual terms unless we accept the biblical version of the origin of man.

Sexual differences are related to the differing roles each plays in the fulfillment of his or her biological function. The uterus is a more efficient organ for retaining the fetus than a rod-like structure (penis) and the vagina is a well-designed passageway to this chamber. The female does not have a vagina and uterus because physiologically she is receptive, but simply because her role is to receive and to retain the fetus which in the primates occurs through the agency of a uterus. Neither does the presence of the uterus or vagina make a person receptive, as far as we know, since the performance of her sexual role requires the penetration of the penis to deposit sperm. To this extent she must receive the male genital organ. To generalize about her passivity and receptiveness from this anatomical design requires an imaginative analogy, and not a collection of data which justifies the conclusion. There are varying social and biological roles which determine and are determined by the nature of the physiological structure of the species. The female is admirably equipped to perform her function as the mothering one and recent studies have brought this more clearly to our awareness. Ashley Montagu, in his book, *The Natural Superiority of the Woman*,[9] has collected this evidence which proves most conclusively that physiologically and psychologically as well as biologically, the female is actually superior to the male in her capacities and potentialities for survival and performance of her biological role. The anatomical configuration and endocrine system of the human female, including the cardiac and respiratory systems, have greater flexibility and resilience than the male. Women are more flexible in their physiological capacity to handle stressful situations and even though they have a limited muscular apparatus, their neuro-muscular apparatus is more highly sensitive and proportioned which enables them to perform finer, more detailed muscular activity. Psychologically, they appear to hold up better than the male under stress, contrary to the popular conception of the fragility of the female. The air raid experiences in the last war have documented the low rate of breakdown of the female compared to the male. The survival rate of the female is greater than the male and while this might reflect on the less strenuous existence they undergo, this is certainly not true where large families are involved. The problem of the aged frequently centers around the widow, who has survived her husband by many years.

Woman must be efficiently equipped to carry out the child bearing role, which in primitive and even recent times, occupied her full existence. When families were not limited, the woman was in a constant state of pregnancy, delivery, or recovery and preparation for the next pregnancy. This required a physiological constitution that was capable of withstanding repeated crises. In addition to the child bearing role, the woman also performed a great deal of the work involved in running the household. Thus, it is not surprising (except to those who refuse to acknowedge these facts) that except for muscular capacities the female equipment may be more efficient and serviceable than the male counterparts. Or, to put it another way, it appears that the female is as well equipped to perform her role as the male. At least, one should not automatically assume that the male has characteristics, both physiological and psychological, which clearly set him apart as the natural and superior individual. Each sex is adapted to carry out its role and this is a more valid approach to understanding their psychological problems than an assumption of a superior role versus an inferior one. The adaptational approach to understanding the female and femininity may be more useful than the motivational or instinctual approach. It avoids teleology as well as the necessity for multiple hypotheses.

From an adaptational point of view, we would recognize the special characteristics of the female which are not items in a race with the male for some superior status, but merely adaptive mechanisms to perform the tasks for which she is biologically ordained. While the male might well envy the female capacity to be available sexually at all times without special preparation, it is simply a recognition of the necessity to be accessible when the male is ready, since his capacities are limited. This is particularly true in Man, and in the primates generally, where the erection and ejaculation is periodic and requires a refractory period in order to accumulate sperm. In a teleological or hedonistic sense, the woman has greater potentialities for sexual pleasure since she is open and available at all times. To counteract this unpleasant fact, the male has created the myth that the female has less sexual desire and less capacity for enjoying sex, since orgasm is less common in the female. Until very recently, the enjoyment of sex was a male prerogative and the free and uninhibited involvement in the sex act was denied to the female. In recent years, the woman has put aside most restraints in pursuing her lustful interests. This has enhanced her sexual freedom in the sense of not only permitting more involvements than heretofore, but also in letting herself go, in participating actively and energetically in sexual activities. Since it is no longer a source of shame or an indication of debauchery for the woman to enjoy sex, she has demonstrated great powers in this regard. It becomes clear that not only can she enjoy the sexual act to the same extent as the male, but can do so more frequently and consistently. The question of orgasm in the female has been a much abused notion which was not clarified by Freud's complicated scheme of the development of sexuality in the female. Freud believed that the female needed to progress from a clitoral orgasm to a vaginal orgasm, and that the vaginal orgasm indicated greater maturity and was a source of greater pleasure. This conclusion was supported only by the theoretical constructions which required this kind of hierarchy and not by any clinical data. There is no evidence of any such progression or that the vagina is capable of erection with tumescence or detumescence and ejaculation analogous to the male orgasm. In addition, there is no evidence that the vagina has nerve endings capable of producing sensations of pleasure, except those as sensations involving dilation of the circular musculature. On the other hand, Dr. Judd Marmor has shown in a most interesting paper on the female orgasm that the clitoris is endowed with numerous nerve endings and is capable of tumescence and detumescence and is probably the sole source of orgasm pleasure in the female.[10]

Sandor Rado has pointed out that:

As is generally known, the sexually most responsive areas of the female organ are the clitoris, the minor labia, and the entrance to the vagina. These are at best supplied with nerve endings responsive to touch are most frequently used in orgasmic self-stimulation during childhood, puberty and later life. In most women, the vagina itself, notably its upper half, is practically without nerve supply. In the absence of sensory innervation there can, of course, be no sensation. And, yet, most healthy women insist that in coitus they can achieve complete orgasmic gratification only through deep vaginal penetration. The reason for this remarkable conviction appears to be chiefly motivational. In the healthy woman maternal feeling is the strongest motivational system. She feels intuitively that deep penetration may bring her closer to the fulfillment of her ever-present though often repressed desire to conceive. And, she knows that deep penetration is a prerequisite of optimal gratification for the male whom she desires to please. Her statements about deep sensation (including the allegedly pleasureable impact of the seminal fluid on the cervix) appear to reflect illusions derived from a folklore of ancient origin.[11]

Consequently, if this is true, the female does not have to take additional physiological steps to enjoy the sex act, but is as capable as the male in achieving it under proper circumstances. The quest for orgasm in the woman is a recent adventure, made possible by allowing the woman to discover that such pleasures are available and possible. This search has taken on great momentum in recent years, and may be responsible for many of the psychiatrist's patients. This has been further complicated by the notion of some women who feel that they can only experience a clitoral orgasm and want to achieve a vaginal one. This distinction, incidentally, must be related to a hangover from the masturbatory period when the clitoris was used to stimulate orgasm. Since masturbation is viewed as a second-rate substitute for intercourse, clitoral orgasm was also considered to be a second-rate achievement which could be overcome by therapy which would produce a vaginal orgasm. This is also related to the tendency to deprecate the orgasm which is obtained through the help of manual manipulation in the sex act. It is considered to be deficient and immature and particularly unnatural since no manual assistance should be needed or is needed in the sexual activity of animals. Although it is clear that intercourse produces a qualitatively different orgasm from masturbation, this is due to the presence of another person and the intimacies involved rather than the achievement of a vaginal orgasm. At the same time, sexual activity in man is strikingly different from the most closely related animals in that instinct plays a lesser role in man. This allows for greater freedom and variation. In humans, foreplay, sexual experimentation and manipulation by the hands as well as the mouth and the innumerable variations in position, etc., play a major part in the sex act. Sex plays a much broader function than mere reproduction. At best, the male assumption that he has greater capacities for enjoying sex is limited to the notion that he has had a longer time to learn how to. The female, in recent years, is learning very rapidly how to maximize her sexual pleasures.

An intrinsic aspect of child bearing is the element of creativity that the woman experiences in the process. This has been underrated by most men and even women, but has nevertheless been noted by many mothers. The fullest expression of creation, the nurture and delivery of a human being, is the sole power of the female. The male, in many primitive cultures, acts out his envy and desire to replace the female at this time by elaborate rites and rituals. More recently, man has dealt with this issue by attempting to share the experience involved in childbirth. But the act of creation and child bearing is a privilege only women have and which they cannot share. Horney, Thompson, Rado, and others have highlighted this aspect of female sexuality which Freud and a male-centered psychology overlooked.

There are other special characteristics of the female which relate directly to her role as mother. These have to do with the woman's particular sensitivity to the significance of human life and its values and relationships. Consequently, the female is frequently characterized by the capacity to live with a more unified value system, although she appears to have greater flexibility and capacity for change. One can argue this contention, but it is a justifiable assumption on the basis of the peculiar biological role that the woman plays that such qualities might be present. In addition it is clear that certain characterological qualities are related to the female because of her biological role. In this dual recognition of the psychology of the female lies a great deal of the dissension with Freud. Freud predicates a psychology of the female on the presence or absence of certain organs. Thus, penis envy is envy of an organ, an anatomical implement that plays a functional role in procreation.

It is not the functional element that the female envies, but rather its symbolic significance. The contemporary theorists take full account of the biological sexual differences and how they influence the psychology of the sexes. However, we must distinguish the roles which biology imposes and the intrinsic value of the sexual organs. It is clear that the menstruation cycle introduces new factors in the work-life of the female. On the other hand, it is only an assumption and an entirely gratuitous one that the female biologically and ubiquitously desires to have a penis, since it is a preferred organ in a preferred sex. Freud's views imply a permanent scarring which in therapy could only be slightly alleviated through a major process of giving up any hope of ever achieving a penis and compromising this with the substitution of a child. The female was biologically scarred, innately neurotic, and described by Freud in a rather unflattering fashion. In therapy they had less potentialities for benefit and change. In practical terms this appears to be entirely inaccurate since the female patient has great flexibility for change and appears to benefit from therapy equally with the male. At the same time, it is noted by most contemporary theorists that the female is neurotic only to the extent that she is caught up in the same neurotic web which entraps both male and female in our culture. They do not postulate separate psychologies and differing milieu that need to be confronted and overcome. In the past fifty years we have witnessed great cultural advances in the status of women with remarkable alterations in what was once considered to be biologically inherited characteristics. As the opportunities for employment have increased and the burden of the housewife and homemaker decreased, the female has become increasingly independent and assertive in her approach to the fulfillment of her own rights. Although this has been partly responsible for the high divorce rates, it indicates at the least that the woman no longer feels utterly dependent on the male and insecure to the exent that she had no choice but to remain fixed in a relationship, no matter how bad it might be. She no longer needs to move about carefully and quietly to avoid distressing the male, and, consequently, she gets involved in extra-marital affairs to an increasing extent. As her role is not exclusively limited to child rearing, she has entered many professions and industrial jobs which not only guarantee her security, but make her co-equal in the world which heretofore was considered the private domain of the male. In many ways the biological differences which Freud felt were all detrimental, now serve to give her many advantages in her new tasks. The capacity for dealing with people and making decisions has produced many successful executives while the skill in the finer, more detailed industrial operations have made her sought after in the more discriminating tasks in machine industries. The increase in her sexual freedom has brought about new demands on the male for more adequate and satisfactory performances, where previously she had no right to complain. This has produced new problems for the male. The increased demands for more lusty sex activity coupled with the demand for orgasm for the female has placed a large part of the burden for satisfying the woman on the man. In addition, the woman who is no longer passive in her cultural role is becoming less and less passive in her sexual activity. She more actively initiates and participates in the sex act and does not look upon it as "masculine protest" or "penis envy" but as sound participation in an activity that can be highly pleasurable.

Although it is clear that the muscular power of the female is clearly less than that of the male, it is no longer a critical factor in terms of status as it once was in primitive societies and expanding frontiers. The value of bulbous muscles decreases very sharply in the machine age when not only a woman but a child can cut down a tree with an electric saw. The advent of the machine age and push-button civilization has decreased the gap between the male and the female and demonstrated that the status of the sexes rests on cultural issues rather than biological ones. Women are interested in essentially the same things that men are; satisfaction and security. The different biological roles dictate varying adaptational techniques for achieving these basic needs. However, the physiological requirements in both sexes are precisely the same, with very minor differences to the extent that they determine the techniques for achieving security rather than in affecting the goals. The psychology of the female, then, must be approached not from the focus of the male but through a study of the psychology of the human being and the peculiar problems produced by the differing roles of the sexes under varying cultural conditions. It would then be possible to get away from the notions of superiority-inferiority of the female or the question of passivity or aggressiveness and simply recognize differences dictated by function.

NOTES

1. Freud said, in an article on character types met with in psychoanalysis, in his collected papers, "As we learn from our psychonalytic work, all women feel that they have been injured in their infancy and that through no fault of their own they have been slighted and robbed of a part of their body."

Also, in *The Psychology of Women* (p. 69), he said: "Nature has paid less careful attention to the demands of the female function than to those of masculinity. And, speaking teleologically, this may be based on the fact that the achievement of the biological aim is entrusted to the aggressiveness of the male and is to some extent independent of the cooperation of the female." In this connection Freud was poorly informed; otherwise he would surely have been aware that rape in approximately the same age group is impossible except if the female is drugged or otherwise immobilized.

2. Viola Klein, in an article entitled: The feminine character, New York, International Universities Press, Inc., said: "The implicit assertion of man's primary superiority which was in strange contrast to contemporary changes in the cultural role of women, has been a stumbling block to many psychoanalysts and has evoked doubts and divergencies among some of Freud's disciples." Ernest Jones, for instance, said in 1927 (Early development of female sexuality, Int. J. Psychoanaly., 1927), "There is a healthy suspicion growing that men analysts have been led to adopt an unhealthy phallocentric view of the problems in question, the importance of the female organs being correspondingly underestimated." This note appears in E. Jones' Life and Work of S. Freud Vol. 1, p. 177.

3. Deutsch, Helene: Female Psychology, 2 vols. New York, Grune & Stratton, 1944, 1945.

4. Zilboorg, Gregory: Masculine and feminine. Psychiatry 7: 257, 1941. In this article Zilboorg suggested that woman envy on the part of the male is probably psychologically older than penis envy on the part of the female.

5. Freud, S.: Civilized sexual morality and modern nervousness, in Collected Paper, Vol. 2, 1924.

6. Thompson, Clara: The role of women in this culture. Psychiatry. 4: 331-339, 1941; also Cultural pressures in the psychology of women. Psychiatry 6:12-125, 1943.

7. In an article called: Some effects of the derogatory attitude towards female sexuality, Psychiatry 13: 249, 1950, she said: "I hope I have emphasized the fact that, the problem of a woman's sexual life is not in becoming reconciled to having no penis but in accepting her own sexuality in its own right."

8. His views on the psychology of the female were presented in some unpublished papers which will soon be available.

9. See bibliography.

10. Marmor, J.: Some consideration concerning organism in female. Psychosomatic Med. 16:240-245, 1954.

11. Rado, Sandor: Sexual anaesthesia in the female. Quart. Rev. Surg. Obst. & Gynec. 16:251, 1959.

IX

Homosexuality

HOMOSEXUALITY has been a major problem for personality theorists
for many years. Until Freud attempted a psychological explanation
it was believed to be evidence of degeneracy caused by physiological
changes, or due to some hormonal inbalance, or caused by the presence of a homosexual brain center. The prevalent medical view of
homosexuality has coincided more or less with the social attitudes
towards this disorder. The social atmosphere has affected the medico-
legal issues regarding this illness as well as influencing the goals of
treatment. As long as it was thought to be due to some constitutional
or inherited degeneracy it was beyond the possibilities of treatment
and cure. At the time when Freud was developing his sexual theories,
the work of Magnus Hirschfield and Krafft-Ebbing dominated the
thinking about sexual perversions, and the disease was thought to
be of physiological origin, probably hereditary.[1]

Freud developed his theories about homosexuality in the framework of the libido theory and the bisexual theory of sexual development. Freud assumed that every individual passed through a
"homosexual" stage on his way to heterosexuality, and since homosexuality was considered to be a fixation at the homosexual level it
was the direct expression of a sexual impulse. Since initially Freud
considered it to be a perversion, it was theoretically untreatable.
However, his clinical observations did not always bear this out.
The development of homosexuality was intimately related to the
bisexuality theory of personality development.

If the predisposition to femininity was excessive in the male, his
subsequent identification to the male might be weak. As he passed
through the Oedipal phase, he would then remain permanently identified with the masculine figure, and homosexuality would result.
Freud's views rested almost entirely on the innate libidinal resources
of the individual although environmental influences could have some
effect.

199

Homosexuality in the male, then, was due either to some constitutional weakness which produced fixation at the homosexual level of development or to regression and identification with the mother because of a fear of castration. Freud also visualized a homosexual development based on repression of competitive strivings in the Oedipal period which forced the individual to forego interest in the opposite sex. Although this model was developed for the male, it applied equally to the female with some significant modifications.

This conception of homosexuality was more dynamic and meaningful than any previous formulation and was accepted with considerable enthusiasm by psychiatrists and sexologists. It encouraged a tremendous amount of interest in the developmental history of the homosexual and encouraged the possibility of influencing his mode of existence. Psychoanalysts filled the literature with numerous case reports documenting and substantiating these formulations. It is only in recent years, however, through the work of the "cultural" psychoanalysts, like Horney, Sullivan and Rado, and others, that major modifications have been made in the dynamics of homosexuality. As the libido theory was abandoned and doubts about the bisexual theory of sexual development were raised, the problem of homosexuality was thrown into a new light. Homosexuality was viewed as a neurosis rather than as a perversion, or inversion, as Freud called it, and merely a symptom in the overall problem of relating to the opposite sex. The environmental factors in its development were stressed more than the biological issues, and lately it has been viewed by some psychoanalysts as an adaptational mechanism of defense designed to avoid heterosexual intimacy due to problems of dependence and strivings for power, rather than as a symptom primarily due to sexual problems. Consequently, many homosexuals can be called pseudo-homosexuals since they have no sexual interest in the same sex but display fears of homosexuality and experience difficulty in heterosexual adjustment.

Karen Horney described the homosexual as a neurotic who manifests his symptomatology in all spheres of his living, including the sexual. If he is the type of neurotic who has a great fear of being trapped or who is so overwhelmed with uncertainty about his competence, sexual and otherwise, then he might avoid any relationship with a woman which would endanger this position. This avoidance might be extreme enough to produce justifications and rationalizations for his behavior in terms of hating women whom he might describe as tricky and covetous. Ultimately, it might force him into a relationship with a man that might involve sexual contact in order to insure the relationship. An example of this type of homosexual occurred in a male who made his first attempt at heterosexual intercourse while in therapy. The sex act went off extremely well, and the patient was quite pleased with his performance. He enjoyed the sex play as well as the orgasm. When he prepared to leave the girl, she asked him why he was leaving so soon and whether he did not like her enough to stay longer. This question threw him into a panic and he had many phantasies of being trapped by the girl. He left quickly in great agitation and could not sleep all night. Although the sexual aspect of the experience went very well, he became panicky about the possibility of intimacy and responsibility, and he felt particularly uncomfortable regarding the tender exchanges which occurred during the evening. Although he felt sexually adequate in this heterosexual adventure, he was totally unprepared for the interpersonal elements in the relationship. This incident illustrates Horney's thesis that homosexuality is an aspect of the general problem of neuroses, and is not necessarily involved in sexual difficulties as such.

Sullivan amplified Horney's ideas and presented alternative views about the so-called homosexual era in personality development. He described those years in which there is interest in the same sex as part of the developmental process of maturing into heterosexuality. The initial attempts at intimacy and relationship with other humans were necessarily involved with individuals who were most like ourselves, that is, of the same sex, which made these relationships easier to develop. In addition, he felt that the motivation for homosexual contact was lacking since the gonadal apparatus had not yet matured. For Sullivan, the ultimate homosexual adjustment arose primarily out of the difficulties entailed in initiating and sustaining heterosexual companionship. This situation might be due to genital phobias or to premature attempts at heterosexual adjustment with profound scarring in the process. It might also be the result of intimacies with the same sex set up in an earlier period of life—particularly in the juvenile era, because they are safe and secure and because of severe anxieties the individual cannot overcome.[2] The problem of homosexuality becomes primarily one of distorted interpersonal relationships. Clara Thompson applied this conception to female homosexuality and demonstrated the same dynamics. Sandor

Rado, in a critical examination of bisexuality, demonstrated the fallacy of predicating a theory of homosexuality on the basis of this concept. From his point of view homosexuality was an attempt at repair of a disordered sexual function initiated through some genital fear or phobic avoidance.

When homosexuality is viewed in this new perspective, it becomes clear that the term *homosexuality* has been applied to many aspects of behavior other than the sexual. This raises many interesting questions, and it becomes necessary to distinguish between sexual activity and activity which utilizes the genitals for purposes other than sexuality—such as the pursuit of power, prestige or vindictive retaliation. Freud's efforts to distinguish between libido and sexuality are not sufficient to answer the criticisms raised by these theorists. The clarification of genital activity as sex in contrast with its use for other purposes has held out great promise in a broadened conception of personality development. Since there are direct social implications of a legal kind in the sexual deviations, the classification and definition of these disorders, particularly homosexuality, is of paramount importance.

Although the legal statutes do not distinguish between the use of the genitals for sexual or non-sexual purposes, a distinction is significant in attempting to comprehend the dynamics of a sexual crime and in planning a therapeutic attack on the patient. Recent legal opinions, however, as in the Durham decision, have opened the way for the alleviation of some of the judicial abuses in the handling of sexual deviations and sex crimes.[3]

It might simplify further research in this area if we agreed that the term sexual be limited to behavior which has as its motivational aims some orgastic satisfaction. All genital activity which is pursued either to orgasm or as preparatory to orgasm would thus be viewed as sexual activity. Genital manipulation, then, would be considered sexual if it were motivationally directed to orgasm as in masturbation. It could be distinguished from the exploratory activity of children which does not have orgastic pleasure as its goal, and consequently, would not be considered sexual. This would also apply to the variety of activities such as manipulation of the orifice of other so-called erotogenic areas. Such activity, when part of the activity motivationally directed to orgastic satisfaction could be considered sexual. However, such behavior, according to the libido theory, has been considered sexual at all times, whatever its origin.

The label of homosexuality on the basis of some of the older theories was applied to anyone who has had contact with the same sex, no matter how fleeting or ancient, as well as to those individuals whose sexual relations are limited exclusively to individuals of the same sex. At times, any closeness or intimacy with the same sex whether it occurs in drinking parties or sport matches would be considered to be evidence of homosexual interest or latent homosexuality. Other theorists would refer to any variant sexual activity with the opposite sex that does not involve the genitals as homosexual. Still others would use the term for any person who avoids the opposite sex, even though he may not have any sexual contacts with the same sex. The looseness of the definitions of homosexuality derives largely from Freud's views which assume the existence of latent homosexual trends in everyone. These trends are manifested in a variety of ways in relationships with the same sex even where sexual contact is entirely absent. In these instances, it would be presumed that sexual contact is absent because of the fear of homosexuality which is in itself indicative of such interest. Consequently, homsexuality has encompassed a multiplicity of behavior which may have varying significance, some sexual but most non-sexual.

It has been demonstrated most effectively by Sullivan, Rado, and their students that competitive defeats and dependency strivings can be symbolized in homosexual terms when the culture considers weakness or failure as evidence of lack of manliness which becomes synonymous with homosexuality. Lionel Ovesey pointed out that the homosexual conflict has three component parts—sex, dependency and power.[4] Only the first category, in which there is a primary motivational goal towards orgastic satisfaction, can be called homosexual. The other two categories are called pseudo-homosexual because they resemble homosexuality but are dynamically different. In this distinction, Ovesey has merely elaborated an aspect of the neurotic structure which is extremely common in homosexuality—the presence of extreme dependent needs in an individual who has marked difficulties in maintaining his status and esteem in an adult world.

It is necessary to the further development of our knowledge about the dynamics and therapy of homosexuality that a more refined, operational definition replace the broad, overly generalized and unprecise definition which now prevails. If we limit our conception of homosexuality only to those instances where the primary motivational goal is orgastic satisfaction with the same sex, we will have reduced the confusion considerably. However, some looseness will still obtain in the delineation of what constitutes orgastic satisfaction.

It would be more desirable to speak only of homosexual behavior rather than homosexuality. This would imply that homosexuality was only a symptom in a behavioral disorder, a notion that is current in the theoretical views of recent behavioral scientists. Such a description would allow for more operational statement about homosexual behavior even though we would still need a definition of what constituted homosexual behavior. However, from this framework, we could visualize a continuum from the most extreme to the least evident homosexual behavior. It would also accommodate the notion of occasional versus persistent homosexual behavior rather than an "all or none" situation which implies that a person *is* or *is not* homosexual. This approach would also allow for the phenomenon of homosexual behavior as a situational problem.

Since homosexuality is apparently not a single, integrated, psychiatric syndrome, it would be limited to those individuals whose difficulties in relating to the opposite sex are of such an extreme nature that they forgo any interest and avoid every effort to integrate on a heterosexual level. Their sexual motivational goal is orgastic satisfaction with the same sex. Although they may frequently engage in heterosexual activities for various reasons, their preference is for homosexual contacts.

It would also include only those people who lead an exclusively homosexual existence as well as those who marry but still have as their primary goal sexual orgasm with the same sex. It would not necessarily include those individuals who have managed some degree of intimacy with the opposite sex, and who only occasionally seek some homosexual contact. The criteria, here, would be determined by the primary motivational goal. It would also distinguish those individuals whose goal is primarily homosexual but who, because of cultural pressures, marry and raise families. It would not include those sexual experimenters who dabble in every deviation. Nor, would it automatically include such persons who, because of professional or ideological reasons, choose a way of life that avoids lust and sexual intimacy. It cannot include individuals who, because of circumstances of forced absence from the opposite sex (jail, prison camps, etc), perform the sex act with whomever and whatever is available. It would thus refer generally to those individuals who cannot integrate on any level of intimacy with persons of the opposite sex and are forced to frame their living with what is left—the same sex. Such a definition obviously neglects the assumptions of the homosexual era in the classical theories of personality development, since it requires orgastic satisfaction as implied in its definition.

Even if we were to agree that the individual does traverse a period of homosexuality in his development, it is strikingly different from the manifestations of homosexuality after the maturation of the gonads. Consequently, we should not apply the same labels even if they are intimately related. We still call a seed a seed and not an apple even though after sufficient nourishment and care the seed will produce a tree which will yield apples. It not only confuses our understanding and interferes with a clarity of operation, but it fails to distinguish between phenomena on varying levels of function. This definition of homosexuality might encourage a firmer grasp of the dynamics involved in the development of homosexuality.

Closely allied to the question of homosexuality is that of latent homosexuality which is a widely used concept in the behavioral sciences. The concept of latency is loosely used by Freud in various contexts, such as dreams in terms of latent content, or in anxiety or hostility where it indicates feelings which are in abeyance at the moment but capable of moving into focal awareness at any time. This notion of latency has broad implication for the behavioral sciences. An analysis of this concept is in order, since it has crucial import in any theory of homosexuality.

It should be noted at the outset that latency has two meanings. The first implies dormancy which refers to the presence of fully matured functions or capacities in an inactive state. The second refers to *potentiality*—or the presence of potential capacities in an undeveloped form which can be developed under proper conditions. Freud used the concept of latency almost exclusively in the sense of dormancy and this fact throws new light on many of his views.

Latent homosexuality was a concept which grew out of Freud's clinical experience based on the bisexual theory of sexual develop-ment. The widespread acceptance of Freud's contributions, particu-larly in the area of sexuality, has led to an automatic, uncritical belief in the validity of this notion.

At the present time the concept has become an all-embracing explanation for certain occurrences in normal sexual development and for all varieties of sexual attitudes or performances. Although the concept has never been verified except by *a priori* reasoning, it has been called a dynamic concept since it presumes an endless variety of reactions in response to its presence. However, its dynamic character is often tautological since we find ourselves saying, for example, that latent homosexuality is often the cause of voyeuristic behavior and that voyeurism is evidence of latent homosexual trends. As an explanatory concept, it has become a universal grab bag used to explain all forms of behavior, sexual and non-sexual, in either sex which deviates from the arbitrary and conventionalized standards of behavior for a particular sex. It explains everything and elucidates very little. It presupposes a sexual interest in the same sex which never needs to be manifested in overt sexual action, since the absence of such behavior proves the concept, while the presence of such behavior implies that the latent has become manifest. Consequently, it has practically no operational value, since it can neither be defined precisely nor visualized except by prior acceptance of its presence in the individual.

Freud used the term in a variety of ways without defining or distinguishing the semantic differences. Dormancy implies the presence of inactive ideas, trends, or dynamisms already in existence and fully developed awaiting some physiological or psychological triggering to set them in motion. Potentiality, however, implies a capacity for evolving from one state to another, provided certain events, situations, or stimuli occur. This distinction played a major role in the earliest history of science, when the distinction had to be made between development as the evolution of previously existing states which were pre-formed and preordained and development in which the potentiality was influenced by environmental phenomena and the only preordained state was the existent potentiality for development. The difference, I believe, is amply demonstrated when spring arrives, and, conditions becoming suitable, the dormant bear awakens and becomes a bear but the acorn becomes an oak tree.

This distinction has bothered many scientists, particularly the operationalists, about many of Freud's concepts. Else Frenkel-Brunswick, in *Psychoanalysis and the Unity of Science*,[5] says, "There is nothing objectionable about the notion of latent or unconscious tendencies, at least not so long as we do not insist on assigning them to the mind in a metaphysical sense." She was attempting to reconcile these ideas with Rudolph Carnap's[6] ideas about "dispositional concepts and their value as heuristic postulates." They have become altered from concepts to "things-in-themselves," and the metaphysical idea becomes reified as an existent actuality. This has occurred in spite of Freud's warnings and because of his own loose and unclear delimitation of these concepts. Latent homosexuality is an example of this tendency, since Freud used it in the sense of dormancy, not as disposition.

In his work on dreams, Freud used the term latency to refer to the dream content which is disguised, distorted, and elaborated in such a fashion as to elude the dream censor. In this sense, the ideas, tendencies, or feelings were existent, but dressed up in order to be made acceptable. Latent in this sense did not imply any dispositional element and had no dynamic quality whatsoever. It simply referred to the essence which was dormant in the manifest content and needed to be taken out of it by interpretative skills. Latency, here, involves dormancy, in spite of the fact that the idea or attitudes may be alive enough. The contrast of manifest versus latent indicated the true or the real versus the substitute or the disguised.

When we look at the concept of latency as applied to hostility or aggression, we find a mixture of both dormant and dispositional elements. As a result of repression, hostility may lie dormant and reappear in a setting which reactivates the original repression, which Freud called the "return of the repressed." On the other hand, certain developmental attitudes or experiences may make an individual sensitive and predisposed to respond with hostility. This possibility could be called "dispositional." Freud did not make this distinction clear, and for many psychoanalysts this potentiality also involves the issue of repression—hence, dormancy. The postulate of latent hostility has also aroused much philosophical contention, and the notion of dormancy, here, also has been disputed by many behavioral theorists. The concept of latent homosexuality could be both a dormant and dispositional concept. However, it has been used by Freud and subsequent psychoanalysts almost exclusively as a dormancy concept. In this sense, it implies that homosexual needs or drives exist in the individual in the fully developed form and are capable of being called into action by certain stimuli. As a concept of dormancy, it is static, not dynamic; mechanical and not developmental. If it is inferred that it was and is used as a dispositional postulate, then its usage is both superfluous and misleading. However one views personality development, whether as formulated by the libido theory, or by the neo-Freudian theorists, the potentiality for the development of homosexuality exists, provided certain positive conditions are fulfilled or negative conditions altered. This fact is accepted by all behavioral theorists, even though we are unable to define precisely the conditions at the present time. This is the essence of a dynamic conception of personality development and we ordinarily do not assign special names to those areas of experiencing which are potential, provided certain conditions are fulfilled. We do not speak of latent heterosexuality, or latent tenderness, or latent maturity. As a dispositional concept, latent homosexuality contains open and infinite variables, and unless the term "homosexuality" is defined with definite ranges and limits, it becomes too broad and all-encompassing and includes large varieties of related and unrelated items of behavior.

Based on the "concept of bisexuality," Freud stated that in each sex there are not only embryological rudiments of the opposite sex, but the inherent psychological characteristics of the opposite sex. Thus the male, and the quality of maleness, which is biologically associated with aggressiveness, activity, and numerous other characteristics related to the pushing, forcing and penetrating aspects of the male genital, also manifests to a greater or lesser degree the characteristics of the opposite sex. The characteristics which an individual displays, which are opposite to the inherent characteristics of his biological sexuality, are related to the latent homosexual trends in his personality. Thus the female, being the passive receiver and the masochist by biological heritage would in any tendency to become the aggressor, betray her latent homosexual trends. The male who displayed interest in the so-called feminine pursuits (cooking, beauty culture, etc.) would be described as having latent homosexual trends where homosexual behavior was not overt.

On the basis of this theory it is assumed that in every individual there lie dormant sexual needs, attitudes, and psychological characteristics of the opposite sex. This does not mean that homosexual trends are necessarily repressed or dissociated but that they lie dormant, influencing behavior.[7]

Freud, in *Three Contributions to the Theory of Sex,* said: "The unconscious tendency to inversion (homosexuality) is never wanting." On the basis of this statement, there has been an uncritical and widespread tendency in psychoanalytic theory and practice to assume the existence of latent homosexual trends in every individual.[8]

The term *latent homosexuality* is usually applied to those tendencies, attitudes, and behavior which involve some difficulty with mature sexuality and partake of some of the psychological characteristics of the opposite sex. In therapy it is applied to those elements in the character structure of the patient which involve personality traits not conventionally attributed to the sex of the patient. This does not mean that he is actively engaged in homosexual activity. It does not refer to the homosexual who has repressed his homosexuality and tries to live a heterosexual existence, for here it is not latent, but repressed. In the course of our development we must all achieve a satisfactory relationship with an individual of the same sex and make our first real efforts at being social creatures before we can achieve similar relationships with the opposite sex. During adolescence this becomes the main burden of our development. Some manage it successfully and rarely have any problems with the opposite sex. These people may never experience even fleeting notions of homosexuality. Others never manage it, and become overt, active homosexuals. Still others manage it with difficulty, yet still never engage in homosexual activity, or may have only fleeting contacts, or may in varying degree have behavioral traits commonly attributed to the opposite sex. These are the individual to whom the label of latent homosexuality is applied, although it is presumed to be present in all people.

Thus, there is a tendency to characterize every withdrawal or difficulty with the opposite sex as either homosexual, or due to latent homosexual drives. Every evidence in the male of weakness, lack of aggressiveness, timidity, sensitivity, inclination toward non-masculine pursuits, or interest in the arts become evidence of homosexuality or latent homosexuality. The homosexual in our culture is symbolized as the weak, passive male who is incompetent and incapable. His success in the masculine pursuits, particularly that of lust, is woefully lacking. Consequently, any traits or attitudes which resemble or are derivatives of these tendencies such as gentleness, softness, or sensitiveness, are also considered evidence of latent homosexuality, whether they have any relevance to sexual life or interest or not. The term is applied to those females whose behavior inclines toward the conventional male characteristics such as aggressiveness, interest in outdoor activities or skills, and, generally, pursuit of the so-called masculine concerns.

In therapy, so-called latent homosexual attitudes are often described as appearing in the course of psychoanalytic work. At these times, the abortive attempts to relate to people of the same sex, or to the therapist of the same sex, are viewed and described as evidence of latent homosexuality. Such activity may be indicative of growing capacities and desires for more tender and intimate participation of a non-sexual nature. They may only indicate a need for expression of interest and affection from the therapist. The necessity for labeling them as latent homosexuality arises not out of the nature of the activities, but from a preconception of the phenomenon. Often the therapist's own difficulty in dealing with closeness or intimacy from a patient of the same sex receives an acceptable rationalization by his labeling the patient's behavior as latently homosexual. Thus, the tendency to take homosexual phantasies or dreams (manifest content) at face value, while searching for the latent content in other dreams, often betrays this preconception. Too often, the interpretation of behavior in terms of latent homosexuality loses sight of the other conflictual aspects of the problem such as competitiveness, fear of aggression, or identification with the female figures who may play a strong role in the patient's current life.

The concept of latent homosexuality arises out of a dilemma which does not distinguish between sex as biology and the role which an individual's sex assigns him in a particular culture. The role of sex in human behavior is two-fold: its biological function in terms of race survival, and its extraprocreative or interpersonal role. The interpersonal aspect of the sexual function refers to the role it plays in fulfilling Man's need to avoid loneliness and to establish intimate and loving relationships with other human beings. Although this aspect of the sexual function becomes very intimately related to the biological aspects of sex, it is often extremely difficult to determine in a specific instance whether sexual activity is serving the purpose of procreation or of alleviating loneliness or anxiety or to prove one's manliness or to force some demand upon one's partner. Because the procreative function of sex is so intimately (though not necessarily) involved in the extraprocreative function of sex, they are often confused.[9]

For survival as an integrated, functioning individual, some people are willing to give up the procreative aspect of sex. This is characteristic of homosexual behavior. However, they still actively use its dramatic, integrating power for establishing contact with another human being, even of the same sex. Karen Horney and H. S. Sullivan, as well as others, view homosexuality and homosexual behavior in this light. Thus, the potentiality for the development of homosexuality is present in all of us. This potentiality can be fulfilled or by-passed. In adolescence, the final choice must be made. If we accept the bisexual theory of sexual development and the libido theory, then everyone has latent homosexual tendencies. If we view the choice of the sexual object as psychologically determined, then everyone has homosexual potentialities until the final heterosexual mode of sexual intimacy is accomplished. Consequently, whatever the framework, everyone can be considered potentially homosexual in a developmental sense. But because we are all potentially capable of being infected by the tubercule bacillus or the spirochete, we do not refer to ourselves as latently tuberculous or latently syphilitic. Consequently, latent homosexuality is a meaningless term in any new conception of homosexual behavior, since it always will characterize a possibility for behavior when heterosexual intimacy is interfered with—whether in early years by parental injunction or threats, or in later years in prisons or under circumstances where heterosexual behavior is impossible.

NOTES

1. Much of the material for this chapter was drawn from a paper entitled: The Concept of Latent Homosexuality, Am. J. Psychoanal. 17:161-169, by the author.

2. Sullivan put particular stress on the element of differing maturing rates in pre-adolescent chumships which tended to stimulate one of the partners into heterosexual contacts, leaving the late-maturing chum behind. Out of loneliness and lack of readiness for the venture, this inadequately motivated individual might attempt heterosexual relationships and fail miserably, and be too ashamed or frightened to try again. This would be particularly true if he were already timid, anxious, and uncertain about his acceptability. Sullivan felt this to be a potent factor in homosexual development.

See also:

Hall, Radcliff: The Well of Loneliness, New York, Pocket Books, 1959.
Salinger, J. D.: Catcher in the Rye. New York, Little Brown, 1951.
Schaffer, Peter: Five Finger Exercise. New York, Harcourt Brace, 1958.
Anderson, Robert: Tea and Sympathy. New York, Random House, 1954.

3. The inadequate definitions in these crucial times, when a homosexual is considered to be a security risk, can be a source of considerable abuse. For administrative and legal purposes, a precise definition is essential. However, there is no concensus among psychiatrists as to the precise limits of sexuality. While I suggest a workable definition, it must be obvious that this is based on a particular theoretical conception of homosexuality. In view of the expanding knowledge of this disorder which throws doubt on our previous points of view, every instance needs to be examined in its own right and in

terms of its own background and development. In this way we might be able to make more valid and equitable judgments about the nature of the particular case, its potentialities for cure, or its susceptibility to blackmail. The evidence of previous homosexual behavior may or may not signify present potentialities. Our predictions about the future behavior of any individuals depend upon an intimate knowledge of their character structure as well as their past behavior. Under the circumstances of an uncertain knowledge and a marked variety of professional opinion, much damage to an individual's character could be avoided if blanket rules or outmoded definitions made way for more intensive studies of individual situations. This applies not only to homosexuality but also to other vague psychiatric categories like sociopathic or psychopathic character disorders.

4. Ovesey, Lionel: Homosexual conflict. Psychiatry, Part 1. 18: 17-25, 1955. This article is one of a group of articles by this author dealing with this problem. They are all very useful in clarifying the problem of homosexuality.

5. Frenkel-Brunswick, Else: Psychoanalysis and the unity of science. Part 2 18: 163, 1955. Proceedings of the American Academy of Arts, and Sciences, 80: 1954.

6. Carnap, R.: Testability and meaning. In Philosophy of Science, 1936.

7. We indicated earlier that for Freud bisexuality had a distinctly masculine connotation even though it applied equally to both sexes.

8. Miller, James G., in an article: Towards a General Theory for the Behavoral Sciences, (American Psychologist, Sept. 1955) said: "Freud was impressed with the similarities between a number of related types of experiences which he included in his conception of sexuality. He recognized the similarity between physiological sexual gratification on the one hand and sensual gratification from art, music, and other sensory experiences and feelings of love and affection on the other. In stressing these similarities in order to make a generalization, he at times neglected the differences between them although he undoubtedly recognized them and would have acknowledged them immediately if they had been pointed out. There are theorists like Freud, concerned with making broad generalizations among dissimilar phenomena in every discipline."

9. Frank Alexander expresses this idea in more general terms and states that what distinguishes man as a personality is what he does with his faculties after he has secured his basic (biological) needs. He says: "What makes man different from all other species is that he uses his creative forces not only for biological growth and propagation, but also plastically for building different forms of culture which are not solely determined by survival needs. On the contrary, in his playful, non-utilitarian but libidinous, exuberant exercise of his faculties, man makes discoveries the utility of which is only later discovered." Psychoanalysis in Western Culture. Am. J. Psychiat. 112: 1956.

X

Love, Hostility and Depression

Hostility

THE RECOGNITION of the role of hostility and aggression in the development of personality was a second milestone in the history of the development of psychoanalytic theory. Initially, the emphasis on the effects of repressed sexual feelings and attitudes dominated all the theoretical developments. The neuroses were thought to be caused either by fixations or regressions in the development of the libido. After the First World War, Freud found it necessary to expand his instinct theory and to take into account the significant role of hostility and aggression in human behavior.

It had been apparent to Freud for some time that hostile attitudes were frequently repressed in the acculturation process and that such repression produced its inevitable consequences in the psychopathology of everyday life, as well as in the neuroses and psychoses. The significance of such factors were incorporated in his final instinct theory which posed the life instinct against the death instinct. The death instinct theory is a highly controversial conception and is accepted by very few psychoanalysts, orthodox or otherwise. It presumes that a force, instinctual in origin, operates towards the ultimate dissolution of life and a return to an inorganic state. This conception was supported by the prevalence of destructive activities in human behavior (in the individual as well as in a social sense), in wars, persecutions, crime, etc. These manifestations of destructiveness are discharged not only against others but also toward oneself as in the masochistic phenomena. Although Freud originally felt that such hostility was a derivative of the sexual instinct and related to sadism, he later felt that this could not account for the extensive manifestations of destructiveness, and he needed to postulate a separate instinct, that he called "thanatos." He presumed that destructiveness was present in the infant in the form of oral incorporative tendencies as well as on the anal level in the form of phantasies of retention and destruction. The sexual perversions of sadism and masochism were considered to be aim-inhibited expressions of the destructive instinct which were linked with the sex instinct.

The significance of Freud's death instinct theory lay in its theoretical as well as practical implications for therapy. Although Freud himself considered it to be speculation on a "far-fetched idea," some of his more orthodox followers have treated it literally and dealt with this concept as if it were an established fact of human behavior. The concept not only describes what is apparent to all, that is, a tendency towards destructiveness in humans, but insists that these feelings are instinctual in origin. Their presence is a fact of nature, not a result of experience, and is due to a human impulse to destroy. The death instinct theory and the innate destructiveness of man arises out of the extensive traditions of the Christian and pre-Christian theologies. It is best exemplified in the doctrine of the original sin and is supported by the rationalist viewpoint of Thomas Hobbes and the evolutionary theory of Darwin. Freud's theories were developed under the influence of these views regarding the "nature of man" and his formulations reflected the Judeo-Christian-Darwinian concept of man's essential evilness and destructiveness. The implication of this notion has had a broad effect on the classical theories in psychoanalysis in spite of the widespread disagreement with the death instinct theory, both theoretically and practically. The conception has been refuted by numerous theorists in recent years.

Some of the recent developments in psychoanalytic theory stimulated by sociological as well as anthropological studies have presented alternative views of the essential nature of man and his destructive instincts. The evidence for Freud's formulation is heavily documented historically and it would seem to be very difficult to refute his thesis that it must be innate and a basic motivational force in man's living. However, in recent years, it has become much clearer that hate can be a development of the acculturation process which can be accounted for in the same way that other psychological needs, desires and attitudes are produced in the human being. William C. Allee, in an article in *Science,* has said that "human altruistic drives are as firmly based on an animal ancestry as is man himself. Our tendencies towards goodness are as innate as our tendencies towards intelligence."[1] Horney has shown that the presence of hostility in man is the result of an adequate response to a situation which produces it. Hostility can be demonstrated as a response to some experience the individual is undergoing or has undergone. Such hostility while originally adequate and in response to a particular individual may become disportionate and generalized to others, and appear unrelated to the current instigating situation. This fact is understandable through our concepts of defense and transference. The early hostilities which develop in the infant or the child may stimulate defenses which eventuate in widespread sensitivities to attack and produce massive reactions in later years to only slight stimuli. But in essence they are defenses, resulting from threats to security, esteem or value systems. Such hostile or aggressive reactions are attempts to bolster or support a weak and inadequate ego rather than biological or innate drives towards destructiveness. Hatred, for some theorists like Ian Suttie, owes all its meaning to a demand for love. He says:

Thus 'love threatened' becomes anxious that is to say partly transformed into anxiety. So far as it is denied it is transformed into hate, while external interference (supplanting) switches it into jealousy. In the same way its rejection—the conclusive refusal by the loved object to accept or return it—converts it into despair; the feelings of unworthiness of a lesser degree make it guilt or shame; the loss of the object, under circumstances not inspiring resentment induces grief, while sympathy with that object's suffering transforms love into pity. In all these constellations of emotion, we can usually observe a rough quantitative equivalence wherever one form of feeling comes to replace another; and on that account, and because no agreement is possible as to the number of primary feelings which exist, it seems to me better to suppose that we are dealing with a single "fund" of love—energy capable of endless transformations of quality or aim even into the apparent opposite of love—hate.[2]

The extent of these hostilities reflects the low state of security of the individual. If hostility is a response to some threat to our security, then it is capable of being explored and alleviated. The death instinct theories supported the notion that the freeing of hostility and bringing it into awareness was a therapeutic task in itself. It encouraged the un-therapeutic goal of being hostile or being able to express hostility as an index of maturity. This tendency, while possibly freeing the individual of many repressed, hostile feelings, interfered with the further search for the underlying cause of these hostile feelings, which would obviate the necessity for having them.

The freeing of such feelings often endangered the security of the patient and increased his anxiety. At best, it could not improve the impaired relationships of the individual since it would tend to alienate further those individuals toward whom the hostility was directed. It is quite effective to encourage a previously inhibited and placating individual to be more aggressive, outspoken and direct. The recognition of his hostilities may allow him to initiate more effective relationships which heretofore were caught in compulsive patterns of appeasing and exaggerated reaction formations of pseudo-friendliness. However, this is only a first step in the search for the more basic issues which aroused such hostility and required such defensive techniques.

Freud's conception of an innate hostility has clouded the matter of aggression. Freud did not clarify or distinguish between aggression as an activity directed against someone or something which was derived from hostile attitudes based on unconscious elements and self-assertion which is the expression of positive, constructive elements in one's personality based on a sound ego. This distinction is imperative, since the goal of psychoanalysis involves the development and encouragement of self-assertive attitudes and the appraisal and elucidation of the sources of aggressive or destructive attitudes. Horney, Silverberg and other analysts have emphasized this distinction. Horney has drawn clear lines in distinguishing those phenomena, while Silverberg has formulated the very vauable notion of "effective aggression" which is synonymous with self-assertion.[3]

The notion of an innate or instinctual basis for hostility has encouraged the classical psychoanalytic theorists to view all hostile feelings or attitudes as primary and all tender and benevolent feelings as secondary. The friendly or non-aggressive attitudes are viewed in a variety of ways as reaction formations, sublimation, denials, etc., of the underlying aggressive instincts. Tenderness becomes a derivative of the aggressive feelings and is not distinguished from tenderness which has as its basis a productive and loving relationship which develops in infancy. It is obvious that a great many non-aggressive feelings and attitudes do arise in this way. Threats to one's integrity may set up hostile defensive attitudes which may need to be repressed, to allow the individual to function in his environment. The issue, then, is one of investigating the source of the hostility by exploring the threats or supposed threats to the individual.

In a system where tender feelings are defensive reactions to aggressive attitudes, therapy would necessarily focus on origins of the tender feelings. However, in the neo-Freudian framework, tenderness, except when it is a pseudo or exaggerated response, is not subject to critical scrutiny but recognized as a primary attitude which experience can distort rather than vice versa.

For many analysts, the source of man's neurotic and psychotic developments lie in the repression of hostile feelings. The dynamics of many disorders, such as schizophrenia, depression, and a multitude of neurotic states, originate in the inability to adequately deal with one's ambivalent feelings, particularly the hostile ones. It was Freud who emphasized the significance of the aggressive instincts by noting its widespread and overt manifestations in the World War. But Freud, who was the father of the notion that unconscious and repressed feelings are responsible for the development of psychopathology, overlooked the fact that if aggression was so actively present and manifest in the lives of human beings, then it would be less likely to be involved in producing neurotic and psychotic states. One might reply that the overwhelming overt evidence of such aggression only pointed to even greater sources in unconscious. This might well be. However, if Freud's observations are to be credited, then it is the aggressive instincts which have been responsible for man's destructiveness through the ages. These hostilities have been expressed not only in the perpetual wars which have plagued man, but also in the gross cultural practices of primitive man as well. Early myths and rituals and a cultural disregard for human life as in the Roman spectacles have spoken clearly of such mass destructive tendencies. Picaresque literature and the modern detective story with all its variants attest to the infinite and more subtle techniques for expressing such hostile feelings. Consequently, we are impressed not only with the extent and variety of man's destructiveness but with his capacity to express it through the ages. It would be difficult in the face of such massive evidence to the contrary to develop a thesis demonstrating that hostility has been repressed in man. Rather one is struck by the ease with which it is expressed, not repressed. In the face of this, we might well ask why it should be such a strong factor in the development and maintenance of neurotic and psychotic illnesses. It is likely that, in spite of the endless opportunities for releasing aggression, much remains repressed. This is the experience of every psychoanalyst.

However, the key to understanding the neuroses lies not in the repression of hostility but in the repression of tenderness, benevolence and human warmth and friendship. This is the thesis of the neo-Freudian psychoanalysts who are more impressed with the inability to acknowledge and express tenderness than with man's ability to recognize his hostilities. In our culture, and in most of the cultures of the centuries before and after Christ, the cultural ideal was framed in terms of the aggressive, powerful male who made free with his powers of destructiveness. Christ's teachings produced a revolution because they spoke of the powers of love, tenderness, and non-aggression. However, the revolution was only skin deep and our present cultural ideal still remains the same—an individual who is manly, determined and hard, an individual who does not yield to his softness and tenderness and who restricts his loving attitudes and feelings to a limited group of people, his family and close intimates. This has necessitated a massive repression of man's soft, tender and kindly feelings in order to achieve esteem in his cultural milieu. This is strikingly apparent in the neurotic states where the individual utilizes aggressive attitudes and hostile feelings not only as expressions of his anxiety and insecurity but also to fulfill his preconceptions of the acceptable cultural ideal. The price of maintaining some of the tenderness which characterizes the female has been to reduce her, at least in Freud's psychology, to a second-rate citizen. It is precisely those character traits which are a result of her having retained strong emotional feelings and dependent passive attitudes which were characterized as neurotic.

The present trend in psychoanalytic theorizing is towards recognizing the inability to express and experience tenderness as a basic factor in the neurotic and psychotic development. Hostility is never lacking in our patients. They experience it freely and express it freely before and during treatment. An increase in their capacity to recognize heretofore repressed or unexplored areas of hostility adds little to the resolution of their neurotic difficulties except to open the way for the development of the capacity to love. In our culture, tenderness is more strongly tabooed than sex. Freud pointed out very correctly that hate is more adhesive and more strongly clung to than love. It binds relationships more strongly than love, and hated objects are given up with greater difficulty than loved ones. This is, however, an aspect of the neurotic entanglement and not a manifestation of a healthy affectionate relationship. This tendency to hang on to hostile relationships only underlies the crucial role that hostility plays in supporting the neurosis and the anticipated uneasiness about the possibility of an emerging loving attitude. The basic problem in neurosis is the inability to love and live productively, which is deeply repressed but available to almost everyone. This puts an entirely new light on the problem of hostility which does not minimize its role in human behavior, but places it in its proper adaptational framework. It denies the instinctual nature of hostility and aggression and sees it as a consequence of a frustrated search for love and a need to love others. Some critics of the neo-Freudian views on hostility refer to this idea as a hangover from Romanticism. Such criticism has its roots in the thesis that man is essentially evil and destructive. It accepts the Darwinian view of man and the innate destructive capacities of man which are biologically inherited from his animal existence. However, current contributions to anthropology and biology emphasize the cooperative nature of the animal kingdom including man's innate capacities for love and participation in a collaborative fashion. It is hardly romantic to postulate that the new born has no hostile or destructive attitudes except those which arise out of his contacts with the environment. It may not be any more valid than the reverse postulate but it develops a system of psychology that in most ways is as explanatory and heuristic as the "basic destructiveness of man." In many ways it is a more accurate portrayal of man and his potentialities. Because it is more optimistic it does not imply that it is less realistic. The issue in psychiatric terms must rest on which hypothesis is most fruitful in understanding man and his distortions, and which theory has the greatest potentialities for uncovering the still undiscovered sources of man's inability to achieve a greater productive capacity in his living.

Love

The problem of love and its role in man's psychology has been considerably advanced by the cultural psychoanalysts once the concept of the death instinct and the libido theory had been abandoned.

Love for Freud was a matter of genital maturity. If the libidinal development pursued a clear course from the oral to the genital area, the capacity to love would follow directly and automatically. The newer theories visualize maturity in terms of a need for closer relationship and an intimacy based on loving relationships. This orientation places the maternal role more in the forefront of the forces acting on the development of personality, since it is more a matter of intimacy and trust, as opposed to Freud's emphasis on the authoritative, paternal figure who played the key role in the resolution of the Oedipus complex as well as in the development of the superego.

Freud visualized love and its associated qualities like tenderness, sympathy, affection, etc., as derivatives of the libido. Since the human has fixed quantities of libido, love for oneself becomes impoverished when one loves another and vice versa. Freud said that "Love for oneself knows only one barrier—love for others, love for objects."[4]

This notion, which comprises the concept of narcissism, sees love as the investment of others with libido which is withdrawn from oneself. This has resulted in an unfortunate tendency to confuse love of self with egocentricity or selfishness or self love.

Fromm has clarified this question by distinguishing loving relationships from sado-masochistic symbioses. In truly loving relationships, love for others and love for self are not alternatives or contradictory but complimentary and conjunctive. The capacity to esteem oneself and regard oneself with respect, concern and affection allows the individual to respect and esteem others. Freud in his concept of love was describing a variety of relationships which only loosely could be described as love, in which the partners have a mutually exploitative arrangement which allows for exchanges which are almost all selfishly motivated. A truly loving relationship is the expression of the maximum potentialities for giving and taking and is derived from the earliest experience in the nursing period, where there is the maximum unfettered and unqualified giving and getting in infant and mother. Ian Suttie has developed this thesis at length and is impressed with the notion that love is the first formed and directed emotional relationship, and the search for restoration of this maternal love inspires a great deal of man's activity, in art, science and religion. He makes a clear distinction between love and sex although a completely loving relationship integrates sex in the genital sense. Love, he states, is quite different from the organic appetites. Love does not question who gives and who gets. Rather, it is a culmination of mutually reciprocal feelings. When this does not occur anxiety results. This explains the capacity of love and sex to dissipate anxiety as well as the capacity for anxiety to interfere with sex and loving relationships. He places great stress on the taboos of tenderness in our culture which makes love and tenderness qualities that need to be repressed rather than expressed.

Love has been defined by recent theorists in interpersonal terms rather than as a biological development. Nelson Foote[5] defines love as "that relationship between one person and another which is most conducive to the optimal development of both." This definition makes no reference to any biological requirements except as it implies that a loving relationship will be optimally suited to fulfill all the needs of the partners. This definition is very similar to the definition of H. S. Sullivan, who in his *Conceptions of Modern Psychiatry* describes love as follows: "When the satisfaction or security of another person becomes as significant to one as is one's own satisfaction or security, then the state of love exists."[6] For Sullivan, love entered the life of an individual in the preadolescent era. At this time, another individual becomes equally important as oneself in all areas. Love was an expression of intimacy devoid of lust at first, since it has its beginnings prior to the maturation of the sexual apparatus. Although Freud described this as the homosexual era, Sullivan viewed it exclusively as an era of intimacy, tenderness, and collaborative companionship. After the maturation of the gonads, sexual intimacy complicated the picture. In those instances where intimacy was established with people of the same sex, the change over of interest to the opposite sex was smooth and basically sound. This allowed for the development of sexual and non-sexual intimacy towards the opposite sexes and encouraged the development of loving relationships. Love thus becomes a factor in patterning sex behavior and a conjunctive force in satisfying the need for intimacy. This is clearly the converse of Freud's view that genital maturity permits a loving relationship to exist.

Sullivan was not unaware of the beginnings of intimacy and the rudiments of love in the infant-mother relationship. He believed, however, that it did not flower into love as a responsible human activity until preadolescence. Fromm[7] has expanded the concept of love and described its role in productive living. He recognized that there is a positive striving for love in all humans which is qualitatively different from dependency, even though dependent needs are mutually satisfied in a state of love. Masochistic dependency or exaggeratedly dependent needs are derived from feelings of insecurity and scarcity. These dependent relationships are exploitative without mutual respect or integrity. Fromm says that to love a person productively implies that one feels responsible for his life; not only for his physical existence but for the growth and development of all his human powers. Love is then an expression of intimacy between individuals where the integrity of each other's individual self is preserved. Selfishness is not the absence of love for others with an enhanced self-love, but is an indication of an emptiness and inability to love oneself. This emptiness interferes with loving others. To love another person requires a sufficient degree of self-affirmation in order to respect and intelligently affirm the worthiness of the other person.

It is necessary to distinguish love and lust and to see it combined in mature healthy loving relationships in order to get a proper perspective of the difference between love, sentimentality, and dependency. In this light, aggression can be identified as a striving for love and as a defense against the loss or threat of the loss of love.

Love is a focal point in most of the neo-Freudian theories. Neurosis is described as a disease characterized by the inability to love productively, and the neurotic is seen as an individual who has an increased need for love and a decreased capacity to achieve it. Love supplies the incentive for growth and development and establishes the conditions for such growth.

Montagu summarizes this view when he says:

> Love is the principal developer of the potentialities for being human, it is the chief stimulus to the development of social competence and the only quality in the world capable of producing that sense of belongingness and relatedness to the world of humanity that every healthy human being desires and develops. Love is creative both for the receiver and the giver. Genuine love can never harm or inhibit, it can only benefit and create freedom and order. Love has a fairness and a discipline of its own for which there can be no substitute.[8]

DEPRESSION

Freud's theory as well as Karl Abraham's concepts regarding the origin of depressions were a direct application of their views. The modification of these views by current theorists derived from the objections to the death instinct has enabled us to get a clearer view of the depressive process. The earliest dynamic view of depression was presented by Freud in his classic study, "Mourning and Melancholia," published in 1917. In this paper Freud likened the process of melancholia to that of mourning where the process consisted of the patient's ego replacing the lost object by an identification which could then serve the ambivalent feelings towards the lost object. In this way, the depressed individual could express his hatred towards the lost object by acts of hostility towards himself. Mourning and melancholia were similar except that in melancholia the loss was unconscious, while in mourning the loss was conscious. Melancholia was thus the response to a lost object to which there were ambivalent feelings. This loss could be real or imagined and the symptomatology could be understood by noting that the patient accused himself of the very things he hated in the lost object.

In 1924 Karl Abraham expanded this notion and noted that the identification amounts to a forceful devouring and destroying the lost object. This helped explain the preponderance of oral factors in the depressive illness. In 1927 Sandor Rado recognized that what was considered to be a lost love was in reality the feeling of loss of love and that the depression was essentially a "desperate cry" for love. This took the emphasis away from the question of hostility and self-punishment in the process of mourning and highlighted the depressive search for the lost elements of love in the relationship. Later, he began to view the reaction as a miscarried process of repair where the individual was attempting to overcome the loss or threatened loss of love. This formulation was the forerunner of many views which took the focus away from melancholia as a process related to mourning where there is no actual loss and emphasized the element of loss of love even where the individual was present and available. It did more than that, however. Viewing the depressive process as motivated by a threatened loss of love rather than as based on hostility permitted us to examine the process as an individual's attempt to restore a loving relationship rather than as a vindictive and aggressive attack by the individual who feels he has been abandoned. The destructive aspects of the depressive process lies not in any basic hostility, but in the excessive, exaggerated, and almost pitiful plea for the recovery of the essential elements in a lost relationship. Horney viewed the depressive process as an accompanying mood to all neurotic states and not a specific syndrome, since the fear of loss of love was present in all neuroses. She indicated that the self-accusations could not be accounted for by the process of introjection which Abraham emphasized. In addition, she felt that this was not the usual picture in melancholia.

Sullivan viewed grief as a process of detaching oneself from a significant person and he thought of it as a constructive process. The depressive process, however, was essentially destructive and binding and only superficially related to grief.

A close examination of grief or mourning and depression or melancholia reveal that the relationships between them is based only on the presence of the affect of grief, but otherwise they are quite dissimilar in their purpose, dynamics and effects. Mourning occurs following the loss of a person, value or cause, where the relationship to the person or value was primarily positive and based on tenderness, love or productive interest. In these instances the neurotic elements in the relationship are minimal and the process of grief allows the mourner to detach himself and sever the relationship and reintegrate his personality without that person, value or thing. It is a constructive process and involves no loss of self-esteem but rather often produces a heightened self-esteem through identification and retention of the virtues and assets of the lost person or cause. Hostility is usually not present, but a warm, poignant and inspired recollection of the lost object is notable. It is fairly brief and allows the mourner to continue his active participation in his current living.

Melancholia, on the other hand, is the exaggerated response to the loss or threatened loss of a person or a thing and is characterized by hostile recriminations towards the lost object, with threats and demands for the reinstatement of the previous relationship. This relationship was not exclusively a loving one but an ambivalent relationship based on neurotic sado-masochistic ties and exaggerated dependencies. Thus, the depression is a response which binds rather than separates the individual and may persist for prolonged periods until some new integration is established generally with another person or thing on the same neurotic terms. There is considerable diminution of self-esteem and the loss is felt as a rejection. The lost person or object was generally intimately involved in the melancholic's neurotic integration and the loss of the person or thing endangered the neurotic structure. Since the original relationship was one of mixed hatred and love the bind is great and the detachment more difficult. This process, consequently, is not subsumed under the dynamics of love, but is rather a process designed to reinstate a neurotic integration. In this sense it is destructive.

In a scholarly article on the "Manic Depressive Psychosis" by Mabel B. Cohen et al.,[9] findings similar to the above were obtained in an intensive study of the life history and the character structure of the depressive patient. They discovered that the depressive reaction occurs in response to the patient's inability to live up to his parents' and his own expectation of himself. His inability to deal with others as a whole, separate individual perpetuates his tendency to deal with others in extremes as good or bad, black or white, and his response to frustration or loss is also in the extremes of depression or mania. His relationship with others is generally in terms of an exploitative dependency gratified by his manipulation of them. They noted that the hostile factors in depression were overstressed and were not the major element in the illness. The depression was found to be a response of a person with a particular constellation of character traits who, when frustrated or denied, responds by exaggerated tendencies to reinstate the lost "neurotic relationship."

This study, by implication, described the illness as an attempt to repair, reinstate, or revive a relationship which by the very nature of the symptoms of the reaction prevents its possibility.

If depression is a "cry for love" or an attempt to force the return of a lost love, then it should be closely related to anxiety which is a response to the loss or threat of loss of approval from a significant other person. Anxiety in broader terms could be defined as the apprehension produced by the threat to some value regarded as essential to the integration of the individual. Consequently, anxiety should result from the same issues which produce depression. This is strikingly so, and anxiety and depression are frequently coexistent and possibly always present together. For some people they are indistinguishable. This confusion was particularly important in the era of the physiological therapies where electric shock, for example, was particularly useful in depression but contraindicated for anxiety states. Although closely related they can be distinguished. Anxiety is the apprehension of the threat of loss of love, while depression is the reaction to a real or supposedly real loss of love or something held essential to the individual. Depression could thus be viewed as a particular kind of defense against anxiety designed to reinstate the lost object. If it can be viewed as a defense, then it has its origins in the ego and not in the id as

Freud and Abraham had visualized it. The question of hostility would thus be a secondary manifestation and its presence could be understood as a reaction to being denied or abandoned. The depressive process is characterized by preoccupation with one's worthlessness coupled with a deep resentment and open hostility towards the environment. While bemoaning his miserable state, the depressed individual is engaged in attempting to force the environment to fulfill his unsatiable needs for reassurance, interest and attention. This he achieves by emphasizing the great loss, by the appeal of utter despair and helplessness, and by an angry demand for the return of his lost values. Because of his failure or supposed failure or defeat, he feels that he can never be loved again. It is an all or none reaction, since he cannot visualize any acceptance in spite of or because of his failure. The feeling that he will never be loved again is reinforced by the actual rejections he receives due to his increasing insatiable and hostile demands on the environment. This forcing, manipulating and exploiting is very apparent in the depressive process and has been the issue that has received the greatest attention by the older theorists. Recent theories and clinical studies have deemphasized this factor.

The hostilities which are manifested in the depression arise to a large extent from the frustration of the dependency needs which are prominent in these individuals. In the depressive process this is manifested by their clinging and demanding attitudes. However, we quickly discover that this dependency is covert while the need to be totally independent and omnipotent is a major personality characteristic of depressed patients. The display of independence is a technique for covering up the marked dependency they experience. This plays a prominent role in the illness where the patient rejects or distorts any sympathetic reassurance because it is evidence of weakness and dependency. The need to be entirely independent underlies most depressions, and a great deal of the hostility is a response to displays of weakness and dependency; hate is directed precisely at those individuals who try to fill these needs. This is the dilemma in the patient and in the therapy of the illness. It clarifies Rado's notion in describing depression as a process of miscarried repair, since the techniques used to repair the damage are those most likely to exaggerate it, and the symptoms of the depression are the adaptational technique designed to overcome the loss.

A patient who became depressed six weeks after the birth of her child demonstrated the problem of dependency versus independency. She responded to the birth of a child as a threat to her value system which involved being a successful business woman. She secretly avoided taking the tranquilizing drugs which were given to her and avoided calling her physician until she became panicky about thoughts of killing herself and her baby. She considered it a weakness to be ill and to take medication to overcome her illness. Her phantasies assumed that people would be contemptuous of her for being ill. She required to be omnipotent and only in her illness could she justify her extremely demanding and whining attitudes which forced total compliance from her husband. She was alternately hostile and self-derogatory, but what was most prominent was her inability to adjust and compromise her ideals which she felt were lost in the necessity to mother her new born baby.

What was originally described as evidences of introjection and hostile incorporation of the object is now viewed as the manifestation of the obsessional mechanism where the depressed person attempts to control and exploit the environment through force, intimidation and threats. Such activities are interpreted by the environment as hostile and are attributed to the hostility of the patient. The patient, however, is searching for love and the return of the lost values through the use of power operations. The environment, feeling attacked and tormented, responds with anger and *retaliation*. Thus, the process is more often one of hostility from the environment produced by a demanding despair of the patient rather than vice versa.

The relationship of depression to the obsessional dynamism has been noted by many theorists. The obsessional need for magical control which is frequently frustrated may result in brief or prolonged despressive episodes. The failure to achieve the impossible standards of the obsessional neurotic is often felt as a loss of an essential value. Depression may supervene in an attempt to recover them. When the power operation of the obsessional succeeds or the magical omnipotence is fulfilled then the individual may become grandiose to the point of a manic response. Lewin[10] and others have described the manic reaction as a defense against the depression through furious distractions and exaggerated feelings of worthlessness. However, it might also be regarded as an aspect of the same process of attempting to retain a value essential to the neurotic integration. When it succeeds mania results and when it fails we get a depression. Depression may precede or follow the mania, depending on the course of events in the experiences of these individuals who respond to their anxiety through a defense of depression.

The explanation for the success of the physiological therapies like electroshock or insulin sometimes suggested that the patient responded because he was receiving punishment which relieved his super-ego harshness. This interpretation was a logical outcome of the theory of depression in which hostility was expressed toward the introjected ambivalent loved object. The shock treatment was experienced as punishment for the hostility which relieved the patient of the necessity for expressing hostility toward his own self. This explanation received only limited acceptance since it was evident that only few patients viewed shock therapy as punishment. The value of the tranquilizing drugs in the depressive states destroyed all the rationale for the above interpretation.[11]

For many theorists the depressed patient is not looking for punishment, but for love. His value system has been endangered by the loss of something essential to his integration and he demands that it be reinstated. The value of shock therapy and the tranquilizing drugs may be due to the temporary disruption of the patient's value system which results either from the cortical confusion following the electroshock or the lessened interest in any value systems which follows the use of the tranquilizing drugs. Cortical confusion was considered to be a necessary condition for benefit to be derived from shock therapy or lobotomy procedures. Recovery from the confusion frequently resulted in a return of the depressed condition when the old value systems were maintained. However, the confusion and sedation often allowed for temporary disruption or at times prolonged alteration of the patient's value systems with relief from the depressive symptoms. The high incidence of spontaneous recovery from depression could be attributed to the same reason where an adjustment of his values permitted him to abandon his previous values or standards.

Consequently, a theory of depression can be formulated which supplies most of the answers to the clinical data present in the depressive reactions without postulating a death instinct and without a mechanical application of the libido theory. Ego psychology has focused on alternative aspects of the process which yield more operational data and in many ways are more explanatory and heuristic than Freud's conceptions.

In summary, it states that depression is a technique of dealing with anxiety where the apprehension of loss of some value essential to the personality integration has become a conviction. The depressive maneuver ensues in order to force the return of such a value. It is a process of repair, misdirected to be sure and destructive in its configuration, but an effort to prevent even greater disintegration of the personality structure. Dynamically, it is a power operation and utilizes the technique of manipulation and exploitation in order to force the environment or a particular individual to restore or replace by some gesture or attitude the lost or supposedly lost value. Whether the loss is conscious or unconscious, the symptoms attempt by coercive, insistent demands and angry rebukes to force the return of regard, affection or acceptance of these values. In some instances the loss is clearly apparent, such as the reaction to repeated failure, the failure to win a loved object, or in the involutional period where the loss is expressed in terms of loss of potency. In other instances the loss is not so easily apparent. The environment is antagonized by the depressive's insistent demands and concern or regard from the environment is interpretated as hostile or degrading and is rejected. This produces the vicious circle so familiar in all neuroses. The implications for therapy in a revised theoretical framework are extremely significant. Rather than an encouragement to express hostility which would be the logical response of the old theory, there is an attempt to reduce the hostile demands and rebukes. An effort must be made to identify the lost value or values without a generalized overindulgence and reassurance. This encourages the patient to feel that the loss is replaceable and that the old neurotic values can be revamped. The lost object is invariably an exaggerated, overly idealized value or goal incapable of ever being actualized and this must be brought down to a reality level. This involves the subtle mixture of regard for the patient's real worth and a firm denial of his extreme demands and pressures. It is essential to recognize that the patient feels that something vital has been lost or denied him and he generalizes this feeling into one of worthlessness and unworthiness to be loved. At the same time, by his hostile reproaches, he interferes with the possibility of altering this evaluation. Thus, it takes a careful sense of timing and sensitivity to determine when one should be firm without being rejecting and when one must be sympathetic without seeming to be indulgent. Too often, the therapist responds either with exaggerated concern or hostile rebukes toward the patient. We feel sorry for him, yet angry with him. Although both these reactions are necessary and useful they can be used at the wrong time. Anger can be a useful tool for the therapist, but it must be accompanied by a conviction regarding the patient's essential worthwhileness and a rejection of his destructive activities. Such a therapeutic approach recognizes both the patient's loss and his tendency to utilize destructive techniques to repair the loss.

Our notions about suicide have been greatly expanded as an outcome of the neo-Freudian views on depression and the death instinct. It has become clearer that suicide is more than an act of revenge inspired by hostile feelings towards another person. While this does occur, the act of suicide more clearly represents an act of despair and an expression of the hopeless efforts to recover or regain some lost values or needs. Consequently, suicide is most prominent in depressions where this issue is paramount, but it also occurs under circumstances where depression is not the major factor. Despair not depression is the most prominent element in suicide, and it may arise from a hopeless resignation or a failure to achieve an exaggerated idealization which accounts for many of the suicides in adolescence. Although it can be a hostile gesture, it is mostly the despair over the impossibility of fulfilling some exaggerated standards and requirements. It occurs frequently during the recovery or in the early stages of a depressive process where there is intense preoccupation with the lost values. It rarely occurs in the depths of the depression. Although suicide is frequently characterized as a turning in of the hostility previously overtly expressed, this interpretation arises out of the notion of depression as a problem of hostility. More often, the hostile elements in suicide are accidental consequences of the act. Primarily, however, they are expressions of disappointment in the search for love or the possibilities of fulfillment in loving relationships.

Suicide which follows financial loss, disappointment in love, or following the awareness of fatal illnesses, etc., can be better understood in these terms than from a "hostility theory." The motives for partial or slow suicides in the persistently masochistic person can also be understood in this light.

The cultural theorists by reorienting the conceptions of hate, love, aggression and hostility, have taken greater cognizance of man's need for positive loving relationships of intimacy and companionship rather than his essential destructiveness as implied in the death instinct or in his aggressive impulses. Hate is a response to a frustrated search for love and the consequences of this failure to achieve loving relationships produces a multitude of defensive reactions subsumed under the rubric of hostility. The emphasis is neither trivial or semantic, but crucial to the development of personality theory. It has a marked effect on our therapeutic research designs as well as on our overall philosophic view of the essential nature of man.

NOTES

1. Allee, W. C.: Where angels fear to tread. A contribution from general sociology to human ethics. Science, 97:251, 1943. There are in addition a large number of articles dealing with an emphasis on the altruistic and cooperative drives in man as opposed to his destructive drives. Ashley Montagu, in his book: On Being Human, New York, H. Schuman Co., 1950 deals very extensively with this problem and quotes a great deal of source material. See his book: The Direction of Human Development, New York, Harpers & Co., 1955.

also, LaBarre, Weston: The Human Animal, Chicago University of Chicago Press, 1954.

Dai, B.: Socio-psychiatric approach, to personality organization. Am. Sociological Rev. 17:44-49, 1952.

Allee, W. C.: Cooperation among animals with human implications. New York, H. Schuman & Co., 1951.

2. Suttie, Ian: The Origins of Love and Hate. New York, Julian Press, 1952. This is one of the early efforts to examine Freud's concepts regarding love as they grow out of his instinct theories. It is an excellent analysis of this vital subject and supported many of the neo-Freudian conceptions regarding the primary role of love and tenderness in neurotic development as opposed to sex or hostility.

3. Silverberg, W. V.: Childhood Experience and Personal Destiny. New York, Springer Publishing Co., 1952.

4. Freud, S.: Group psychology and analysis of the ego. In Collected Papers. pp. 54-57.

5. Foote, Nelson N.: Love. Psychiatry 16:245-251, 1953.

6. Sullivan, H. S.: Conceptions of Modern Psychiatry. Washington, D. C., William A. White Foundation, 1947, p. 20.

7. Fromm, E.: Man for Himself. New York, Rhinehart and Co., 1947. This book deals with the problems of man in achieving a productive way of life which is synonymous with loving. By productiveness Fromm does not mean producing in quantitative terms or just doing or keeping busy. He attempts to describe a way of life and a type of character structure that utilizes all of one's capacities in a concern and interest in the welfare of others which is the result of concern and interest in one's own welfare.

8. Montagu, Ashley: Direction of Human Development (see Bibliography) pp. 293-294.

9. Cohen, M. B., Baker, G., Cohen, R. A., Fromm-Reichman, F., Weigert, E. V.: An intensive study of 12 cases of manic-depressive psychosis. Psychiatry 17:103-132, 1954. This is an excellent study that indicates the manner in which statistical studies, using the psychoanalytic method of study can be highly rewarding and can clarify a great deal of psychoanalytic theorizing.

10. Lewin, Bertram: Psychoanalysis of Elation. W. W. Norton & Co., 1950.

11. Although drug therapy is never viewed as punishment since it produces relief from anxiety, it does, however, produce a mildly confused state and a capacity to abandon the rigid standards and demands the depressed individual tends to make on himself. By reducing his tendency to "care too much," and to accept himself without undue self criticism, it permits the individual to revise and possibly abandon previously fixed positions regarding his role and his status. In this way, the tranquillizing drugs may be curative rather than simply ameliorative, as are the other types of physiological therapies. Anything, whether it be rest, removal from sources of anxiety, drugs, electroshock, sea voyages, or psychotherapy which allows the depressed individual to diminish his spastic rigid grasp on his standards can allow for a re-examination and possibly reorientation of these standards which will relieve the depression. Ataractic drugs, as well as the stimulating drugs, are useful in depressions for this reason, I believe, rather than for their specific action on the neural centers.

XI

Masochism

MASOCHISM was originally described as a sexual perversion in a novel, *Venus in Furs*, by Leopold von Sacher-Masoch. Freud originally used the term to describe a variety of perversions closely related to sadism and later extended the meaning to include a variety of activities other than sexual, in which an individual was abused, humiliated or degraded.

Masochism, Freud believed, was related to the death instinct. He described it as a secondary development in the attempts to deal with one's aggressive or hostile impulses, and when linked with the sexual instincts, it produced the masochistic sexual perversion. This formulation was descriptive and in line with the libido theory. However, it required further elaborations in order to encompass the other varieties of masochism which Freud called feminine and moral masochism.

Masochism has been on the human scene for a long time and has been understood in a variety of ways. Man has abused himself from time immemorial, and at certain times and under certain circumstances this was highly regarded. It was particularly true in religious movements where it became institutionalized. Under these circumstances it was called mortification and was regarded as highly virtuous. Thus, the significance of masochistic activity was intimately related to the cultural setting. In recent centuries, and particularly with the advances in psychology, it has come to be regarded as a pathological phenomenon and subsumed under the discipline of psychiatry.

Recent alterations in classical psychoanalytic theory have stressed its role in human behavior as adaptive rather than instinctual. Thus Wilhelm Reich, who was a dedicated classicist in most respects, first described its role as an adjustive maneuver designed to deal with disastrous personal or social conditions. Karen Horney agreed with his views and recognized that masochistic behavior attempted to deal with these conditions by ridding the individual of his "own self." And thus the individual was able to achieve some satisfaction in his living. Erich Fromm viewed it as an extreme technique of relating in which an individual with unbearable feelings of aloneness and powerlessness engaged in a relationship even though he suffered, if it were the only one available. Frequently, this involved the establishment of a sado-masochistic symbiosis, since no other variety of relationship could be established. These interpretations emphasized the adaptational function of masochistic behavior and clarified the motivational elements in the phenomenon. They also stressed the reparative role rather than the destructive aspects of the process. Jules Masserman saw the process in even simpler terms as "an experientially derived pattern of current sacrifices for eventual gains."[1]

The problem of masochism has interested many behavioral scientists because of its universality. In the past twenty or thirty years masochism has been seen as the inevitable result of the neurotic process and not the cause of it. The neurotic's inability to fulfill his exaggerated and idealized demands stirs up his hatred for his weaknesses and inadequacy and produces a variety of self-derogatory activities extending from disgust and contempt for himself to actual physical abuse. In this framework it is always pathological. However, some philosophers and psychoanalysts view it as an inevitable accompaniment of human existence, since man's potentialities can never fully be realized and, thus, a feeling of powerlessness is inevitable. This is most clearly expressed in existential philosophy and its applications to psychoanalytic theory.

For Freud, masochism was a process of achieving pleasure through pain through the fusion of the aggressive and libidinal instincts. Fromm, Masserman, Rado, Sullivan, and others see it as an attempt to achieve some satisfaction as do other human activities, except that pain and discomfort are either prerequisites or unavoidable accompaniments to these efforts. However one views the genesis and dynamics of the masochistic process, certain elements in the process are mutually agreed upon. These include the tendency to berate, belittle or to actively destroy the self or part of the self in order to obtain some psychic reward or relief from tension. Sullivan, in his *Conceptions of Modern Psychiatry* (see Bibliography), said it in this way: "A large number of people appear to go to rather extraordinary lengths to get themselves imposed on, abused, humiliated, and what not, but as you get further data you discover that this quite often pays; in other words, they get the thing they want, and the things they want are satisfaction and security from anxiety. Those people who get themselves abused and so on are indirectly getting the other people involved in doing something useful in exchange."

In the process of self-degradation the individual achieves several goals at the same time. First, he manages to escape *real* responsibility for his actions and to present a justifiable excuse for his failures. It allows him to manipulate and exploit others through his display of utter powerlessness and this may fulfill his secret needs or else obtain some good will through a demonstration of his suffering. However, we usually discover that the individual, through his suffering is fulfilling some value or set of values which he holds essential to his integration, while degrading the opposite set of values. The values which are cherished are not only moral but frequently refer to certain personal qualities, attitudes or standards which are considered essential for survival. Often, these values are incorporated into a code of ethics or personal philosophy which are supported by numerous moral or intellectual rationalizations. Thus, the process which at first appears to be one of suffering, is soon noted to be an adaptational device designed to maintain the individual's integrity in his goal for survival. Masochism can no longer be viewed primarily as a sexual perversion or as a derivative of the aggressive instinct. It must be seen as a universal technique employed by man throughout the ages to deal with basic problems of existence. It is present in all humans and is prominent in neurotic and psychotic states. Only when it forms the core of the psychodynamic process, or is the major integrating technique can it be called masochism, which connotes a particular syndome, distinct and separate from other neurotic states.

The symptomatology of this disorder has been extremely difficult to comprehend since it seems counter to the pleasure principle as well as the reality principle. Until it was visualized as an adaptational technique it appeared to be an utterly destructive human activity which controlled hostile feelings by directing them towards oneself. From this point of view, if the individual directed his hostile feelings toward the external world, the masochistic development would be minimized and averted. The effects of directing hostile feelings outwardly, however, often produces more damage than it alleviates and may even aggravate the guilt feelings which are an intrinsic part of the masochistic process. Consequently, the older theories based on the presence of aggressive instincts, while explaining the phenomenon, were not useful in therapy. Masochism became one of the refractory problems in therapy and was the basis for Freud's conception of the negative therapeutic reaction. He felt that the masochistic process was essentially antagonistic to successful therapy and considered most of these patients untreatable. He was referring to the masochist's tendency to respond to a decrease in anxiety by new outbursts of anxiety-provoking behavior. Freud in *Analysis Terminable and Interminable* said: "There are certain people who behave in a quite peculiar fashion during the work of analysis. When one speaks hopefully to them or expresses satisfaction with the progress of the treatment they show signs of discontent and their condition invariably gets worse. One becomes convinced not only that such people cannot endure any praise or appreciation, but they react inversely to the progress of the treatment. Every partial solution that ought to result, and in other people does result in an improvement or temporary suppression of symptoms produces in them for the time being an exacerbation of their illness." They have a need to face and defeat therapy.

The revisions in the theories about masochism involved the recognition of the ego elements in its production. Wilhelm Reich emphasized the characterological aspects of the masochistic process and saw the symptomatology as a defense. This fact was noted by many analysts who commented on the masochist's craving for love and affection. This was pointed out particularly by Trygve Braatøy and Bernard Berliner. Berliner highlighted this exaggerated need for love (and bodily contact which Braatøy emphasized) which is thwarted by the masochists' inability to receive and accept such offerings. This issue was very clear in a young professional woman who wanted therapy because her marriage was failing. She presented herself as an impossible person who was eventually disliked by anyone who got to know her. In the face of her self-derogatory appraisal, she was extremely demanding. The bulk of her activity could be described as the acting out of the adult who demands a continuing supply of love because she feels she was denied it in childhood. Her demands were always either plaintive and whining or else angry denunciations of the world's lack of benevolence. By virtue of her extreme demands and suffering, she felt that she should receive a bountiful, and benevolent response from the world. However, she could not accept any help or affection when offered gratuitously, since this was degrading. Any affection which she managed to get by force or extortion was depreciated because it was not gratuitous. This is characteristic of the masochistic cycle, which makes it inevitable that every contact or exchange be viewed as degrading and derogating. The masochist in his extreme need and desperation attempts to secure affectionate interest, but his adaptational techniques either alienate the world or else the final achievement is belittled because it has been forced. Even where benevolent interest and affection is present, the masochist can easily twist it into an unfriendly exchange and feel abused and denied.[2]

The masochist succeeds in converting every situation into a rejection of his needs which justifies and perpetuates his patterns of behavior. Freud interpreted this behavior as a need to fail, but the ego psychologists have emphasized the element of the "need to succeed" and have demonstrated how excessive and compulsive needs for success can by themselves produce failure. Currently, there is a tendency to view the masochistic process in terms other than defined by the death instinct hypothesis. Masochism and masochistic tendencies whether extreme or minimal are viewed as ways of dealing with certain problems of existence—particularly guilt, helplessness and powerlessness. Although masochistic behavior often appears to be "unconscious guilt seeking punishment," the guilt is frequently secondary to the brazen exploitative and righteously indignant behavior of these individuals. Such behavior is often met with rebuff or condemnation, which increases the feelings of guilt.

The utilization of this defensive technique for dealing with feelings of powerlessness depends upon man's continued belief in primitive magic and its power of expiation as well as the belief that one can stimulate another human being to benevolent action by the appeal of helplessness. It is one of man's favorite delusions and Jules Masserman has called it "an *Ur* defense of Man." This belief has its roots in the prolonged state of helplessness which characterizes the human infant. The helplessness of the infant does stimulate the environment into benevolent efforts designed to fulfill the infant's needs. We call this maternal love or affection, and the utter helplessness and powerlessness of the infant plays a large role in the extensive care and support which accompanies infancy. Such helplessness in the adult, however, is not productive of the same response. The masochist never relinquishes the conviction regarding the appeal of helplessness. Consequently, the masochist maneuver is essentially a primitive way of adapting. It is analogous to the behavior of some animals, who at moments of grave danger either freeze or present their most vulnerable areas to the enemy. Such behavior frequently terminates the danger to the animal who can then escape.

In humans it is one way of dealing with the hopeless despair which man faces in his awareness of his ultimate powerlessness and inability to control his destiny. Its ubiquitous involvement in all human affairs can be understood in terms of the universality of these feelings. If this thesis is correct, the developments of science and technology which enhance man's power to control his environment should decrease the prevalence of masochism. Masochism, like other psychological concepts, is related to standards and practices within a culture and is related to the level of the technological and scientific development of a culture.

The depressive maneuver is similar to the masochistic defense in many ways. In depression we have noted the angry rebukes and hostile recriminations against the environment associated with self-derogation and denial. In the extreme, suicide may occur, which is the ultimate of self-denial and hopeless despair. The depressive maneuver is a defense against the loss or supposed loss of a person or value held essential to the individual's integration. As a process of repair it attempts to replace or restore these lost values by a variety of maneuvers (among them the masochistic defense) in which the individual insists that he cannot live unless these lost objects are restored. The masochist, on the other hand, demands that he gets what he is entitled to, never admitting that he has lost anything or that he needs anything. One is an overt expression of weakness and despair, while the other is an overt expression of strength with covert manifestations of helplessness and despair.

The process and goals of masochistic behavior represent the tendency to maintain the psyche-soma or body-soul dichotomy, in which one elevates a set of needs whether they be valid or not, above and in opposition to other bodily needs. Sacrifices must be made, suffering endured, rewards and gratifications denied while fulfilling this value established at some early period of one's life.

The mortification phenomenon so prominent in religious systems, both East and West, reflects this notion of masochism as a body-soul phenomenon. It also supplies us with a valuable historical source of understanding of man's self-destructive activities, philosophically acceptable, and rationalized and ritualized in religious dogma. Mortification represented the goal of fulfilling higher needs and values by expressing contempt for bodily functions through mutilation or neglect of these functions. The essence of mortification in the Christian ethic was the denial of one's worldly, material, biologic existence in order to leave the soul pure and unsullied and available to the divine.

Consequently, there was cultural support for acts of mortification which had its greatest flowering in the fourteenth and fifteenth centuries. What was the mortifier attempting to achieve? He was trying to kill nis old self, the natural man and his self-regarding instincts and desires. The natural needs and functions of man interfere with the fulfillment of his more spiritual, divine goal, and so they needed to be denied or extirpated. Mortification became elevated into a more ethical and spiritual process than the base fulfillment of man's biologic needs. Mortification is still current in some flagellant sects as a means of identifying with Christ by assuming that in the sharing of his suffering they can share his martyrdom. The masochist, like the mortifier, fulfills some higher need by a process of active denial or self-punishment. In order to fulfill some values, sacrifices must be made and baser needs denied. Fritz Wittels, in his article, "The Mystery of Masochism," says: "The masochist wishes to prove the futility of one part of his person in order to live the more secure in the important other part."[3]

In the masochistic process the individual is attempting to fulfill some higher ideal as visualized by him. It may be simply the ideal of independence or freedom, and although the accompanying effects may be self-destructive, the individual views it as a positive program. While putting aside his striving for strength, pride and dignity, the masochist abandons himself completely to weakness and dependency, achieving a false sense of strength and grandiosity through his power to control, dominate and manipulate the environment. Thus, we cannot conceive of the masochist as gaining pleasure from his activity. He is interested exclusively in the effects of his activity, not in the activity itself. His performances are esteemed only as they fulfill the value which he conceives as the major goal of his behavior.

The ritual of expiation, or propitiation, which is so universal in the masochistic process, is an acknowledgement of the threads of unity or totality of the personality. They represent the patient's awareness of some distortion in his goals and a recognition of his unsatisfied needs. Thus, the masochist is actively searching for some contact while he denies it. Yet, he can accept it only at the extremes of his performance, which then requires the expiation ritual.

Essentially the masochistic ideal is to be a person who is loving and universally loved. Since this cannot be achieved by the miracle of just wanting and so getting, he is forced to deny his need entirely and presents himself to the world as someone who needs no one. However, such supreme isolation is unattainable and is approached in the sado-masochistic symbiosis.

The magical belief that by suffering one can claim higher rewards is based on the infantile notion that one can arrest attention and obtain fulfillment only in extreme states. It assumes that rewards and fulfillments can come only from an authority who demands to be appeased and placated, and whose attention can be gained only through extremes of misery and suffering. It believes that things must get worse to get better, or that only the exceptional will arrest the attention and interest of the significant adult. If it cannot be achieved by positive, satisfying performances, then it will be done by negative, destructive and self-thwarting activity. The concept of extremes leads to the Christian notion that "man's extremity is God's opportunity." It has become so widespread a belief in the Judeo-Christian culture that suffering, pain, anguish, etc., have been considered as necessary preludes to salvation. The existential philosophies of Kierkegaard, Heidegger, Tillich and Reinhold Niebuhr have emphasized this aspect of the human predicament.[4]

Any hypothesis about masochism must account for the masochistic sexual perversions as well as the fact that the sexual apparatus rarely plays some role in the masochistic process. From the point of view described here, it is apparent that any tendency, impulse or activity which is potentially pleasurable but culturally disapproved, could be made the object of the masochistic dynamism. This may account for the universality and timelessness of masochistic phenomena, since the disapproval of certain pleasurable activities has always accompanied the human situation. Sex is peculiarly suited for this purpose, since it is potentially a great source of pleasure while it is an object of much disapproval. At the same time, unlike any other biologic function, it is capable of being denied or permanently abandoned. Since sex can be the source of the greatest pleasure, it should produce the greatest rewards in the masochistic process.

Although self-denial can serve positive purposes and be a stimulating constructive force, it is qualitatively different from masochism. Unrestricted gluttony is not the converse of masochism, but another mode of the masochistic process, since it overemphasizes the sensory requirements of man. An exaggerated emphasis on the biologic needs, as in physiologic hedonism, is also masochistic. The masochist attempts to enhance certain values, whether spiritual or somatic, by denying or destroying those aspects of himself which seem in opposition to those values.

This description of masochism has clarified the genetic basis for the development of the particular techniques of dealing with anxiety. Genesis is neglected to a certain extent when adaptation is emphasized in psychological theory. Yet, such investigations are not closed off but rather stimulated and fresh hypotheses regarding symptom choice can be formulated. Although Freud recognized that the problem of symptom choice, that is, why a particular person selected a particular defensive technique, was largely an unresolved issue, his formulations tended to discourage such inquiries. Genesis was largely a matter of acknowledging the preconceived notions of libido and instinct and observing their transformations through some traumatic incident in the course of development. Such formulations tended to obscure questions of genesis while pretending to answer them.

The formulations which arise out of an adaptive cultural orientation towards human behavior emphasizes the individual's behavior in action as he attempts to deal with his needs. The genesis of the distortions of these techniques are not the primary concern of the therapist. However, the genesis of neurotic techniques like masochism is neither unimportant or secondary, but at the moment the least understood of all the problems in psychoanalytic theory and therapy. Ego psychology has not been very enlightening so far, on this question.

Notes

1. Masserman, J.: Principles of Dynamic Psychiatry. Philadelphia, W. B. Saunders, 1961.

2. This thesis is amply documented in: Masochism, a review of theory and therapy. In Science and Psychoanalysis; Individual and Familial Dynamics, ed. by J. Masserman, New York, 1959. Case material is presented to support this view of the masochistic disorders.

3. Wittels, Fritz: Psychoanalytic Review, 14.139-149, 1937.

4. James, W.: The Variety of Religious Experience. New York and London, Longmans Green, 1902. See also, Pratt, J. O.: The Religious Consciousness, New York, MacMillan, 1920.

   Starbuck, E. D.: The Psychology of Religion. New York, Scribners, 1903.

   De La Croix, Henri: Etudes d'Histoire et de Psychologie du Mysticisme; de Sanctis, Sante: Religious Conversion. New York, Harcourt Brace, 1927. and, Les Grands Mystiques Chretiens. Paris, Alcon Press.

XII

Therapy

PSYCHOANALYTIC THEORY grew out of Freud's experience in the treatment of the personality disorders, particularly hysteria. Although he first utilized the prevailing techniques for the treatment of these disorders such as rest, massage, hydrotherapy and electrical stimulation, he found them unsatisfactory and abandoned them in favor of hypnotism. His experience with hypnosis influenced many of his theories as well as his techniques for the treatment of the mental disorders. Originally, the data he derived from the actual treatment process provided the basis for his theorizing. Later however, theory influenced and determined the techniques and treatment behavior of the therapist. This progression is inevitable in the development of a healing science which must be applied directly to ameliorate suffering and distress. However, one should never lose sight of this fact, otherwise certain technical principles which are appropriate to one stage of the theoretical development of the science and not to another may become reified, sacrosanct and beyond human alteration. The techniques of the psychoanalyst vary with his theoretical background even though there may be underlying principles accepted by all. The goals as well as the technical operations of therapy are intimately related to the theoretical conceptions regarding personality development and its distortions.

Freud altered his therapeutic goals and techniques whenever he revised his theories. These revisions were logical outgrowths of the altered views regarding the dynamics of personality development. In recent years there has been an unhealthy tendency to freeze certain theoretical principles and therapeutic tools, and to consider them as unchangeable primary facts beyond critical appraisal. Freud would have none of this during his own development, and even though he considered certain issues in psychoanalysis such as transference, for example, to be indispensable to

243

the science, he was open and available to changes which occured frequently during his own lifetime.

Modifications in theory by the ego psychoanalysts have produced alterations in technique which are applications of these theoretical changes. Some of these changes are trivial and purely technical, while others involve more significant questions such as the nature and process of insight and change. Although some issues may seem petty and contentious, a more careful appraisal will reveal that crucial questions underlie these changes. One must exercise great caution in revising any established therapeutic technique unless a solid basis of data can support and justify such alteration. In a science as young and unformed as psychiatry and psychotherapy, a flexible attitude must be allowed for speculation and experimentation. At the same time there must be a judicious limitation of unscientific therapeutic programs which seem to be supported largely by the enthusiasm of the discoverer rather than by his theoretical and therapeutic documentation. Unfortunately, we have seen too much of such "magic" in the guise of therapy which has in the long run only served to discredit the slow and serious developments in the field.

The most distressing aspect of this problem is the difficulty of determining the value of a particular therapeutic approach by an investigation of its effects. It is commonplace in psychiatry that the application of any new treatment measure is rewarded by a high percentage of beneficial results. The initial success, however, is not often continued. The validity of a therapeutic approach must be examined from a long range point of view, with a careful appraisal of its rationale and justification in terms of the prevailing knowledge in the field, as well as the goals which the therapy sets up. From such a position dianetics, scientology and even the more acceptable alterations of therapeutic techniques are found to be either nonsense, chicanery or the oversimplified and exaggerated applications of isolated fragments of theory.

Therapeutic techniques, arise out of the theoretical formulations regarding personality development, and in turn the technique may influence the data obtained in the therapeutic work. Freud's earliest efforts in treating hysterical patients utilized his experience with hypnosis, and in 1887 he began to use hypnotic suggestions, and several years later, hypnotic catharsis. This procedure consisted of the patient lying on a couch and the hypnotist giving suggestions designed to achieve some catharsis in order to alleviate the patient's symptoms. Although this technique proved to be quite successful, it had many drawbacks, and Freud soon abandoned it. Freud had difficulty in hypnotizing all his patients, and at the same time he recognized that in order to achieve more lasting effects it was necessary for the recall to occur in the waking state. This led to the use of the technique of hypnotic suggestion, in which the therapist sat behind the patient who was prone. When recall became difficult the therapist would touch the patient's forehead and suggest that the memories would return. After a while, he merely touched the patient and in 1897 he stopped that as well. At this time psychoanalysis was born. The theories of repression and resistance arose from the early years of his work and were closely identified with hypnotism. The problem of resistance led him to utilize the technique of free association which was designed to bypass and overcome the reluctance to reveal the painful thoughts and feelings which had been repressed. This technique became the basic tool for elucidating the repressed and unconscious elements in the neurotic states. Although Freud at first supported the concept of the sexual etiology of the neurosis, he later abandoned the notion of an actual sexual trauma in favor of the effect of phantasy on personality development. With this profound alteration of theory, the technique of psychoanalysis changed from the goal of discovering the sexual trauma and aimed at releasing the sexual and aggressive instincts which had been repressed during the development of the individual. This still required a recovery of childhood memories to allow the emotions which accompanied the repression to be consciously experienced. The goal of therapy was still symptomatic, however, and was directed toward recovering the repressed memories which initiated the symptomatology. Dream interpretation was also utilized as an additional and valuable tool for elucidating the contents of the unconscious. Dream interpretation became a widely used instrument for exploring the unconscious and often became the major focus of all the therapist's activity in the treatment process. This technique of dream interpretation was very important in dealing with the transference reactions which Freud felt to be an essential aspect of the psychoanalytic process. Transference for Freud referred to all the feelings the patient manifested toward the therapist which were essentially childish attitudes toward the parental figures. These feelings were merely transferred to the therapist and could become a source of resistance as well as a basis for insight. Although Freud first considered it to be a nuisance, he later acknowledged that it was essential to the process.[1] It was this concept that led to many practices in the orthodox psycho-analytic technique which has become rigidly enforced. One of these issues was the necessity for anonymity in order to minimize the opportunities for clouding and confusing the transference relation-ships. The notion of anonymity not only required that the doctor not be visible during the therapy session, but also forbade any social contacts outside of the sessions. It purportedly minimized any realistic attitudes and thus made for purer irrational trans-ference attitudes. It encouraged the analyst to believe that it was possible to reduce the patient's attitude to the therapist to those referring exclusively to his childhood feelings and attitudes.

The early techniques were all related to Freud's notions regard-ing the genesis of neurotic disorders. When neurosis was due to the repression of certain experiences which occurred as traumatic events in the individual's life, it was necessary to encourage and produce the recall and conscious elaboration of these incidents. A prone position was indispensable to the hypnotic process, and concerns about anonymity or too much activity were at that time not the issue. When Freud abandoned hypnotism for free associa-tion, dream analysis and interpretation, he was still trying to effect a recall in order to make the unconscious conscious. During this period, however, he recognized the role of resistance and transfer-ence which required technical changes and new rules in carrying out the therapy. The role of resistance necessitated the use of interpretations which would overcome the resistance. At first these interpretations were restricted only to those occasions when re-sistance ensued, but later they were utilized to enhance insight. The concept of transference not only produced many technical innovations but revised the primary objective of the genetic re-construction of the patient's illness, since the concept of transference involved the emotional re-experiencing and reliving of the past situations. In order to limit the transference difficulties, anonymity and a strict policy of maintaining only a therapeutic attitude toward the patient was encouraged. The analyst sat behind the patient in order to avoid a face to face encounter for eight hours a day and to encourage revival of current feelings and attitudes toward the therapist. The position of the therapist and the prone position of the patient was rationalized on theoretical grounds. The rule of the therapist's silence and inactivity was maintained to allow the patient's free associations to focus on his unconscious undisturbed by the therapist's activities. The therapist's silence was expected to stimulate recall, stir up latent hostilities and avoid influencing the patient's productions. It was aimed primarily, however, at accelerating the genetic reconstruction of the illness. Dream interpretation was energetically pursued as the "royal road to the unconscious."

It is clear that the principles of therapy were outgrowths of the assumption that the neurosis was the result of repressions which, when allowed to enter consciousness, would result in the relief of the symptoms. Thus, from 1900 to 1920, therapy was mainly designed to encourage an emotional reliving of past situations in which repression occurred.

From 1920 onwards, Freud altered many of his theories. He developed many metapsychological formulations which, although highly questionable, intruded themselves into the technical problems in therapy. One major addition at that time was the recognition of varieties of defense other than repression, such as regression, sublimation, projection, etc. This encouraged the therapist to study the ways in which the patient defends himself against unconscious forces and led to a study of the external factors which were brought to bear on the individual. This required a more intensive study of the patient's current activities in order to more fully comprehend his resistances and defense, which was the beginning of an ego psychology in contrast to the earlier focus on the id.

The therapeutic techniques which are an integral part of traditional psychoanalytic method include the revival of childhood experiences—particularly those related to sexuality and the libidinal development, and the interpretations of the unconscious by dream analysis and free association with special reference to transference and ego defenses. These techniques are directed towards an elucidation of the regressed or fixated libidinal cathexes which are the causes of personality deformation. The subsidiary issues of the use of the couch, frequency of interview (four or five times a week), anonymity, use of interpretations only, and the virtue of passivity in the therapist, derive from these two basic premises in the therapeutic technique which arise out of the theoretical constructs in orthodox theory.

Since 1925 there have been many alterations and variations in theory as well as technique. These alterations have been the product of Freud's students and not Freud himself, and center around the primary alteration of therapy from a symptom analysis to an analysis of the character structure. The shift of emphasis from the genetic reconstruction of the past to the emotional re-experiencing in the therapeutic situation was more fully exploited by Ferenczi, Rank, Alexander, and the ego or cultural psychoanalysts. This process, while not belittling the value of the historical reconstruction, placed greater emphasis on insight and learning which resulted from the repetition of old patterns in a therapeutic setting in which the therapist behaves differently than the parental figures. The concept of development as adaptation was implicit in this notion and, although Freud never fully accepted this view, it has become the dominant, overriding concept in the philosophy of dynamic psycho-therapy.

Neurosis in this framework was visualized as the result of the development of certain defenses against anxiety which manifested themselves as characterological attitudes. The patient's character structure was thus the center of the resistance to change and be-came the focus of the therapist's interest. Neurosis was thus broad-ened into a problem of character structure rather than a series of symptoms. Thus, the character structure of an individual, which is the special way he organizes his defenses against anxiety, became the predominant focus in analytic therapy.

In this framework therapy was an attempt to comprehend the character structure and elucidate its origins and function in main-taining the neurosis. The tendency to establish simple casual rela-tionships between character traits and certain childhood experiences, however, can be very misleading and not conducive to change. The initial impact of the development of character analysis was to alter the stress from the reconstruction of the past to the elucidation of the present modes of behavior of the individual. Although it does not obviate the need for genetic reconstruction, it is primarily concerned with the analysis of the structure of the defenses which support the neurosis. The clarification of character traits, however, frequently serves to clear the way for the recall and clarification of early childhood experiences which can reinforce the insight. Many of the technical alterations in therapy derive from this con-ception of the neurosis. In elaborating the character structure of an individual, it is necessary to get a comprehensive view of how he functions and adapts in the present. This calls for a detailed presentation of his current experiencing in order to identify areas of anxiety and the ways the individual deals with these anxieties. Consequently, therapy proceeds in a more directed fashion with immediate goals that are clear to the patient. The therapist is generally more active and may direct the patient to areas which he feels might be illuminating. Such activity is manifested by more frequent questions and interpretations and a variety of devices, both verbal and non-verbal, designed to encourage the patient to see how his present patterns of behavior are contributing to his difficulties in living. The therapist's role becomes more than a mere facilitant to reliving the past; he becomes a collaborating partner in examining the neurotic structure. Activity also permits the patient to recognize his distortions regarding others which arise out of his transference attitudes.

In this novel give-and-take framework, transference becomes more than a mere revival of infant-parent relationship. It is viewed as a collection of distortions or characteristic attitudes toward a variety of people who have played meaningful and determining roles in one's life. Irrational attitudes can thus be explored through an understanding of their current adaptive value. Transference in this approach is also a major tool for therapy since it allows for the most direct observation of the distorted attitudes which are developed in the course of maturing. In the relationship of the "here and now," the patient is forced to acknowledge that some of his attitudes toward the therapist do not arise out of a response to the therapist as he is, but to the therapist as the patient personifies him. Such an observation can open the way for a clarification of the distortion. The more current views on transference involve the recognition that many individuals aside from the parents share in the development of these distortions. A patient's irrational hatred of the therapist arises not only from a hatred of his father, for example, but probably because of a series of relationships in which the patient has been abused and mistreated by authority figures. This leads him to expect malevolence from the analyst. In the intimacy of the therapeutic relationship many opportunities will occur to produce this resentment. Transference would then be more than a mere repetition or transferring of feeling; it would be a dynamic process which represents and reproduces the effect of early experiencing on present behavior. The activity and lack of anonymity which characterizes this type of therapeutic approach arises out of the theoretical conception that transference attitudes are more meaningful and revealing when they are produced through contact and experiencing than when they occur in a vacuum of pure phantasy.

Thus, the present tendency is not to limit or inhibit the therapist's activity or to prevent him from revealing facets of his own personality. Face to face encounters in terms of patients sitting up are more frequent and there is not such a strong taboo against activities outside the analytic hour. The role of activity has also been understood from another point of view by Frieda Fromm-Reichmann, who stressed the fact that we know enough about the therapeutic process to actively intervene and encourage productive areas of inquiry and discourage endless and only vaguely useful meanderings. She was not only attempting to accelerate therapy, but she was attempting to obviate the necessity of dealing with every patient as if we had learned nothing from the last one. It certainly reflected a greater therapeutic rather than research interest, but it was based on a conviction regarding the validity of many psychoanalytic concepts. Often, such directive activity involves a limitation of the free association technique which, while undoubtedly useful, can be abused by the patient and the therapist, thus destroying its value as an uncovering instrument. This notion has been supported by most ego analysts who use the free association technique with caution and judgement rather than as a required routine.

When the therapist takes a more active position and role, it becomes apparent that not all the patient's attitudes toward the therapist are irrational. Some of the patient's responses are realistic and rational attitudes toward the therapist in terms of the kind of person he really is. While this was considered an artefact in orthodox analytic therapy, it has become apparent that the most stringent efforts of the analyst to remain incognito are largely impossible to achieve. In spite of all the safeguards, patients are able to discover many important pieces of data regarding their analyst through contact with him. The analyst does lead a public life, and patients are particularly adept, when interested, in discovering a great deal about him. The office habits and practices of the therapist do stir up responses which are related to the therapist's own character structure. These responses were called transference reactions and were always assumed to be a result of previous attitudes or feelings. However, there is a current tendency to distinguish transference responses from realistic responses. Such a distinction can serve the important function of increasing the patient's convictions regarding the significance of the transference reactions. It avoids the difficult task of convincing the patient that his attitude is irrational when objective factors prove otherwise. Indirectly, it has lessened the authoritative atmosphere of the analytic situation and has permitted a realistic appraisal of the analyst, which is a vital need of the neurotic who already is overburdened with distorted conceptions about others. The practice of using chairs rather than insisting on the routine use of the couch has aided in realistically appraising the therapist. The use of the couch, which grew directly out of the early history of analytic therapy, was recognized as a valuable facilitant in producing regression and stimulating recall of childhood experiences. When the theory required such childhood reconstruction it was a rational tool. However, as the necessity for genetic reconstruction became subordinate to the elucidation of a patient's character structure, the use of the couch could not always be justified. It may even become an obstacle when it encourages regression and dependency which may strongly reinforce current character trends and serve as a resistance to analysis. Under such circumstances the couch is frequently dispensed with and used only when rational considerations justify it.

A most important outgrowth of the increase in activity of the therapist was the recognition and exploration of the role of countertransference in the therapeutic process. Freud, very early in his therapeutic work, recognized the potential influence of the therapist's own personality on the therapeutic process. This led to the requirement that every therapist be analyzed in order to become more aware of his own distortions and neurotic difficulties. This has remained as a most important element in the therapeutic process, since it is clear that the therapist can influence the outcome of therapy in a striking fashion. The analysis of the therapist tends to minimize the hazards. So, while Freud was aware of the possibility of countertransference, he hoped to minimize or eliminate it by a cloak of anonymity. More and more it has become apparent that this cloak is a thin veil and the countertransference elements which are inevitable in the therapeutic process can be utilized to good advantage.

The attitude of the therapist towards the patient can be a very powerful tool in elucidating the character structure of the patient. When the therapist is free, flexible, and willing to become involved and committed to the therapy, his reactions to the patient can illuminate character trends which otherwise would go unnoticed. Such reactions are most helpful in learning about the subtleties of the patient's activities. When brought to the patient's attention, such observations can open up major lines of inquiry, and the effect of the patient's behavior can be examined in the here and now as it effects the therapist. Such reactions on the part of the therapist can infuse new meanings to the therapeutic process and are most valuable in overcoming resistances and impasses. The therapist's responses can also be used as a check on the patient's progress and movement by the frank recognition of his feeling for his patient. It is obvious that the therapist does not like all his patients equally or at all. With some he can recognize interest and affection while he may be annoyed or simply unimpressed by others. Such attitudes do not offer any clues to the possibilities of successful therapy. They do present many opportunities to the keen and competent therapist to make rapid and fruitful formulations about his patient's patterns of operations. The utilization of countertransference feelings in the therapeutic process, however, can be equally detrimental to the therapeutic process as an ill-advised or poorly timed interpretation. It takes considerable skill to decide when it is safe to make observations which might produce a strong response from the patient. However, when wisely used it can accelerate therapy considerably and inaugurate a contact with the patient which becomes invaluable for the further progress of therapy. The utilization of these countertransference reactions is becoming more widespread and is an essential part of current psychoanalytic practice—particularly among neo-Freudian analysts. The value of countertransference phenomena has reopened the important problem of acting out versus verbalizing in the therapeutic process.

As the notion of therapy as an educational process continues to grow, it becomes less valid that all insight must be verbally achieved, and acting out discouraged. As many neurotics try to deal with anxiety by activity, since they are incapable of tolerating anxiety for any length of time, it is important to get them to refrain from acting out. This enables both the patient and the therapist to examine the anxiety in order to discover its sources. However, with the achievement of some insight, living and experiencing is essential to a consolidation of the insight. This notion is embodied in Alexander's ideas of the "corrective emotional experience" and is stressed by Robbins in his concept of cure versus insight. Consequently, in current analytic practice there are few rules regarding abstinence or the insistence on foregoing making decisions or major alterations in one's life. Living must continue even though therapy is in process, and when we consider how long therapy can continue, we should be very cautious in advising our patients to retain their status quo until a signal to go ahead is given by the therapist. It requires wisdom and resourcefulness from the therapist under circumstances where such rules are avoided, since it is frequently necessary to restrain the activities of patients who, in the enthusiasm of certain discoveries, tend to make premature and unwise decisions. This is particularly noticeable in the patient who attempts to solve his problems by "doing" rather than "inquiring" as to what he intends or is about to do. On the whole, however, it is becoming more frequent to encourage the patient to continue his living, with the express undertanding that all major changes and decisions be a subject for investigation and examination. The authoritative atmosphere of the analytic process and the dependency on the therapist is decreased in this way.

The problem of dependency has produced many technical alterations which involve frequency of visits as well as the use of the couch and other formal requirements of abstinence. The trend is towards decreasing the dependency through less frequent visits and variations in frequency depending on the progress of therapy as well as in the avoidance of the couch in very dependent individuals. The need to encourage the patient toward more self-reliant activity is the purpose of such technical devices. Such dependent patients are encouraged to make more decisions rather than less and to force the examination of their dependency by removing some of the support that is traditionally involved in the more classical techniques. This has, in many instances, shortened the process of therapy and produced striking results.

The concept of psychiatry as the study of interpersonal processes formulated by Sullivan has produced many significant technical innovations. Sullivan saw therapy in terms of an interview which had a structure and a goal of elucidating the individual's techniques for dealing with anxiety. These techniques were defined by Sullivan as the self-system or the personality. Consequently, therapy was a process of discovering what the individual was like and how he came to be the person he is. This procedure utilized the techniques of the interview and the therapist attempted through questions or interpretations to illuminate the characteristic defenses of the patient and so explore his neurotic way of functioning. In this way the distortions in the neurotic process would be clarified. In removing these distortions the patient would come to see the world as it really is, that is, a consensual validation of the world, and a cure could result. In pursuing the process of therapy as a variety of the psychiatric interview, Sullivan introduced many technical devices and maneuvers which have been widely incorporated in the therapeutic armamentarium of clinicians of all types. He made particular use of the technique of the surprise encounter by a direct and pointed question or interpretation. This would highlight a defensive maneuver which then could not be avoided. This type of intervention cut through a great deal of obsessive rumination which was mostly a source of distraction designed to avoid major issues. It is in the treatment of the obsessive and the paranoid that Sullivan was an undisputed master. The use of the caustic or sarcastic comment and the value of a sharp but cogent interpretation was a technique Sullivan used to great advantage. His techniques cast a new light on the role of free association, passivity and the preoccupation with early experiences in the treatment process. He demonstrated how the free association technique could be used to avoid a confrontation with anxiety. This was true in the patient's tendency to focus exclusively on childhood recollections as a way of staying on grounds which were comparatively painless and where there could be a transfer of blame to the parents. He acknowledged the difficulties an individual has in dealing with his present anxieties but showed that the preoccupation with childhood experience in the classical techniques was actually an avoidance reaction. The value of the direct confrontation, surprise and novelty as a factor in maintaining patient interest and participation has been widely incorporated in current therapeutic techniques. Communication, rather than symbol interpretation, became the main device for developing insight, and this encouraged new exploration in the significance of the non-verbal communicative devices which has greatly expanded our understanding both of the verbal and non-verbal patient.

In recent years, existential philosophy, by broadening our knowledge of man has been of interest to psychiatrists and psychotherapists. Existentialism stresses the nature of man's existing not only as a biological entity but also as a being who functions in a world in which he has created the problems and conditions which affect his attitudes and behavior. It has stressed the significance of man's relation to his fellow man and to the world and, thus, it has focused on the problems of loneliness, time, love and death. It has emphasized the significance of contact, exchange, interaction and mutuality in the therapeutic process. These issues which have been elaborated by psychoanalysts like Binswanger, Boss, Bally, Ernie Strauss, etc., have produced some interesting innovations in the therapeutic process. The notion of therapy as an interaction or dialogue, which is directly attributable to Martin Buber and Paul Tillich, has encouraged such techniques as confrontation and the direct assault on some issues which may result in exchange with the patient that classical theory attempted to avoid. Some of these notions correspond closely to Sullivan's views which advocated the necessity for involvement and decision in the therapeutic process. Therapy becomes more than an objective scrutiny of another individual, it becomes a mutual process; an integration in which the elements of trust and courage play a crucial role. However, when existential philosophy itself becomes translated into a therapeutic framework with its own methodology, it becomes cumbersome, entirely unscientific and only vaguely useful as a psychotherapeutic technique. Current developments in theory and practice to the extent that they draw on the insights of the existential philosopher have broadened our therapeutic skills and techniques.

Therapeutic Goals—The Role of Values in Therapy

Originally, the goal of therapy was symptomatic cure. This involved making unconscious material conscious and stimulating the emotional re-experiencing of repressed feelings or attitudes. During this phase of the development of psychoanalysis the problem of values played no role in psychiatric theory or practice except through a deliberate attempt to exclude it. Therapy was a matter of releasing repressed material which would then allow the libido to unfold in an unimpeded fashion and permit the individual to develop. It soon became evident that this concept of cure was limited, and produced only temporary relief of neurotic suffering. It was based on a conception of personality development which did not take into account the fact that the neurotic symptom is a defense against the anxiety which maintains the neurotic structure. Freud's alterations of his concept of anxiety as a warning signal and the recognition of the function of resistance in the character structure broadened the goals of therapy. Now, therapy involved a recognition of the defenses which maintained the neurotic structure and the reorganization of the personality to obviate the need for such defenses. This was called character analysis.

Character analysis required an understanding of the way the patient functions in the present as well as a history of his childhood in terms of his libidinal development. While the focus of therapy remained on the historical reconstruction of the experiences in the early years, its purpose was to illuminate the distortions of character structure. In spite of all efforts to avoid value judgments about behavior and personality, a normative system of ethics was inevitable. This involved the acceptance of certain values, standards and cultural norms which were part of the therapist's own cultural heritage as well as the normative systems that were part of personality theory. For example, according to psychological theory, infants and children were expected to develop certain capacities and forego others at appropriate times in their development. Playing with feces was considered normal or expected at certain ages while abnormal at others. At the same time, stealing, lieing, destruction of property, etc., were always viewed as evidences of some disturbance in the face of moral attitudes which are derived from a Judeo-Christian heritage. Although moralizing was and is always inappropriate to the healing process, particular values and judgements of what is right or wrong, good and bad, depend upon the cultural setting of the therapy as well as the cultural heritage of the therapist. Thus, activities about the genital would produce various responses in different cultures at different times. What is appropriate and acceptable by the Dobu Indians is quite different from what is viewed with equanimity in the Western cultures or by the Alaskan Indians. This implied assumption about values played an integral part in the therapeutic process in spite of all the disclaimers which Freud and his students made. What was generally meant was that there should not be judgemental attitudes toward any variation or distortion of development; and rather than criticize or moralize, efforts should be made to overcome the blocks and resistances to the development of "normal" behavior. The values were inherent and assumed, and consequently, did not need to be explicitly formulated. The tendency to deny the presence of cultural standards promoted the notion that classical therapy tended to accept the existing cultural situation as the normal and to encourage the patient to adjust to the prevailing conditions, regardless of how distorted the culture might be.

The values of the therapist subtly but inevitably intrude themselves into the therapeutic process. Since neurotic distortions can be viewed as deviations from the cultural patterns, one aspect of therapy could involve the ability of the individual to conform to the cultural demands. This would constitute cure. For example, in a culture where aggressive, energetic competitive strivings were considered normal for the male, a passive, uncompetitive pattern would be indicative of a neurotic incapacity. The index of maturity would be measured by the strength of the aggressive strivings.

The goal of therapy in such a setting is inevitably one of adjustment and conformity. This is a potent source of criticism against the therapeutic goal of the orthodox psychoanalytic process. Although this criticism is largely incorrect, the tendency to theorize in terms of the need to conform to cultural norms supports this view. It arises out of the concept of society as a restricting and repressing force which requires that the individual submit to the culture in order to relieve his repression.

When the goal of therapy extended beyond symptomatic relief to an attempt to reorganize the total character structure, the significance of the current functioning of the individual in his cultural setting became most important. The past becomes important to the extent that it is experienced and reproduced in the present. A new concept of neurosis and mental illness developed which affected the technique and goals of therapy. From a characterological point of view, a patient is ill not because of experiences which occurred in childhood, but because such experiences still operate in the present to affect his personality and character structure. A patient may be unhappy, insecure, or compulsive, not because he was unloved in childhood or infancy, but because his early experiences had so shaped his personality that in the present he is unable to love and be loved or to trust others in their readiness to love him. Consequently, the index of cure is not the degree of recall of early experience or certain traumatic events like primal scene, etc., but the capacity to function adequately in the present. Some theorists express this capacity in terms of an ability to relate to others without serious perceptual or conceptual distortions. Sullivan described this end state as the capacity to relate with a minimum of parataxic distortions where there is consensual validation of the patient's perceptions. Others describe health as the capacity to love and be loved, or the expression of the full potentialities of the individual. Such goals reflect a value system that conceives of man as capable of fulfilling the potentialities of a humanistic philosophical view of man's capacities. It does involve an ethic of good and bad, which, however, is quite different from the theological or authoritative judgement of morality. "Good" is whatever is fulfilling or unfolding of man's innate potentialities while "bad" is whatever contains or restricts this fulfillment. Since good-bad have had such a long semantic attachment to theological norms, the therapist strictly avoids such terms and speaks only of destructive or constructive, or integrative and disintegrative or conjunctive or disjunctive activities. In addition, there is the necessity to distinguish between the total person and his behavior, which is only a reflection of his neurotic difficulties. This avoids the tendency of the neurotic to feel rejected or condemned while it is his behavior or activity which is not acceptable. It has become increasingly evident that a major concern of the neurotic is a question of values; what he is doing with his life and how he is utilizing his capacities. Difficulty in establishing his identity, which implies an inability to recognize who and what he is in the face of the cultural requirements and his own ideals, has been the expressed complaint which draws more and more people to seek therapy. Concern about symptoms are frequently only reflections of this concern with moral issues. Consequently, therapy can no longer evade the issue of values but must recognize its significance in the life of every human being. In addition, the current theoretical formulations recognize that the therapist, being a product of the established mores and standards himself, cannot erase them from his own personality, nor should he attempt to do so. This accounts for our current extensive interest in countertransference phenomena. The therapist, being aware of these reactions, can refrain from imposing them on his patients.

It is from the viewpoint of values that psychoanalysis finds itself no longer in an active war with religious feelings, even though the therapist himself may be devoid of such feelings. This new outlook permits the therapist to distinguish between false values which are used as defenses and true values which can be used for productive purposes in the patient's life. Fromm has had much to say on this matter which has been of inestimable value to the development of a rational therapeutic program for the treatment of the neurotic disorders.

The current goals of analytic therapy can be expressed in terms of aiding the patient to achieve his potentialities through a process of overcoming the obstacles to a full and loving relationship with his fellow man. Such a goal has had its effect on the techniques of therapy which stress the reconstruction of personality rather than the repair of certain disordered elements of behavior. It distinguishes sharply between the physiological therapies such as electroshock and drug therapy and the psychological therapies which attempt a reconstruction of the personality towards a more effective control of the environment. Clara Thompson states this in the following way:

> Today in addition to relief from neurotic suffering a person is considered cured when he is capable of relating to other people with a minimum of parataxic distortion in his behavior and when he is free to develop his power as far as his education and life circumstances permit. The second arises out of the first. When the life situation is good, and the culture predominantly constructive, the healthy person achieves relationship to the group free from neurotic dependency. When the culture is less favorable, he may have to acquire the ability to endure relative isolation. Cure is not synonymous with conformity, nor with happiness as happiness is conventionally understood. A person may remain healthy in adverse circumstances in which he is suffering if he does not have to blind himself to his situation by various escape mechanisms of neurosis.[2]

Such goals in therapy require holding a patient to adult levels of cooperation and encouraging aspiring and self reliant motivations in the patient. It discourages the regressive tendencies of the patient and refrains from any treatment activity which increases dependency and parentifying behavior on the part of the patient.[3] It has also stimulated new investigations regarding insight and its value in the therapeutic process.

INSIGHT

It has long been noted that insight alone is not capable of effecting change in a patient's behavior. This led Freud to distinguish between intellectual insight as opposed to emotional insight which was assumed to have the power of altering the neurotic process. Such a distinction proved very useful in getting a patient actively (emotionally) involved in his treatment. It was clear that treatment as an intellectual exercise only served as an additional and more effective means of defense. It could also become a powerful resistance to treatment. Freud emphasized the necessity of reviving the emotional aspects of the repressed experiences in order to ensure emotional insight. Recent theoreticians have raised many relevant questions about Freud's views and have concluded that the distinction between intellectual and emotional insight is artificial. What is significant is how the insight is used and what motivation lies behind the achievement and utilization of insight. The emphasis needs to be placed on the capacity and encouragement to put the insight into practice in one's living. Change is the essential ingredient in therapy, not insight. Freud was aware of this necessity when he spoke of the "working through" period where transferences were resolved and the patient was encouraged to utilize his insight. However, this was seen as a terminal phase of therapy and often omitted because of time factors. This additional dimension in therapy is intimately involved with the question of the activity of the therapist and the continuous encouragement of the utilization of insight which could then effectuate change. Change, not intellectual or emotional enlightenment is the true goal of therapy. Unfortunately, it is not as true as we hoped or would like to believe that once a patient recognized his neurotic pattern and uncovered its genetic roots, he would then be free to experience his new powers. Thus, the "working through" or the utilization of insight is a crucial aspect of therapy and frequently a most difficult one. Most important is the recognition early in therapy that the possibility of making a discovery about oneself might effectuate a productive change in one's living. This is a most powerful incentive towards enhancing the patient's motivations and overcoming the inevitable resistance to change. When change rather than emotional insight is the goal of therapy, a more rational and organized treatment plan can be formulated. Under these circumstances a therapist's activities can be more clearly planned and interpretation and intervention can be measured by its effects in activating change rather than its elucidation of a symbolic construction of the patient. This was the constant appeal of Sullivan in his therapeutic work when he would ask the therapist, "Why did you say that? What did you have in mind? Where did you expect to go? And, what effect do you think it has or will have on the elucidation of the patient's way of living? Will it effectuate a change?" It forced the therapist to re-examine his activities with an eye always toward his goal of producing a change in his patient's living. Such a therapeutic attitude stimulates the patient to examine *most clearly* the effects of his current patterns of behavior on others and to notice the changes in others produced by changes in himself.

Franz Alexander was greatly impressed by this conception of analytic treatment when he formulated his conception of the corrective emotional experience. Recently, he summarized his views in the following way, which highlights the current views on the goals of psychoanalytic therapy.

It is obvious that from this perspective the cognitive act, namely, the intellectual recognition of the difference between past and present is secondary to the actual experiencing of this difference in interacting with the therapist. In this view, the emphasis shifts from insight to experience, although the role of insight as a secondary but often powerful consolidating factor is by no means denied. This emphasis on emotional experience has been earlier made by others, particularly Aichorn in his treatment of delinquent youth. The therapist's permissive, yet involved, behavior is perceived by the patient as a quite novel experience, and induces him to change his own responses. The old controversy between Plato's and Aristotle's learning theory, learning through logical insight versus learning through practice, is revived in this current argument, It appears to me that we deal not with a question to which the answer is either/or. Both principles, experience and insight, are operating in every form of learning, also in the specific form of re-education we call psychonalysis, and if I may add, also in dynamic psychotherapy. If some analysts choose to call this new emphasis on emotional experience a dilution of the true concepts of the classical theory, I can only answer them that the phenomenon in nature seldom can be understood from one single principle. Even the phenomenon of radiation could not be adequately described by the undulatory theory alone and required the revival of the older corpuscular theory. Certain aspects of radiation require undulatory, other aspects of it the corpuscular theory. The emphasis on the emotional events during treatment may dilute the purity of the single-minded emphasis on insight, but only the two together do adequately describe the actual therapeutic process.

Here is the point where the aims of etiological research and treatment begin to diverge. As long as insight into the origins of the disease were considered as the principal therapeutic factors the aim of genetic research and psychoanalytic treatment indeed coincided. The stress on emotional experience alters the absolute validity of this contention. It is quite possible that by focusing attention upon the emotional interaction between therapist and patient, the cognitive reconstruction of past events will lose its primary significance, although I believe that in many treatments this will always remain a potent factor. At present it would appear to me that intellectual insight follows, rather than precedes, corrective emotional experiences. It is made possible by the latter. Bluntly stated, profound therapeutic results may arise from merely corrective experiences, even if they are not followed by the revival of repressed memories. Cognitive reconstructions alone never have penetrated therapeutic effect. The appearance of repressed memories is the sign rather than the cause of an emotional change which has already taken place.[4]

This states very succinctly the problem of insight versus experience, as well as the relevance of technical procedures designed to produce both. Alexander has, incidentally, raised a question that plagues the field of psychotherapy, that is, the definitions, distinctions and delimitation of psychoanalysis versus other exploratory theories. There has been a distinct tendency to sharply differentiate psychoanalysis from all other forms of psychotherapy. This tendency derives partly from the notion that the process of psychoanalysis is different in essence from other varieties of psychotherapeutic endeavors. It also arises from a need to distinguish the so-called "deep therapies" from the more "superficial" ones, which carries a value judgement as to the ultimate value of psychoanalysis as being more basic and curative than the other psychotherapies. This question can only be decided by the future conceptions of personality development and the nature of change in human operations. However, psychoanalysis is a specialized form of psychotherapy based on its own theoretical system and defined by the utilization of certain technical procedures such as transference, etc. Its value as a therapeutic procedure does not rest on its presumed ultimate truth regarding the motives and organization of human experience. Its value must be determined by its greater capacity to increase the knowledge of human behavior and encourage research in the pathology of personality development. In many ways this is strikingly true, yet the past thirty years has shown that there is not a "true psychoanalysis" versus a diluted variety called intensive psychotherapy or dynamic psychotherapy, etc.[5] Psychoanalysis is a subdivision of psychotherapy which is a method of influencing human behavior by the verbal and non-verbal application of theoretical principles which are constantly expanding and developing.

In some circles there is a notion that all the psychotherapeutic procedures and techniques are merely semantic alterations or superficial applications of the classical principles of dynamic psychology. These individuals emphasize the essential similarities and propose an integration which would incorporate all the deviant theories and practices. It is my belief that this is not only premature but doomed to failure since the ultimate truths of personality development and pathology lie somewhere in the future. Each theoretical approach with its therapeutic applications should be developed and studied in order to enlarge the parameters and factors which come to bear on human development. Some of the therapeutic applications of the ego psychoanalysts are at variance with some of the practices of the orthodox analysts and can never be integrated into a common approach unless the theoretical premises are also modified and integrated. Enlightenment and exploration should be the goal rather than rapproachment. It is clear that there are no single avenues to nirvana and many roads lead to Rome. We have yet to discover the shortest, most appropriate and most illuminating avenue to the comprehension of human development. Psychoanalysis is one of the royal highways which must be repaired and remodeled and even abandoned if it does not serve its true purpose. It cannot claim any special virtue because of its noble history and must justify its claims through a continuous demonstration of its value. At any rate, the energy and time which is spent in differentiating other therapies from psychoanalysis could be better spent in determining what is the essence of the process of change and cure, since it occurs demonstrably in such varied and unscientific activities as in faith healing, magic and sorcery as well as in the rational procedures called scientific psychotherapy. Cure is not necessarily a sufficient criterion of the truth of the theory which produces it. Change can occur from the most diverse and paradoxical theoretical formulations. We still do not clearly comprehend what transpires in the process of change. Our theory, however, is most important in arriving at the ultimate truth, with a minimum of false and misleading side tracks.[6] In this sense, psychoanalysis, if viewed as a subdivision of the broad subject of psychotherapy, can allow us to investigate the whole psychotherapeutic process without a preconception about what is deep or superficial, permanent or transient, basic or secondary, and worst of all, true as opposed to a false view of man's psychology.

DREAMS

Freud's work on the dream and its significance in the mental economy is firmly established in the behavioral sciences. The function and meaning of the dream, theoretically and practically, has been considerably modified in recent years. The dream when adequately interpreted constituted "the royal road to the unconscious" and gave the therapist the clearest and most expansive view of the id contents. So long as the focus in therapy was to make the unconscious conscious or to free the repressed feelings, the dream was a fruitful source for discovering these repressed or unconscious forces. The free association process which also served this purpose was long and tedious. Dream analysis early became an integral part of psychoanalytic therapy and played a large part in the process. However, it became clear that intensive dream analysis was too time consuming and did not yield sufficient returns to justify all the expended time.

Dream analysis was a useful instrument for validating Freud's theoretical conceptions. Although theoretically valuable, it began to play a more modest role in the treatment process. More and more only parts of the dream were analyzed and soon only a limited amount of free association of the dream material was permitted. On other occasions the dream would only be heard and not interpreted although the therapist took account of its message. Finally, the analysis of dreams took its place in the therapeutic process as an expression of the mental life of the patient which at times could be very revealing. However, since its message was disguised, at times the overt verbalizations were more efficient communications about the patient's neurotic problems. Although the use of the dream in the therapeutic process has been sharply reduced during the past thirty years, its value in illuminating many aspects of the individual's covert and prelogical processes is still unchallenged. The meaning of the dream content, its structure and function in the mental economy has been revised by many theorists, particularly Jung, Adler, Fromm, Rado and some physiologists who have experimented with the dream process.

Freud made a systematic study of the dream and concluded that it was a product of mental functioning rather than a random, accidental phenomenon. Whatever the validity of his description of the dream mechanics and its purpose or function, his recognition of the dream as a meaningful communication will remain an epochal milestone.

Freud's interpretations of the dream content rested on his view of the psychic apparatus and its model of functioning. The dream was an outlet for unconscious needs or desires which could not be fulfilled during the waking hours because of cultural prohibitions.

Consequently, he stated that without exception, dreams were wish fulfillments disguised by elaborate distortions using various devices such as condensation, displacement, secondary elaboration, and other techniques. Ultimately, the needs or desires expressed in the dream were libidinal in nature. Freud established an elaborate coterie of symbols which represented the sexual organs and sexual activity. For a long time there was an undisciplined tendency to interpret symbols as if they all had universal meaning rather than distinguishing between the accidental or personal symbol as opposed to the universal symbol. There has been a more cautious application of symbol interpretation following some work by Fromm on dreams which has enhanced the value of dream interpretation.[7]

The meaning of the dream for Freud then, was always concealed in its distortions and the dream as described by the dreamer was thus only the manifest dream which disguised the latent content. The dream was derived from infantile, instinctual sources and was always a hallucinatory fulfillment of irrational wishes, particularly sexual wishes. The function of the dream is to preserve sleep. The dream according to Freud was always stimulated by a present event which evoked early infantile experiences. The resulting dream was a product of this interaction.

Freud's interpretation of dreams was challenged very early by Jung, who indicated that dreams also had a protective function which was oriented to the future. A dream could, in addition to dealing with the past, also deal with the goals and ideals of an individual and represent an attempt to overcome conflict regarding future wishes and desires. Jung gradually reduced the use of free association of dream material and utilized his archetype symbolism to interpret the dream meaning.

Adler saw the dream as an attempt to face an actual difficulty in the life of a dreamer which dealt with rational problems in the present. Fromm broadened the meaning of the dream by viewing it as "a meaningful and significant expression of any kind of mental activity under the condition of sleep."[8] This implied that the dream could concern itself with a variety of issues, in addition to its wish-fulfilling function, and could be drawn from many sources, both conscious as well as unconscious. The dream is a meaningful kind of mental activity and differs from waking thought and activity in several important ways. First, the dream is a product entirely of the individual's own making. The dreamer writes his own script in which he casts the characters and directs and produces the show. The characters are all of his making, and it must be recognized that the figures who play roles in his dream may represent live or real persons, but they are in the show by virtue of the dreamer putting them there. They do not get into the act by themselves. Since it is all played out in phantasy, the dreams disregard the physical laws of time and space, and consequently do not follow any of the laws of logic. Symbolic representation is a common vehicle for relating the drama. Freud made a good deal of symbolism, particularly as it involved sexual material. There are three kinds of symbols: the conventional, the accidental or personal, and the universal symbol. The conventional symbol is represented by the familiar name we have for objects, like chair or table. These symbols are understood only by convention in particular cultures. The accidental symbol is one that has meaning for a person because of personal associations and particular experiences. The sea may be a symbol of joyous peace and contentment or intense danger and anguish, depending upon one's experiences with water. Although some aspects of water have universal significance, they may also have private or personal significance. This is an extremely common occurrence, and such use of symbols must be distinguished from the universal symbol in interpretation of dreams. The universal symbols, like fire, or "outskirts of town" have meanings for all peoples in all cultures throughout history. Although they may also have personal meaning, they have a generally accepted meaning for all. Freud implied that all symbols have sexual significance. He described large numbers of such symbols, for example, spires, sticks, pointed objects, etc., as representing the male genital, and cavities, boxes, open spaces, as representing the female genital. While such objects can be sexual symbols, they do not have the universal significance which Freud attributed to them. Fromm has emphasized the necessity of interpreting each symbol in the light of the patient's own experiences before accepting them as having a universal meaning.

The clear difference between the dream and waking activity lies in the fact that in the waking state there is an active changing of the environment. In the dream state there is only mentating or phantasying. Thus, change never takes place in our environment, only in ourselves. Because we have no need to conform to physical laws or to be burdened by the requirements of waking life, we make long trips in our dreams without buying tickets or allowing sufficient time to elapse before we arrive somewhere. We simply decide to go and we are there. If we keep this in mind, the dream content is not as bizarre or peculiar as it often appears. The same features occur in our day dreams which allow us to overcome enormous obstacles by a mere decision. We need never concern ourselves about time, space, or the problems of everyday living unless we especially want to in our dreams. The dream is all imagery, whatever provokes it, and whatever its physiological origins might be. From this point of view, Fromm considers the dream as being capable of dealing with all kinds of mental activity, wish-fulfilling, problems solving, phantasy planning, etc. Like Jung, he points out that the dream represents the activity of the individual during sleep, with all the limitations of being in the sleeping state. The activities, like those of the waking state, derive from conscious as well as unconscious sources and can express and deal with the more tender, decent, and intelligent feelings than are represented in the id. In fact, Fromm points out that dreams may be purer expressions of personality since there is no need to be concerned with reality confrontation, and thus are more honest expressions of feelings and attitudes. While in the waking state an individual may be forced to be sweet and pleasant to his boss in order to preserve his job, in his dreams he may be able to express his true resentments and hostility. Dreams, therefore, may not be entirely irrational, in spite of the fact that they need not be logical.

Essentially then, Fromm's contributions to dream theory are an elaboration of Jung's idea that the dream is more than wish-fulfilling and may represent the more positive, creative and constructive aspect of man's development. In addition, one must be careful in interpreting symbols not to assume universal meanings for all symbols since often enough a cow may simply be a cow, and a stick may represent something to lean on rather than an implement to be used in sexual intercourse even when it is straight, long, and hard. Dreams need not necessarily be distorted, and the clearest, most convincing examples of Freud's interpretations are those dreams in which he recognizes the least distortion. Dreams are very useful in the process of therapy because they give strong hints about what is really going on inside a person who may be reluctant or unable to communicate in the waking state. To be truly useful, dreams should be self-propogated or spontaneously produced rather than a response to the therapist's requests—implied or explicit. One receives a truer picture of what a person is really like, because in the dream the necessities of reality are removed.

With the development of an ego psychology and an increased emphasis on the conscious and rational elements in the neurotic process, there has been a greater tendency to view the dream statement as an expression of these rational attitudes that are kept out of awareness because of neurotic defenses and cultural prohibitions. This view has been developed by Sandor Rado, who views the dream as an adaptational process which attempts to deal with unresolved emotional conflicts. He sees it as the product of the action self or the total organism in action, which is enfeebled in sleep and allows certain problems to be tackled which cannot be dealt with in the waking state. Here, the question of manifest or latent content becomes secondary to the adaptive activities attempted in sleep and expressed in the dream. The necessity for such elaborate disguises is not considered crucial, and consequently, there is less concern about symbolism and the other techniques of dream distortion.

The dream for Freud was a beautiful demonstration of his theoretical views and his interpretation tended to confirm his views through a skillful examination of the dream content and the emphasis on certain elements in the dream while overlooking others. It is extremely interesting and illustrative to note the varying interpretations given the same dream by observers of differing theoretical orientations. Fromm illustrates this in his examination of Freud's interpretations of a dream of nakedness as well as his famous, "Dream of the Botanical Monograph."[9]

Freud's interpretations of dreams tended to be static statements about the contents of the unconscious. They pointed up a repressed idea or need that was in conflict with the ego and which the individual was not aware of in his waking state rather than a struggle in which the total personality was involved. These interpretations were largely cathartic in that they rarely revealed anything that was not already known in the conscious state. They reflected Freud's views that therapy was simply a process of uncovering and that the insight itself would then be curative. The use of the dream in recent years has been extended to reveal not only the content of the conflict, but the individual's struggles, goals and desires. The atmosphere and emotional climate of the dream is often more important than the content since the nature of the conflict is generally known to the dreamer prior to the dream. What is not available to the individual are his true feelings and attitudes toward the elements in the conflict. Often this is not hidden in the latent content but is revealed in the actions, feelings and symbolic use of the dream content. Although Freud claimed that those who disagreed with his dream interpretations generally made the error of confusing the manifest content with latent content, it is striking that his most convincing evidence of the wish-fulfilling thesis of the dream rested in the manifest content of the dreams of children which were frankly and manifestly wish-fulfilling.

The difficulty with Freud's technique of dream interpretations was in its elaborate detail which was impractical, while a more limited interpretation revealed little that could not be discovered elsewhere.

Dream interpretation in the hands of neo-Freudian psychoanalysts, particularly Horney, Sullivan, Fromm and Rado becomes a motivational analysis of a life situation in which a conflict is occurring. The conflict is expressed in terms of the patient's current activities and in the way his sensitivities, pressures and tensions are revealed as an aspect of the neurotic process. The dream may represent an illusory fulfillment of frustrated desires, but it generally expresses much more. It is viewed as an active process which is an attempt at communication of the adaptive struggles the patient is undergoing. It is more than a fresh or novel discovery of infantile or repressed data. It is seen as a new conceptual attempt to deal with a current live conflict and is viewed as a process as living in the dream state with its physiological limitations rather than a statement of a conflict of the past stirred up by a present association. In therapy, then, it becomes an invaluable source of information regarding the activities, conflicts and attitudes of the individual which he may have difficulty in expressing in his waking state. A dream, then, is interpreted only to the extent that it reveals some motivational and adaptational data about the patient's living inside and outside of the analytic situation. Thus, the dream is more versatile than Freud ever believed. It can be wish-fulfilling, revealing hitherto unrecognized anxieties and conflicts as well as prospective, predictive, restrospective and a combination of all of these. The dream process becomes another mental operation drawn from conscious as well as unconscious sources which attempts to deal with conflicts through the peculiar modality of the dream with its free use of symoblic, visual imagery and the freedom of the imagination unhampered by actual realistic restraints. Some distortion in terms of condensation and displacement may be necessary if these conflicts are too stressful or anxiety provoking to be viewed directly. On the other hand, they may be clear and undistorted and a communication unhampered by conventional limitations. It is very helpful to recognize that a dream is a script written and acted by the dreamer and thus reveals not only his views and attitudes but is peopled and acted by characters that he directs.

The dreams can then become an intergral part of the therapy to be utilized as the treatment situation allows and not used simply to reconfirm the therapist's theory of personality development. It can often be a corrective to a misleading hypothesis about the patient's problems. Its interpretation should rest on the examination of the motivational intent and thesis of the dream as related to the dreamer's current living. The dream must be viewed in its totality, as a complete story, parts of which may be clear and undistorted and other parts disguised and requiring associations and symbolic clarification in order to be made meaningful. In this context latent versus manifest content loses its prime significance. The latent becomes simply disguised elements of the dream which need to be understood through interpretative skills rather than evidence of unconscious material. In essence, the dream is a communication of a process of living and a dynamic encounter rather than a memory feat provoked through some fortuitous association of a current event which exposes a repressed wish or desire. The analysis of the dream can expose new aspects of a conflictual situation which not only illuminate the problem but also present the dreamer's efforts to adapt and overcome these issues.

The following example might illustrate some aspects of the practical application of the dream in the therapeutic process.

A 54 year old compulsive patient was in treatment because of a phobic inability to practice his professional craft which required his speaking in front of audiences. Our work has clarified the phobia to the extent of revealing that it was involved with his necessity to be correct and in control of himself under all circumstances. Public appearances in which he might be called upon to perform produced panicky fear in the anticipation of these events. One evening, he had a dream which was clear and distinct but which he only vaguely understood. He dreamt: "I was driving in my Thunderbird in the proper lane and at a very reasonable speed when a car alongside of me sideswiped me. The whole side of my car was smashed in. We stopped and I went to the other car to exchange licenses and insurance information. The other car was an old beaten up one and there were two people in it. I recognized one as the dean of my son's college and we got into friendly conversation. We exchanged licenses and departed on very friendly terms. As I went back to my car I wondered if I had done the right thing, if I had gotten the correct information and I reviewed in my mind whether I had said anything that could be held against me."

The patient recognized several aspects of the dream that related to that day's events. He had driven a friend in his Thunderbird to keep an appointment at a country club. He had first picked up his car from the garage where his radio had been repaired and had a slight tussle with the repair man who tried to charge him for a job which they had been responsible for. Unlike his usual placating and dignified behavior, he raised his voice, requested to see the service manager and managed to successfully correct the error. However, this delayed him and he was concerned about being late for his appointment. He added that he was very delighted with his Thunderbird which did not have a scratch on it and felt that since its production was being discontinued he had a rare car that he wished to keep in perfect shape. He had some associations with the dean who had talked to him sometime ago regarding his son's college status. He had been a charming, helpful man, whom he felt he had impressed favorably. He had no other associations to the dream until I pointed out to him that he seemed to take the accident very calmly, unconcerned about the damage, even friendly to the occupants of the car who had been clearly wrong in the accident. I highlighted this discrepant attitude, and he added that he was very angry about the damage but in the dream he was unconcerned and cheerful. I then inquired about the only feeling he had felt in the dream, that of being uncertain whether he had performed well and gotten all the relevant information. I suggested that he acted as if he were guilty, trying to befriend the people in the other car and being concerned about whether he would be held responsible. To this he replied that he was certain he was in the right and that all the evidence was clear in this regard, but that his behavior towards the other men was typical of the way he acted in many instances. This reminded him of many incidents in his life which he had not described before. These were occasions when even though he was clearly in the right, he acted guiltily and was afraid that he would be found guilty. It reminded me, I said, of the story of the man who went to his lawyer, having found his wife in bed with another man and having him ejected from his house. He was asking the lawyer if this man could really sue him. The patient responded to this story with a clear assent that this was precisely how he himself always behaved, and then he related an incident when he was nineteen. He was teasing a driver who was trying to pass him on the road. When the other car caught up with him at a red light the driver of it started to get out of his car. The patient was frightened sick and drove off in panicky fear. He never forgot this incident although he never mentioned it to anyone in his life.

It is clear that this dream represented a problem for the patient that was involved in his phobia. It exposed an aspect of his personality that had not been revealed before. This was his tendency to feel guilty and open to danger and abuse even when he was in the right. In the dream the patient calmly reviews some damage to a very prized possession under circumstances in which he is entirely innocent. There is no evidence of anger, fury or any emotion other than the need to placate and be charming. Actually, he was furious, a fury which in the dream is kept under strict control, as opposed to the incident in the early afternoon when he allowed some anger to be made public for practically the first time in all his adult life. The dream indicates the reaction to the afternoon incident about which he was both proud and ashamed. In the dream he is again the man in control, proper and decent and noble. This problem of nobility has been the pressing issue in his life and has prevented him from being publicly aggressive and self regarding. His hated view of himself is the man in the dream who cannot be human and angry. This is the idealized phoney individual who does not allow him to appear in public for fear that he will not maintain this idealized perfectionistic status. The dream not only reveals this conflict, but does more by indicating clearly that the fear of retribution as exemplified in the incident when he was nineteen prevents him from being unpleasant even when he is within his rights. The dream revealed a new facet of this patient's problem as well as demonstrating in a most graphic way the extent to which he degrades his own values and needs to maintain the neurotic status of the controlled, disciplined man. It portrayed the essence of the conflict which was being investigated in the analytic situation where the patient felt he was being pushed to being other than the sweet, proper person. The dream was telling him how dangerous this was. The interpretation of the dream was then obvious to him; he must be sweet, genial and controlled at all costs, even when his prize possessions are damaged. Even when he is so controlled there is still the danger of his being hurt in some way. The afternoon's event frightened him and he is saying that it is extremely dangerous to change and to give up the need for total control.

In addition to the message which seems so clearly delivered in this dream, it should be noted that whatever symbolic elements were involved in the automobile, the dean, the damage to his prized possession, etc., it was profitable to deal almost entirely with the manifest content. A deeper interpretation would only extend the meaning of the feared damage to a prized possession. The interpretation is limited to the current issues in the therapy and the validity of the interpretation was enhanced by the evidence from the patient's waking life.

Another patient's daydream reveals several aspects of the same tendency to utilize the manifest contents of a dream, emphasizing the emotional atmosphere of the dream as the focus of the interpretation.

The patient phantasied a situation in which a collection agent went to his home and his wife handed over a radio the agent asked for. The patient became furious, told his wife off, calling her stupid and ineffective, and recited a collection of grievances he had against her. After a long tirade, he decided to leave his wife who had just given birth (actually this had occurred three weeks before) and divorce her.

This patient was amused about this daydream and could not account for it at all. He was concerned about the violence of his feelings and actions since he rarely lost his temper. When asked about the events leading up to the phantasy, he suddenly said, "Oh, yes," and proceeded to describe in detail a swindle in which he had been involved. A friend of his had bought a camera for him, but instead of paying cash had bought it on time. He had given his friend the total amount, but recently he was informed that the camera would have to be returned, since the payments had not been kept up. His friend had taken the full amount and had only made a down payment on the camera. In order to clarify the situation, he had made an additional payment to his friend to dispose of the debt with the promise of repayment in the near future. Following the second payment the friend left town leaving the patient minus camera and money.

It was clear that this daydream was a simple reversal of the situation in which the patient had been swindled and had acted in a simpleminded, naive fashion. In a transference of blame he portrays his precise difficulty as occurring to his wife. What is of interest in regard to the theory of dreams is that the phantasy is not disguised at all (except in the displacement of the people involved) and that the emotions experienced in the phantasy were completely denied by the patient as representing the feelings he felt towards himself. He had not felt angry at himself, just sorry for his poor friend who needed to steal. He had not considered pressing charges or making any real attempts to reclaim his loss. He had the need to maintain the picture of himself as a clever man of the world who was generous and without malice. The daydream revealed the extent of his anger and disgust at himself and the need to conceal from himself the picture of an individual who was easily taken advantage of. The essence of the dream lay in the undisguised, manifest content which was the current topic of the analytic situation. In this dream there is no element of a repressed wish or desire, but an attempt to work through the humiliation in connection with an incident in the patient's life of which he was entirely conscious. It allowed him to recognize his need to remain perfect and his anger at himself for the manifestation of a weakness. It also demonstrated very dramatically his tendency to transfer blame to avoid recognizing his own deficiencies.

Another brief dream illustrates how the prospective aspect of the dream precedes developments in the therapeutic process and frequently informs the patient of major movements in his life.

This dream occurred in a paranoid female who had a brief psychotic episode without hospitalization. She was seen during the psychotic episode and the work proceeded very favorably. The dream occurred after one year of therapy. During this time we had examined her fear of intimacy and the tendency to translate every friendly gesture into a threat. She was finally able to consider the possibility that my goodbys following our hours were perhaps only conventional gestures and not attempts to subvert her into friendliness. She dreamt shortly after this occasion, "You were staying at my home. In the morning when you left for work you asked me to take care of your clothes. I gave you a warm, 'uncle kiss' when you left."

Unlike all her previous dreams which were frightening and nightmarish accounts of being exploited, this was a situation in which she could feel exploited but reacted in a warm, friendly manner. She recognized that this very situation had occurred with her husband, and she felt she still needed to see me as her husband to allow herself to be friendly. It was a clear statement of some trust in me, and an indication of a possible break in her paranoid system. It was more than wish-fulfilling or even problem stating. It expressed a feeling which could not yet be formulated openly and which needed to be said in the dream even though there was a minimum of distortion.

A dream of a severely obsessive young lady demonstrates the value of the dealing with the manifest content as a device for accelerating the current therapeutic endeavor. She dreamt of hanging on to an airplane in speedy flight by her finger. She was doing acrobatics and felt no fear—she had a long standing phobia of high places and her only association to the dream was the pointing finger in the Michelangelo fresco; God pointing his finger as he makes Adam. The patient was astonished at the interpretation of her godliness and extraordinary presumptiveness. It was a completely new view of herself which had been suggested in therapy on many occasions and which she had rejected out of hand. However, as a result of the dream she was strongly impressed and finally recognized that her phobia of high places involved her fear of being helpless and her need to be superhuman in order to guarantee her safety at all times and in all places.

Dreams are viewed by the ego theorists as products of mental activity of all kinds and not only wish-fulfillment. The mechanics of the formation of the dream as described by the classical work of Freud on dreams remains largely undisturbed. Although some theorists do not make a clear distinction between manifest and latent content, other theorists limit the associative material until they recognize a clear statement in the dream which can be usefully employed in pursuing the work of therapy. Neo-Freudian theorists see the dream as an adaptive process which states a problem as well as indicating some attempt at solving it. Freud's use of the dream, however, was usually only a statement of the conflict. The adaptational view sees it not only as a statement but also as an attempted solution. In utilizing the dream in therapy, the therapist must ask himself not only what the dreamer is trying to say, but also what he is trying to do. A dream which is familiar to all, and which was used to demonstrate the wish-fulfilling character of the dream illustrates the adaptive function of the dream. This dream occurs in a variety of ways but essentially is triggered by the somatic stimulus of a full bladder. In this type of dream the dreamer goes through the act of urinating or searching for a urinal. Eventually, however, the dreamer awakes, unless he has already disposed of the problem and is awakened by his wet bed. After he wakes he still needs to urinate and will proceed to do so. The dream process attempts to deal with a physiological need by hallucinating the performance of the function. In this sense it is fulfilling a need. However, the dream is also attempting to adapt the organism to a full bladder without awakening the sleeper. It succeeds up to a point, yet the physiological tension is not relieved and so the dreamer awakes. Such a dream is not a fulfillment of a wish, nor even a representation of the desire to remain asleep since the dreamer must ultimately awaken. The dreamer is attempting some adaptation to a somatic stimulus by a hallucinatory performance which is unsuitable and unable to satisfy the physiological requirements. Such is the nature of the dreams of starving, deprived or imprisoned individuals. These dreams appear to be wish-fulfillments but are actually the attempts to adapt to stressful physiological situations. They state the problem and the attempts at solution. They are prospective in that they express the goals and needs of the individuals as well as retrospective in pointing up the frustrated desires. They are often simple and undistorted by complicated symbolism and are excellent examples of how a dream can be utilized in the therapeutic process.

Technical Alterations in Therapy

The effects of theoretical alterations on therapeutic procedures can be demonstrated in the examination of the therapy of typical neurotic and psychotic disorders. An examination of the effect of recent theoretical alterations on therapy might be seen in a study of the changes in outlook regarding the so-called negative therapeutic reaction. While all the neo-Freudian theorists will not accept the formulations presented here, most of them would agree, more or less, with the major premises. It is being presented not to indicate a definitive position but rather to suggest how greatly the therapeutic atmosphere might change as our theory is altered. This situation was dramatically portrayed in the work of Frieda Fromm-Reichmann who did such astonishing and successful work with schizophrenics when she concluded that the concept of primary narcissism of Freud was inaccurate.[10] She concluded that schizophrenics were capable of marked transference reactions and could be treated through the psychoanalytic process if significant changes in technique were made.

The problem of the negative therapeutic reaction is selected for presentation because it involves a large group of patients who were also considered untreatable in classical psychoanalytic theory by virtue of their overpowering need to fail. The therapeutic atmosphere with regard to this group of patients was prevailingly pessimistic and the therapist's failures were supported by the theoretical formulations. A fresh look at the theory and the phenomenon produces a more optimistic attitude towards therapy in these circumstances.

Freud concluded that the negative therapeutic reaction represented active resistance to the progress of therapy based on the patient's need to fail, rather than on some defect in the therapist's theory, or in his grasp of the problem or in his technique. On the assumption that such patients, in spite of his best knowledge and efforts, refused to alter their pathology, he interpreted their resistances, blocks, and negativism as involving primary instinctual defects.

The authority of Freud and the relief from responsibility had the unfortunate but not unexpected result of encouraging the therapist to overlook and disregard his possible role in the development of this response. The therapist was thus supported by a theoretical formulation which supplied all the answers and even provided a rationale for some of his therapeutic failures. This attitude interfered with any serious investigation of these therapeutic failures for a long time and encouraged an unduly pessimistic view of the therapeutic potentialities of the analytic method. But its most serious effect was to encourage the therapist to be inclined to view his role in any therapeutic impasse or failure as blameless, perpetuating the myth of his infallibility and the patient's obstinacy and permanent inadequacy. This attitude strengthened the authoritative role of the theorist and made the clarification and resolution of the transference ultimately more difficult and frequently impossible. Failures in therapy represented inherent weaknesses of the instinctual apparatus and so no revision of theory or technique was necessary. On the contrary, such instances reaffirmed the theory and was another example of the self-sealing, self-perpetuating tendency of some of Freud's original theoretical formulations.

An examination of the problem could be facilitated if negative therapeutic reaction was not conceived as a single phenomenon which has distinctive characteristics and as produced by a single set of factors. There are many kinds of negative therapeutic reactions which, when studied individually, reveal a multitude of causative factors. They are essentially varieties of resistance of a massive kind.

The progress of a therapeutic situation may be examined from three points of view:

1) The nature of the patient's defenses, or his character structure.
2) The personality and therapeutic techniques of the therapist.
3) The nature of the relationship or interactions between the two. This could be defined as the interpersonal, or field aspects of the therapeutic process.

From this framework we will find that a therapeutic impasse can result from a particular type of defensive structure whatever the personality of the therapist. In addition, we will find that certain defenses produce negative reactions only with certain kinds of therapists. At the same time, we might find that some therapists experience a therapeutic impasse with many kinds of neurotic defenses, while other therapists rarely experience the phenomenon. And finally, we will discover that certain character defenses have an overwhelming tendency to produce a therapeutic impasse with any kind of therapist by virtue of the relationship they tend to establish. The masochistic defenses frequently produce the therapeutic impasse which led Freud to describe the negative therapeutic reaction, and we are all familiar with some therapists who have difficulty with any type of patient they undertake to treat.

Consequently, many so-called negative therapeutic reactions seem to arise out of difficulties which can ultimately be traced either to the defenses or techniques of the patient or to the deficiencies of the therapist or his techniques. Above all, the impasse lies in the faulty therapeutic relationship which is established between them. At the same time, if this thesis is correct, there are no negative therapeutic reactions which cannot be overcome when the patient-doctor relationship is altered or ameliorated. Such impasses can be overcome when we understand the nature of the defenses which have instigated them and either alter the technique or change the therapist. We can no longer attribute the difficulty to the patient's instinctual defects or his uncooperative attitude. It is in the nature of the patient's problems to have characteristic defenses and resistances while it is the therapist's role to deal with them and, if possible, overcome them.

For purposes of description and clarity, we can describe situations where one of the three factors is most in evidence or at least may be the instigating cause of the impasse.

A. Patients' Defensive Structure

1. There is a large group of patients who are so belligerent, unpleasant, and contentious, that in spite of an active interest in therapy, they alienate the therapist and ultimately produce a stalemate which terminates therapy. They tend to visit many analysts, but therapy is either never established, or it soon bogs down in a negative therapeutic reaction.

2. A compulsory need to appear perfect often produces an impasse by virtue of its not allowing any new insight or understanding to penetrate the personality structure. Such patients will never accept any observation which appears to make them look imperfect. Karen Horney felt that this defense was the explanation for the negative therapeutic reaction. She said: "According to my interpretation the difficulty in leading the patient to acquire real insight into his problem lies in the seemingly inpenetrable front he offers because of his compulsory need to appear perfect."[11] The same situation often develops in the grandiose patient who knows all the answers and can never accept anyone else's view.

3. Utterly independent or utterly dependent patients either resist any help or passively accept whatever is done for them. The defense of needing no one prevents any relationship from ever becoming established, and the passive acceptance of all interpretations and insights gives a false appearance of great movement. However, no change in living seems ever to occur.

4. Some very severely obsessive-compulsive patients cannot relinquish their need to control every event and exchange in their lives. In therapy this pattern can result in the patient's never losing control and in his attempting to dominate the therapeutic relationship with no possibility of benefit. The technique of undoing both during the hours and after the hours negates any insight and change, and ultimately, the negative therapeutic reaction ensues.

5. The paranoid patient deals with every exchange as a malevo-

lent invasion and attack until he can allow some doubt to enter his distorted perceptions and conceptions. In this atmosphere, there is no possibility of establishing a therapeutic relationship and when the therapist is viewed as unremittingly antagonistic, a therapeutic impasse develops which can only be resolved through a change in therapist. This impasse can frequently be avoided by not challenging the distortions until some degree of trust has developed in the therapist and in the possibility of benefit from the relationship.

6. We frequently discover that a negative therapeutic reaction has occurred after prolonged therapy during which the patient has seemingly been working well in therapy. While all goes well, no change occurs in the patient's living. We can sometimes discover that the patient has been secretly maintaining a delusion or withholding crucial data and so has never really committed himself to the therapy. Therapy under these conditions cannot get beyond the therapeutic block until these delusions are exposed and dealt with.

B. *The Personality and Techniques of the Therapist*

(In this category we can detail a great number of characteristics of the therapist which lend themselves to the development of a negative therapeutic reaction. I shall briefly mention a few.)

1. The therapist who theoretically sees the analytic process as endless, and as long as the patient does not complain, therapy continues, although no change occurs.

2. The patient who changes to his maximum potential, but not sufficiently enough to satisfy the therapist's goals or preconceptions.

3. The patient who changes, but not in the direction that suits the therapist's requirements or ideals.

4. The patient who gains insight with some change, but who has not produced the required analytical materials such as primal scene, etc. Here therapy proceeds endlessly, or until such material is produced.

C. *The Patient-Doctor Relationship*

This situation, I believe, is of greatest relevance to the negative therapeutic reaction. In these situations, the patient, by virtue of his prevailing character defense, invariably and immutably becomes involved in all his relationships in a way which ultimately is self-defeating and self-destructive. This is called the masochistic reaction, and an examination of this phenomenon reveals that we are again dealing not with an instinctual deformation but rather a typical, interpersonal, or transference situation which, when sufficiently understood, can be resolved. In a sense, every defense is self-defeating, since it is designed to maintain the neurotic structure which limits personality development. In therapy, the defenses are utilized to thwart the analyst's efforts. However, the masochistic defenses are particularly suited to fulfill all these self-destructive activities. This technique enables the individual to distort every contact, exchange, and involvement with others into a source of self-denial and derogation. Consequently, an impasse is inevitable, whatever the personality of the therapist. Every interpretation or lack of one, every question or the absence of one, every maneuver or its opposite will lead to a feeling of derogated self-esteem and complaints about the lack of benefits received from the therapeutic process. A positive appraisal will be rebutted or denied, while a negative appraisal will be agreed with. Meanwhile, the therapist will be assaulted on either score for being misinformed or plain nasty. Consequently, the very nature of the patient's patterns of interacting inevitably leads to an impasse in which the patient, the therapist, or both agree that an insurmountable obstacle exists to the further course of treatment. Here, we have the clearest expression of the therapeutic impasse which is the essence of the character defense. It is designed to produce impasse, to re-experience failure and defeat, and thus to further derogate the already low self-esteem.

Another instance of this type of impasse is in the psychopathic personality. Here, the patient uses his defense to encourage some trust and conviction in his potentialities for relationship and insight. The therapist, in his earnest desire to be useful, is entrapped in this device, and soon discovers that he has been hoodwinked. Frequent repetitions of such experiences tend to introduce some distrust and cynicism into the relationship which then reduces the possibility of favorable outcome. Eventually a negative therapeutic situation results. If initially the therapist refuses to entertain any trust in the possibility of a beneficial outcome, the basis for successful therapy does not exist. Thus, the therapist is again damned if he does and damned if he doesn't. In a sense, his maneuvers are precisely opposite to the masochistic character defenses, since the psychopath endeavors to alter every exchange or event into a statement about his supreme worthwhileness. Unlike the masochist, he tries to emanate optimism about his potentialities for success. To a large extent, this accounts for the enormous difficulties in resolving the psychopath's defensive structure.

ANOTHER EFFECT OF THEORY ON THERAPY

Another example of the effect of altered theory on therapy is reflected in the problem of the paranoid state. The theory and therapy of the paranoid illnesses has been profoundly influenced by Freud's recognition of the relationship of paranoia to repressed homosexual drives. This grew out of his classic study of the Schreiber case in which he demonstrated the semantic reversals which resulted in paranoid attitudes.[12] On that occasion he showed how the formulation of "I (a man) love (a man) becomes altered to he (a man) hates me" by the homosexual's inability to accept his repressed homosexual drives. This view of the paranoid process was extremely fruitful and explained much that heretofore had been uncomprehensible. Its value as a therapeutic formulation, however, has been largely unsuccessful. In recent years, there have been many new developments in the concepts regarding homosexuality and the paranoid states. The studies of Sullivan, Rado, Robbins, Ullman and Ovesey have suggested new approaches to the whole question of the etiology and therapy of these disorders.

The grandiosity in the paranoid state was thought to follow the paranoid delusion as a way of explaining the special interest which the world focuses upon them. Freud doubted this explanation himself saying, "The development of megalomania is thus attributed to a process which we may describe as rationalization. But to ascribe such important affective consequences to a rationalization is, it seems to us, an entirely unpsychological procedure."[13]

The classic formulation thus states that a paranoid development is a defense against a repressed homosexual wish and the grandiose development is secondary to it. Thus, the emphasis on therapy is to explore and bring into the open the repressed homosexual wishes and make them acceptable to the patient's ego, which would obviate the need for the paranoid development.

An alternative view of this development can be postulated which might be stated in the following way. The paranoid development is secondary to a grandiose structure which develops in order to deal with extreme feelings of low esteem. There is considerable evidence to document this formulation which assumes that the grandiose development precedes the paranoid ideation. Such grandiosity will provoke belittling derogation and openly hostile attacks from the environment which may be sufficiently humiliating and damaging to encourage feelings of generalized rejection and malevolence.

Such a thesis is the reverse of Freud's formulation and does not specifically relate to the feelings of rejection or expected rejection when an individual is overwhelmed with the feelings of inadequacy and unacceptability attendant upon his homosexual interests. It broadens the concept of paranoia and suggests that any feelings of deficiency are dealt with through initial power movements which, if they fail or are undermined, may result in paranoid feelings. Thus, while paranoid mechanisms are sometimes associated with anticipated attacks and retributions which might result from an attempted (or feared) homosexual assault, these expectations are not simple displacements or semantic reversals. These individuals feel that as homosexuals (or suspected homosexuals by their own view) they are looked down on by the community, considered weak, impotent and unable to sustain a competitive struggle. Such deflated feelings may first result in grandiose feelings or an attempt to reinstate the deflated self-esteem by a display of strength or power.

Thus, the emphasis in therapy is shifted. The psychosexual history is no more significant than in any other psychopathological disorder and the adaptive aspects of the individual's living are explored. The therapeutic pessimism which has always accompanied the disorder can be lifted, in spite of the continued difficulties in the treatment process. The grandiosity and its development would occupy a prominent place in therapy. It would then be noted that the grandiosity in such patients is related to early, infantile omnipotence and is based solely on desire and not on performance. These patients require that their wishes and desires be immediately acknowledged and fulfilled. The desires usually represent items of success highly regarded in the individual's family by which they can command immediate recognition. Such persons, because of early experiences, have usually abandoned the possibility of developing any esteem except through magical fulfillment which will astound and stupify the world. This accounts for their feelings of personal uniqueness and thus they feel they no longer require any realistic effort to achieve their purposes.

The paranoid defenses are often more easily explored in therapy through instilling some doubt or uncertainty in regard to their delusional structure. When we have established some element of doubt we can then examine the distorted notions in the light of the alternative possibilities to their interpretation. In order to get the patient to consider his perceptions, he must see the therapist as a disinterested but benign helper. The consideration of alternative possibilities is best done by the direct confrontation and realistic appraisal of his interpretations. When a patient insists that he is being followed, we must recognize that he obviously is, for during any space of time, someone will always be behind him. The issue here is to help him see that the person behind him may be there for a variety of reasons, without forthrightly denying that he is following the patient. While this approach is extraordinarily difficult, it is often successful.

The revisions in psychoanalytic theory has encouraged new therapeutic approaches in the mental disorders which a more rigid theory did not find compatible. In recent years, group therapy, family therapy, milieu therapy, and other therapeutic approaches which take into account the cultural and societal elements in the development of mental illness have been developed. These approaches have expanded our therapeutic horizons and hold great promise in refining our theories regarding mental disorders.

Our therapeutic rationale is intimately related to our theoretical formulations regarding the mental illness. To guarantee a continuing growth of therapeutic knowledge and skill we must insure a free and open atmosphere for the development of new ideas and conceptions about personality development. This book, by detailing some of the formulations of the ego psychological theorists, has tried to indicate the value of these contributions when they are translated into therapeutic maneuvers and techniques. There has been great progress made in our understanding of human behavior since Freud, and most of it has come from the group of theorists who have built on the solid foundations of Freud's contributions without necessarily accepting all his theoretical constructs or frivolously discarding any of them. We honor our teachers by growing beyond them and not by remaining rooted in the past in which they made their epochal discoveries. We must take note of all the developments in the behavioral sciences in order to keep our formulations about human behavior current and responsive to new insights. In this way our therapeutic skills will also expand and will not be based on discoveries and conceptions which were characterized as an earlier phase of the science of human behavior. The great challenge of psychoanalysis to modern man can be met only by the recognition that psychoanalysis, born only recently, is a vital expanding science with a long life ahead it.

NOTES

1. Jones, Ernest: The Life and Work of Sigmund Freud. New York, Basic Books, 1955, Vol. II. pp. 497. In a letter to Pfister he said: "As for the transference it is altogether a curse." This type of remark was characteristic of Freud, who changed his mind frequently and revised his views as his experience indicated that such revision was in order.

2. Thompson, Clara, and Mullahy, P.: Psychoanalysis: Evolution and Development. New York, Hermitage House, 1950. This in essence is the view of most neo-Freudian psychoanalysts on the goals of psychoanalytic therapy.

3. This is an attempt to distinguish between the patient's behavior and the potential goals of therapy. The goals which can be achieved in therapy are intimately related to the patient's goals, which are either expressed overtly, or implied in his covert behavior. This distinction is amplified later on in this chapter. It is fully dealt with by Rado in the collecton of his papers in a volume called: Psychoanalysis of Behavior. New York, Grune & Stratton, 1956.

4. Alexander, Franz: Psychoanalytic therapy. Am. J. Psychotherapy, 116:323, 1960.

5. In recent years the Academy of Psychoanalysis was organized to develop and expand psychoanalysis as a science of human behavior. It has included psychoanalysts of various backgrounds and orientations and has avoided encouraging particular points of view or theoretical conceptions. Its influence is steadily advancing and it may avoid the growing tendency of the psychoanalytic institutes to become trade schools rather than scientific institutes.

6. Frank, Jerome: Persuasion and Healing. Baltimore, John Hopkins Press, 1961. Frank has attempted to discover, in a most interesting book, the essential factor in all psychotherapeutic activity, whenever change occurs in an individual's life.

7. Fromm, Erich: The Forgotten Language. New York, Rhinehart & Co., 1951. He also presents a more generalized theory regarding the significance of dreams.

8. Ibid.

9. This dream of Freud's played a large role in developing his theory of dreams. Fromm analyzes the famous dream in *The Forgotten Language* (p. 73) with most interesting results.

10. Practically all of Fromm-Reichmann's work had clear therapeutic implications. The collection of her writings in Psychoanalysis and Psychotherapy, Chicago, University of Chicago Press,, 1950 are rich with suggestions for the technical handling of both the neuroses and psychoses.

11. Horney, Karen: New Ways in Psychoanalysis. New York, W. W. Norton, 1939.

12. Freud, S.: Psychoanalytic Notes on an Autobiographical Account of a Case of Paranoia, Standard Edition, Vol. XII. These notes constituted a major source for Freud's theory of homosexuality. It was based on the notes of a Dr. Schreiber who was a jurist who suffered from paranoia during his life.

13. Ibid., p. 40.

Postscript

SCIENTIFIC PSYCHOLOGY or the science of the development of man had its beginning in the epochal work of Freud. He firmly established the principle of the dynamic development of personality. The outcome of this work made it possible to comprehend some of the pathological distortions in man's development. Freud developed his theories in the framework of the existing scientific philosophical systems. Under the influence of a philosophy of causality and quantitative mechanical concepts, Freud framed his theories to conform with the best scientific methodology available to him. Although his genius for observation and theorizing remain unparalled, in recent years some of his interpretations and conceptions of the dynamics of human behavior have been revised. Although his instinct theories were extraordinary achievements, they were drawn in the rigid energy mechanics mold and bound by the notions of absolute causality. The students of Freud and the work of psychiatrists and psychologists in the past thirty years have raised practical and theoretical questions as well as philosophical ones regarding his contributions. These developments have occurred in two directions. One was the extension of Freud's id theorizing and the attempts to validate the libido theory. Wilhelm Reich carried the instinct theory to its ultimate conclusion by discovering the libido which he called orgone. The other direction was in terms of the extension of ego psychology, which is the major interest of this book.

The extension of ego psychology was initiated by Alfred Adler, one of Freud's most competent and maligned colleagues. He felt that the libido and the libido theory were not descriptive of the basic motivations in human development. He described the search for power as the major propelling force in the individual's struggle to achieve status, prestige and feelings of superiority. The need to assert oneself and affirm oneself inevitably involved the individual in relationship with others, and his activities were no longer motivated exclusively by inner biological urgings but became sparked by the attitudes, prejudices and standards of the outside world. Although Adler never fully outgrew the biological limitations of Freud, he was the first to recognize that man's development was determined by his relationships with other men as well as to inner biological strivings. He extended the instinct theory by a recognition that, in addition to the dynamism of self-preservation, there also existed a communal need or innate feelings of community which implied existing not only for oneself, but going out of oneself to give to others. By altering the emphasis from inner motivation as a fixed characteristic of man to a recognition of motivation designed to achieve status with regard to our fellow man, he introduced the cultural concept into psychoanalysis.

Carl Jung's contributions extended the instinct theories while also expanding the role of the ego in personality development. While Jung was bound by a too mechanical view of personality in his dualistic notions of opposites and counter-forces (introversion-extroversion, etc.), he broadened the concept of man as a functioning being beyond that of mere animal to that of an individual with special problems of existence. He directed attention to the positive interests and concerns of human activity and recognized the spiritual and aesthetic needs of man. For him, these higher interests were more than sublimated sex needs and arose out of values and needs specific to man. Thus, he expanded libido into a general life force and stressed the positive aspects of the unconscious. In recent years he appears to be a philosopher of semantics and a mythologist who is a master of symbolic imagery and metapsychology, rather than a medical psychologist or psychiatrist.

There are many contributors like Ronald Fairbairn, Heinz Hartman, Ernest Kris, Richard Loewenstein, etc., who have remained in the libido theory farmework while recognizing some of the difficulties in doing so. They have tried to reinterpret Freud's biological view to include the newer insights into the role of culture, perception and child development. Fairbairn, for example, extended the concept of libido from a sexual to an object relation framework. This necessitated expanding biological goals to include cultural forces. Hartman, Kris and Loewenstien simply expanded and redefined new categories in ego psychology while remaining in the biological framework of Freud.

Karen Horney discarded the biological orientation and postulated that personality develops entirely in the parent-child, child-adult, and adult-adult interaction. The motive power lies in the need to fulfill one's potentialities in a self-realization process. The impetus derives from the need to deal with the prolonged helplessness of the infant. Under unfavorable conditions, the anxiety in development is dealt with by such defenses as idealization, withdrawal, attachment, etc. Her theory involves a recognition of the endless vicious circle which occurs in the neurosis where man attempts to achieve some security in his living. Consequently, she emphasizes the importance of the current aspects of an individual's life. This does not minimize the genetic and developmental approach. It simply emphasizes that the recent most available experiences are more illuminating than the faded reconstructions of earlier years. Her contributions to therapy have influenced contemporary practices very greatly. They include the complex integration of the patient's efforts to actualize his idealizations in order to overcome his insecurity. These attempts lead to all the complications of the neurotic and psychotic states, producing such problems as alienation, loneliness, and the constriction of one's living. Horney's therapeutic conceptions are directed towards personality expansion and self-affirmation through a process of unwinding the dictates of the shoulds and claims which maintain the neurotic structure. In this process the individual's capacities for affirming his true self are enhanced with consequent development of greater intimacy and participation.

Erich Fromm has made his most meaningful contribution by stimulating other researchers to take account of man's great need for relatedness and by formulating many insights regarding man's character structure in these terms. The problem of ethics and morality as they involve personality development was viewed in a more scientific manner. His ideas on the effect of culture on personality extended our knowledge of the forces which impinge on man—including economics, politics, religion, etc. In pointing up the specific kinds of relatedness of the individual towards himself and the world, he made explicit the existential dichotomics which plague man. The problems of isolation and separation force man to relate in whatever ways he can, which produces such unsatisfactory destructive ways as sado-masochism, and automatic conformity, etc. He has encouraged the multi-discipline approach to the study of personality by increasing the variables involved in personality development.

Sullivan's personality theory stressed the interrelations of man as necessary for development and, thus, he postulated nothing except that which can be observed in these interactions. It was based exclusively on the notion of man as an experiencing animal who has basic biological needs. The essence of his interpersonal theory is his formulation of the postulate of maternal tenderness which best illustrates his theoretical approach to the study of man. His theorem says: "The observed activity of the infant arising from tensions of needs induces tensions in the mothering one which tension is experienced as tenderness and as an impulsion to activity towards the relief of the infant's needs."[1] No instincts are postulated, but simply the capacity of an individual to respond or produce an effect on another person by virtue of the relationship that exists between them. The same is true of his conception of anxiety which states: "The tension of anxiety, when present in the mothering one, induces anxiety in the infant."[1] This, too, requires no biological rationale. Thus, in adults, anxiety becomes a response to the disapproval (or anticipated disapproval) of a significant adult. The self grows out of the need to deal with anxiety but always occurs in living and experience—even if the experience is only phantasied. This approach of Sullivan's is closest to an operational statement of human behavior that has been developed up to date.

The group of theorists which are dealt with in this book have all taken exception to the instinctivist foundation of Freud's theory. They have broadened personality with the dimension of culture, without relinquishing any of the basic essential validity of the biological nature of man. They all acknowledge the hereditary predisposition of the human infant while stressing that these potentialities unfold in a cultural situation that influences the ultimate development. They, thus, assume a pliable human nature capable of change and being motivated towards change by a drive or urge towards a realization of the innate potentialities of the human being. They all see man as creatively driven, striving to achieve his goals. The anxiety which supervenes in his development is produced by the culture and is amenable to alterations in the culture. While none conceives of human existence without anxiety, they have an optimistic view of the ultimate capacity of man to minimize his anxieties through various devices. Finally, by a revised philosophical view of man and his need to deal with his biological heritage in a social milieu, they have enlarged the scope of the therapeutic techniques for dealing with man's distortions and alienations.

The critics of the neo-Freudian psychoanalysts center their attacks on the notion that these theories merely expand Freud's views on the ego and its defenses. Even if we assume this to be true, it has little merit unless we agree that the id as detailed by Freud is a valid, verified concept that is a permanent element of an ultimate theory of man's psychology. We can, I believe, assume that major change will occur to the original concept of the unconscious, without detracting from the biological heritage of man and its influence on man's psychology. Such criticism derives from the assumption that we have an undisputed conception of personality which will persist for all time.

Criticism of these social psychological theories should be restricted to an appraisal of the weaknesses of these formulations which could be broadly stated in terms of a neglect of the genesis of certain attitudes and behavioral patterns. These theories still have little to offer on the ultimate problem in human psychology, the integration of psychological phenomena on a physiological basis. In this area, Freud made the initial attempt but he was hampered by a physical model which was too limiting. The models of communication theory, field theory, etc., are still inadequate. However, it will become clearer in the next decade that the contributions of the ego psychologists will form along with Freud the bridge to a more comprehensive view of man's psychology.

NOTES

1. Sullivan, H. S.: Conceptions of Modern Psychiatry (see Bibliography).

Bibliography

Abraham, K.: Selected Papers. New York, Viking Press, 1927.

Ackerman, N. W.: The Psychodynamics of Family Life. New York, Basic Books, 1958.

Adler, A.: The Practice and Theory of Individual Psychology. New York, Harcourt, Brace & Co., 1924.

Alexander. F.: Psychoanalysis of the Total Personality. New York, Nervous and Mental Disease Monograph Series, No. 52, 1930.

——: The Medical Value of Psychoanalysis. New York, W. W. Norton Co., 1936.

——: Fundamentals of Psychoanalysis. New York, W. W. Norton & Co., 1948.

——: Psychosomatic Medicine. New York, W. W. Norton & Co., 1950.

——: Psychoanalysis and Psychotherapy. J. Am. Psychoanal. A. 2:685, 1954.

——, French, T. M.: Psychonalytic. Therapy: Principles and Application. New York, Ronald Press, 1946.

Allee, W. C.: The Social Life of Animals. New York, W. W. Norton & Co., 1938.

Appel, K. E.: Psychoanalysis: reflections on varying concepts. Am. J. Psychiat. 112:711, 1956.

Barnett, L.: The Universe and Dr. Einstein. New York, Mentor, 1954.

Bateson, G. and Mead, Margaret: Balinese Culture. New York, William Morrow & Co., 1942.

Benedek, Therese: Psychosexual Functions in Women. New York, The Ronald Press, 1952.

——, and Rubenstein, B: The correlations between ovarian activity and psychodynamic processes. Psychosom. Med. 1:245, 461, 1939.

Benedict, Ruth: Patterns of Culture. New York, Mentor, 1953.

——, and Weltfish, G.: The Races of Mankind. New York, Columbia University Public Affairs Pamphlet, No. 85, 1953.

Bieber, I.: A critique of the libido-theory. Am. J. Psychoanal. 18-52, 1958.

Binswanger, L. M.: Existential Analysis, psychiatry, schizophrenia. J. Exist. Psychiat. 1:157, 1960.

——, Sigmund Freud: Reminiscences of a Friendship. New York, Grune & Stratton Inc., 1957.

Boss, M. Meaning and Content of Sexual Perversions. New York, Grune & Stratton, 1949.

Bowlby, J.: Maternal Care and Mental Health. Geneva. WHO. 1951.

——: The nature of the child's tie to his mother. Int. J. Phychoanal. 39:350, 1959.

Braatøy, T.: The Fundamentals of Psychoanalytic Technique. New York, John Wiley & Sons, 1954.

Brenman, Margaret, and Gill, M. N.: Hypnotherapy. New York, Int. Universities Press, 1947.

Breuer, J., and Freud, S.: Studies in Hysteria. New York, Nervous and Mental Disease Publishing Co., 1936.

Brinton, C.: The Shaping of the Modern Mind. New York, Mentor, 1953.

Brody, Sylvia: Patterns of Mothering. New York, Int. Universities Press, 1956.

Buber, M.: I and Thou. New York, Charles Scribner & Sons, 1937.

——: Distance and relations. Psychiatry 20:97, 1941.

Cantril, H. Perception and interpersonal relations. Am. J. Psychiat. 114:119, 1957.

Cassirer, E.: Determinism and Indeterminism in Modern Physics. New Haven, Yale University Press, 1945.

Colby, K. M.: Primer for Psychotherapists. New York, The Ronald Press, 1951.

Cole, W. G.: Sex in Christianity and Psychoanalysis. New York, Oxford University Press, 1953.

Cushing, J. G. N.: Committee Report. Bull. Am. Psychoanal. A. 8:44, 1952.

Darlington, C. D.: The origin of Darwinism. Scientific American 200:60, 1959.

Deutsch, Helene: Psychology of Women. New York, Grune & Stratton, 1944-45, 2 Vols.

Dollard, J., and Miller, N. E.: Personality and Psychotherapy. New York, McGraw-Hill Book Co., 1950.

Durkheim, E.: Suicide. Glencoe, Illinois, Free Press, 1952.

Einstein, A., and Infeld L.: The Evolution of Physics. New York, Simon & Schuster, 1938.

Erikson, E.: Childhood and Society. New York, W. W. Norton & Co., 1950.

——: The problem of ego identity. J. Am. Psychoanalytical treatment. A. 4:56, 1956.

Fairbairn, R. D.: On the nature and aims of psychoanalytical treatment. Int. J. Psychoanal. 39:74, 1959.

——: Psychoanalytic Studies of the Personality. London, Tavistock Publications, 1952.

Foote, Nelson N.: Love. Psychiatry 16:245-251, 1953.

Ford, C. S., and Beach, F. A.: Patterns of Sexual Behavior. New York, Harper & Bros., 1951.

Forel, C.: The Sexual Question. New York, Physicians and Surgeons Book Co., 1926.

Frank, J., et al: Patients' expectancies and relearning of factors in determining improvement in psychotherapy. Am. J. Psychiat. 115:961, 1959.

——: Persuasion and Healing. Baltimore, John Hopkins Press, 1961.

Freud, Anna: The Ego and the Mechanisms of Defense. New York, Int. Universities Press, 1946.

Freud, S.: The Psychopatholgy of Everyday Life. New York, The Macmillan Co., 1917.

——: Totem and Taboo. New York, Dodd, Mead & Co., 1918.

——: Group Psychology and the Analysis of the Ego. London, Int. Psychoanalytic Press, 1922.

——: Three Contributions to the Theory of Sex, 4th Ed. Baltimore, Williams & Wilkins, 1930.

——: The Interpretation of Dreams. rev. ed. New York, The Macmillan Co., 1933.

——: New Introductory Lectures on Psychoanalysis. New York, W. W. Norton & Co., 1933.

——: A General Introduction to Psychoanalysis. New York, Garden City Publishing Co., 1943.

——: Leonardo da Vinci. Random House, 1947.

——: Outline of Psychoanalysis. New York, W. W. Norton & Co., 1949.

——: The Origins of Psychoanalysis: Letters to Wilhelm Fleiss, 1887-1902. New York, Basic Books, 1954.

——: Civilization and Its Discontents. London, Hogarth Press, 1955.

——: Collected Papers. ed. James Strachey. New York, Basic Books, 1959.

Fromm, E.: Escape From Freedom. New York, Farrar & Rinehart, 1941.

——: The Forgotten Language. New York, Rinehart & Co., 1951.

——: Simund Freud's Mission. New York, Harper & Bros., 1959.

——: Man for Himself. New York, Rhinehart & Co., 1947.

——: Psychoanalysis and Religion. New Yale U. Press, 1950.

——: The Sane Society. New York, Rhinehart & Co., 1955.

Fromm-Reichmann, F.: Principles of Intensive Psychotherapy. Chicago, University of Chicago Press, 1950.

Gardiner, M.: Facts and Fallacies in the Name of Science. New York, Dover Publications, 1957.

Gesell, A., and Ilg., F. L.: Infant and Child in the Culture of Today. New York, Harper & Bros., 1943.

Gill, M., Newman, R., and Redich, F. C.: The Initial Interview in Psychiatric Practice. International Universities Press, 1954.

Glad, D. D.: Operational Values in Psychotherapy. New York, Oxford University Press, 1959.

Glueck, B., ed.: Current Therapies of Personality Disorders. New York, Grune & Stratton, 1946.

Goldstien, K.: The Organism. New York, American Book Co., 1939.

Grinker, R. R.: Psychosomatic Research. New York, W. W. Norton & Co., 1953.

——: A transactional model for psychotherapy. A.M.A. Arch. Gen. Psychiat. 1:132, 1959.

——, and Robbins, F. P.: Psychosomatic Case Book. New York, Blackiston Co., 1954.

——, and Spiegel, J. P.: Men under Stress. Philadelphia, Blackiston Co., 1945.

Halliday, J. L.: Psychosocial Medicine. New York, W. W. Norton & Co., 1948.

Harlow, H. F.: The nature of love. American Psychologist 13:673-685, 1958.

Henriques, F.: Love in Action. New York, E. P. Dutton & Co., 1960.

Hartmann, H.: Comments on the Psychoanalytic Theory of the Ego. Psychoanalytic Study of the Child, Vol. 5. Int. University Press, N. Y.

Hess, E.: Imprinting in animals. Scientific American. 198:81, 1958.

Hoch, P., and Zubin, J., eds.: Psychosexual Development. New York, Grune & Stratton, 1949.

——, and ——, eds.: Depression. New York, Grune & Stratton, 1954.

Hollingshead, A. B., and Redlich, F. C.: Social Class and Mental Illness. New York, John Wiley & Sons, 1958.

Hook, S.: Psychoanalysis—Scientific Method and Philosophy. New York, Grove Press Inc., 1959.

Horney, K.: Neurotic Personality of Our Time. New York, W. W. Norton & Co., 1937.

——: New Ways in Psychoanalysis. New York, W. W. Norton & Co., 1939.

——: Neurosis and Human Growth. New York, W. W. Norton & Co., 1950.

Huxley, T. H.: Man's Place in Nature. London, Thomas, Ltd., 1898.

Jones, E.: Life of Freud. 3 Vols. New York, Basic Books, 1953-58.

Jung, C. G.: Psychological Types. New York, Harcourt, Brace & Co., 1923.

——: The Psychology of Dementia Praecox, 2nd ed. New York, Nervous and Mental Disease Publishing Co., 1937.

Kalinowsky, L. B., and Hoch, P. H.: Shock Treatments, Psychosurgery and Other Somatic Treatments in Psychiatry, 2nd ed. New York, Grune & Stratton, 1952.

Kardiner, A.: The Individual and His Society. New York, Columbia University Press, 1939.

——: Karush, A., and Lionel, O.: A. methodologic study of Freudian theory. J. Nerv. Ment. Dis. 129:11-19, 133:43,207,221,341,351, 1959.

Kierkegaard, S.: The Concept of Dread (1844). Princeton, Princeton University Press, 1944.

Kinsey, A. C., Pomeroy, W. B., and Martin, C. E.: Sexual Behavior in the Human Male. Philadelphia, W. B. Saunders Co., 1949.

——:, Pomeroy, W. B., Martin, C. E., and Gebhard, P. H.: Sexual Behavior in the Human Female. Philadlephia, W. B. Saunders Co., 1953.

Klein, Melanie: Contributions to Psychoanalysis. London, Hogarth Press, 1948.

LaBarre, W.: The Human Animal. Chicago, University of Chicago Press, 1955.

Langer, Suzanne K.: Philosophy in a New Key. New York, Mentor, 1956.

Lennard, H. L., and Bernstein, A.: Anatomy of Psychotherapy. New York, Columbia University Press, 1960.

Lewin, K.: Resolving Social Conflicts. New York, Harper & Bros., 1948.

Lief, A., ed.: The Common-Sense Psychiatry of Dr. Adolf Meyer. New York, McGraw-Hill Book Co., 1948.

Linton, R.: The Tree of Culture. New York, Alfred A. Knopf, 1955.

Loewenstien, R. N.: Conflict and Autonomous Ego Development during the Phallic Stage. Psychoanalytic Study of the Child, Vol. 5. New York, International Universities Press, 47-52, 1950.

Lorenz, K.: King Solomon's Ring. New York, Basic Books, 1952.

Malinowski, B.: The Sexual Life of Savages in Northwestern Melanesia. New York, Liveright, 1929, 2 vols.

Masserman, J. H.: Some current concepts of sexual behavior. Psychiatry 14:67, 1951.

——: Practice of Dynamic Psychiatry. Philadelphia, W. B. Saunders Co., 1955.

——, ed.: Current Psychiatic Therapies. New York, Grune & Stratton, 1961.

——: Science and Psychoanalysis, Vol. 1-4. New York, Grune & Stratton, 1958.
Mead, Margaret: Sex and Temperament. New York, Mentor, 1952.
Montagu, A.: The Natural Superiority of Woman. New York, Macmillan Co., 1953.
——: Direction of Human Development. New York, Macmillan Co., 1955.
Mullahy, P.: Oedipus—Myth and Complex. New York, Hermitage Press, 1948.
——: Contributions of Harry Stack Sullivan. New York, Hermitage Press, 1952.
Muller, H. J.: The Uses of the Past. New York, Mentor, 1952.
——: Science and Criticism. George Braziller, 1943.
Monroe, Ruth: Schools of Psychoanalytic Thought. New York, Dryden Press, 1955, pp. 174-219.
Murphy, G.: In The Minds of Men. New York, Basic Books, 1953.
——: Human Potentialities. New York, Basic Books, 1958.
Nagel, E., and Newman, J. R.: Godel's Proof. New York, New York University Press, 1958.
Nuttin, J.: Psychoanalysis and Personality. New York, Sheed & Ward, 1953.
Oppenheimer, J. R.: The Open Mind. New York, Simon & Schuster, 1955.
Piaget, J.: The Child's Conception of Physical Causality. New York, Harcourt, Brace & Co., 1930.
——: The Language and Thought of the Child, 2nd ed. New York, Harcourt, Brace & Co., 1932.
——: The Construction of Reality in the Child. New York, Basic Books, 1954.
Powdermaker, Florence B., and Frank, J. D.: Group Psychotherapy. Cambridge, Harvard University Press, 1953.
Pumpian-Mindlin, E., ed: Psychoanalysis as Science. Stanford, Stanford University Press, 1952.
Rado, S., and Daniels, G.: Changing Concepts in Psychoanalytic Medicine. New York, Grune & Stratton, 1956.
——: Psychoanalysis of Behavior. New York, Grune & Stratton, 1956.
——: Sexual anaesthesia in the female. Quart. Rev. Surg. Obst. & Gynec. 16:151, 1959.
Rank, O.: Will Therapy and Truth and Reality. New York, Alfred A. Knopf, 1947.
Rawcliffe, D. H.: Illusions and Delusions of the Supernatural and the Occult. New York, Dover Publications, 1959.
Reich, W.: Character Analysis: Principles and Technique for Psychoanalysts in Practice and in Training, 3rd ed. New York, Orgone Institute Press, 1949.
Reichenbach, H.: The Rise of Scientific Philosophy. Berkeley, University of California Press, 1956.
Ribble, M.: The Rights of Infants. New York, Columbia University Press, 1943.
Riesman, D.: The Lonely Crowd. New Haven, Yale University Press, 1958.
Rioch, D. McK.: Current Trends in Psychological Theory. Pittsburgh, University of Pittsburgh Press, 1951.
Robbins, B. S.: The myth of latent emotion. Psychotherapy 1:3, 1955.
Rogers, Carl R.: Counselling and Psychotherapy. Boston, Houghton Mifflin Co., 1942.
Ruesch, J., and Bateson, G.: Communication. New York, W. W. Norton & Co., 1951.

Ruesch, J., and Kess, W.: Non-verbal Communication. Berkeley, University of California Press, 1956.

Russell, B.: Outline of Philosophy. London, Allen & Unwin, 1927.

Salimbone: In A Portable Medieval Reader. James Bruce Ross and Mary Martin McLaughlin, eds. New York, The Viking Press, 1949, p. 366.

Salzman, L. :Spiritual and faith healing. J. Pastoral Care 11:14, 1957.

——: Masochism In Masserman; J. H., ed., Science and Psychoanalysis, Vol. 2. New York, Grune & Stratton, 1959.

——: Evaluation of shock therapy. Am. J. Psychiat. Vol. 103:669-679, 1947.

——: Resolution of a paranoid psychosis. M. Ann. D. of C. 23:489-493, 1954.

——: Psychology of religious and ideological conversion. Psychiatry 16:177-187, 1954.

——: Premature ejaculation. Int. J. Sexol. 8:70-76, 1954.

——: Concept of latent homosexuality. Am. J. Psychoanal. 17:161-169, 1957.

——: Negative Therapeutic Reaction. Psychoanalysis and Human Values. Science and Psychoanalysis. New York, Grune & Stratton, 1960.

——: Paranoid state—theory and therapy. Arch. Gen. Psychiat. 2:679-693, 1960.

——: Masochism and psychopathy as adaptive behavior. J. Individual Psychol. 16: 1960.

Sartre, J. P.: L'Existentialisme est un Humanisme. Paris, Nagel, 1946.

Saul, L. J.: Emotional Maturity. Philadelphia, J. B. Lippincott Co., 1947.

——: Technic and Practice of Psychoanalysis. Philadelphia, J. B. Lippincott Co., 1958.

——: Freud's death instinct and the second law of thermodynamics. Int. J. Psychoanal. 39:323, 1959.

Schachtel, E. G.: Metamorphosis. New York, Basic Books, 1959.

Schlipp, P. A., ed.: Albert Einstein: Philosopher-Scientist. Evanston, Illinois, Library of Living Philosophies, 1949.

Schmideberg, Mellita: Values and goals in psychotherapy. Psychiatric Quart. 32:233, 1958.

Simeons, A. T. W.: Man's Presumptious Brain. New York, E. P. Dutton & Co., 1961.

Silverberg, Wm. V.: Childhood Experience and Personal Destiny. New York, Springer Publishing Co., 1952.

Simpson, G. G.: The Meaning of Evolution. New Haven, Yale University Press, 1949.

Sivadon, P. D.: Techniques of sociotherapy. Psychiatry 20:205, 1957.

Sonneman, U.: Existence and Therapy. New York, Grune & Stratton, 1954.

Strauss, E.: On Obsessions. New York, Nervous and Mental Disease Publishing Co., 1948.

Sullivan, H. S.: Conceptions of Modern Psychiatry. Washington, D. C., William Alanson White Psychiatric Foundation, 1947.

——: The Interpersonal Theory of Psychiatry. New York, W. W. Norton & Co., 1953.

Suttie, I.: The Origins of Love and Hate. New York, Julian Press, 1952.

Szasz, T. S.: On the psychoanalytic theory of instincts. Psychoanal. Quart. 21:25, 1952.

——: Problems in contemporary psychoanalytic training. A.M.A. Arch. Gen. Psychiat. 4:106, 1960.

——: Pain and Pleasure. New York, Basic Books, 1957.

Taylor, O. R.: Sex in History, Vanguard Press, 1954.

Thompson, Clara: Emotional climate of psychoanalytic institutes. Psychiatry 21:45, 1958.

——, and Mullahy, P.: Psychoanalysis: Evolution and Development. New York, Hermitage House, 1950.

Tillich, P.: Courage to Be. New Haven, Yale University Press, 1952.

——: Love, Power, and Justice. New York, Oxford University Press, 1954.

Tinbergen, N.: The Study of Instinct. Oxford, Clarendon Press, 1951.

Walter, W. G.: The Living Brain. New York, W. W. Norton & Co., 1953.

Wheelis, A.: The vocational hazards of psychoanalysis. Int. J. Psychoanal. 37:171, 1956.

——: The Quest for Identity. New York, W. W. Norton & Co., 1958.

Whitehead, A. N.: Science and the Modern World. New York, The MacMillan Co., 1925.

Whitehorn, J. C.: Understanding psychotherapy. Am. J. Psychiat. 112:328, 1955.

Wollberg, L. R.: The Technique of Psychotherapy. New York, Grune & Stratton, 1954.

Index